# GLOBALIZATION AND THE DEVELOPING ECONOMIES

## *Theory and Evidence*

# Globalization and the Developing Economies

## *Theory and Evidence*

*Edited by*
ADITYA BHATTACHARJEA
SUGATA MARJIT

CENTRE FOR STUDIES IN SOCIAL SCIENCES

MANOHAR
2004

First published 2004



ISBN 81-7304-545-3

*Published by*
Ajay Kumar Jain for
Manohar Publishers & Distributors
4753/23 Ansari Road, Daryaganj
New Delhi 110 002

*Printed at*
Lordson Publishers Pvt Ltd
Delhi 110 007

# Contents

# Foreword

The motivating idea behind organizing a conference on the teaching of economics at an advanced level is that economics as a discipline within the broad area of human sciences is necessarily context-specific. The definition of the context in this case would include the delimitation of regions, countries and population groups. Even if there were master concepts which would apply to all situations, the attempt to apply them would itself require context-specific adaptation and interpretation of basic axioms. The branch of institutional economics has grown up with such adaptations in mind. But there are many practitioners of social science with economics as a major component of their practice who would have the humility to admit that they would have to change mental gears as they encounter different terrains of macroeconomic instability, primary and secondary uncertainty, and the sheer weight of malnutrition and poverty even as the marvels of growth are celebrated.

In particular, developing countries all over the world face problems many of which require fresh approaches. The tools of arrogantly imperialistic economics have failed to cure the 20-year-old maladies of stagnation and instability wrecking the lives of hundreds of millions of people all over the world, and these wrecked lives have their counterparts in millions in the developed market economies as well.

In a fast changing world, and with rapidly increasing population, it has become imperative for policy makers and analysts to both analyse the impact of socio-economic changes and design appropriate policies to take care of the educational, nutritional, and health requirements of vast numbers of people. The analysis itself has become demanding in terms of techniques and informational inputs. Much of the education in this kind of analysis is now acquired by professionals in the developing countries going to the advanced and affluent countries of Western Europe and North America. Such education is very costly from the point of view of most developing countries. Moreover, many of the professionals do not return to their own countries after acquiring that education and prefer to stay on in the advanced countries themselves. As a result, the developing countries lost both in terms of the expenditure which they had incurred for initially educating these migrating professionals and the services of some of their best human material. There is yet a third problem associated with getting the professionals of the developing countries trained in a typical university in an OECD country. The information network and positive experiences from one developing country can be adapted to the benefit of analysis and policy making in other developing countries too, and these will not be available in an OECD country.

The conference was organized as a pilot demonstration of the variety of national experiences and experiences of oppressed groups (such as women and labour in a globalized world) that need to be brought into focus with analytical tools, if we hope ever to address the issue of degradation of human beings. Apart from economists from India, economists from Malaysia and South Korea participated actively in the conference and helped to illuminate the problems arising out of the Asian financial crisis for their Indian colleagues. I was enormously impressed and gratified by the seriousness with which the contributors confronted their task. I am sure that other academicians and students of the particular topics taken up by the nine papers in this volume will find them equally instructive.

On behalf of the Centre for Studies in Social Sciences, Calcutta (CSSSC), I thank all the contributors of the papers and all the invited discussants and other participants for their active interest. Thanks are due to the United Nations Educational, Scientific and Cultural Organization (UNESCO) for giving a grant to the CSSSC under their Participation Programme, which enabled us to hold this conference. I would also like to thank the officers of the Indian National Commission for Cooperation with UNESCO, and in particular, Sarvashri P.R. Dasgupta, Champak Chatterjee and D.P. Singh, for their cooperation. Thanks are due to the staff of the CSSSC for rising to the occasion and helping to make the conference a success. Finally, I thank the two editors, Dr Aditya Bhattacharjea and Professor Sugata Marjit for ungrudgingly taking over the task of liaising with the contributors and putting the final editorial touches to the papers.

AMIYA KUMAR BAGCHI

# Introduction

*Aditya Bhattacharjea and Sugata Marjit*

This volume brings together substantially revised and updated versions of papers presented at a UNESCO conference that was held in December 1999 at the Centre for Studies in Social Sciences, Calcutta, on the theme of 'Economics Relevant for the Developing Economies'. The purpose of the conference was to bring to the fore certain contemporary and critical economic issues relevant for teaching students in the developing world. The essays cover various topics, and provide broad surveys of the literature and some ideas for future research. Some of them deal with individual transition economies, and their experience with economic reform and structural adjustment programmes. Overall we aspire for a balanced understanding of important issues in the global economy. The essays in this volume use analytical techniques that can be accessed by students with a fairly basic knowledge of economics and statistics. We are confident that getting familiar with the materials presented here will not cause any undue burden on the students of the Third World, many of whom are deprived of adequate infrastructure for learning.

The volume is divided into three broad sections. The first section begins with a fairly extensive view of contemporary Russia, possibly the most complex and failed example of economic transformation. This is followed by two more country studies, on crisis management and development in Korea and Malaysia. The second section opens with a general theoretical paper on balance of payments and currency crises, as a continuing reflection on the macroeconomic adjustment problem dealt with in the earlier section. Also included in this section is a paper on the contemporary topic of increasing returns and specialization in international trade, focusing on issues that are particularly relevant for the developing world. The next two papers are also on international economics. One deals with the general problem of labour mobility and international trade. It highlights topics such as wage inequality, skill formation, and brain drain in terms of simple analytical models. The continuing debate on the distribution of gains from trade between the North and the South is taken up next, with a thorough and rigorous statistical exercise on the extent and impact of export diversification and terms of trade. Statistical analysis features again in the next paper, which looks at the puzzle of the apparent lack of correlation between income growth, food consumption, and nutritional status in India. The last section consists of a single paper on a topic that has emerged as possibly the most hotly debated issue in development studies. This has to do with the question of 'gender' in economics. An elaborate survey of the voluminous literature in the field is presented, with an equally extensive presentation of open ended research ideas.

Economic reform in the erstwhile socialist or socialistic economies is a matter of great concern to policy makers and world organizations. In these economies, the last decade has witnessed a gradual decline in state control, a drive towards more market oriented adjustments, and most importantly a move towards creating an open trade and investment regime. The experience of the so-called transition economies has been fairly mixed and not very promising. A case in point is that of Russia, which has been passing through an unprecedented economic trauma over the past few years. The Russian case is an example which clearly shows how some textbook style reforms can go wrong in a society which does not have the required institutional structure to back up such an effort. Chapter 1, 'Can Russia Survive the IMF Medicine?', by Nirmal Chandra focuses on three essential issues. First, the problems of carrying out reforms in Russia are elaborately analysed, highlighting the role of corruption, labour problems, and measurement problems. Second, it gives a good idea of what should be the possible concerns while implementing reforms in a typical non-market economy, which we think provide lessons for some mixed developing economies as well, since some of the problems have also cropped up in other economies in Eastern Europe, South Asia, and Africa. Third, the paper provides a fairly interesting and broad range of statistics relevant for understanding the recent developments in the Russian economy which should help researchers in this field. Chandra uses his familiarity with Russian-language sources to good effect here.

It is conventional to argue that less control by the state reduces the scope for corruption. But this has been clearly nullified in Russia. Erstwhile state-owned enterprises were eventually sold to people with criminal connections. Not only were the sales undervalued, but also interested parties misinvoiced their transactions heavily to siphon off funds overseas. In 1997 about one-sixth of the national budget was misspent due to mismanagement and corruption. International Monetary Fund (IMF) credit to Russia went out of the economy through the back door. The Bank of New York was involved in a scam unprecedented in the history of structural adjustment programmes. Chandra suggests, by citing references, that there was indirect political support for corruption in Russia. What emerges as a clear conclusion is that the total absence of an efficient and apolitical regulatory authority, possibly a strong treasury, has led to a disaster in Russia. Chapter 1 also discusses the problem of measuring national income in a barter economy. The measurement of gross domestic product (GDP) in Russia is plagued by the fact that there is hardly any measure available for the informal sector; possibly, the underground economy and barter transactions are difficult to record. Another problem highlighted by Chandra is the general decline in life expectancy in Russia. If the current trend continues, by 2050 the Russian population would be half of what it is now. The root of the problem lies in a continuing rise in the death rate in Russia. It is possible that the hitherto inadequate health initiative of the Russian Government has been further accentuated by a cut in the health related expenditure in the post reform period. There has been a sharp rise in mortality among working age men with a high rate of open unemployment, low wages, and alcoholism. Chandra agrees that the roots of such crisis have to be traced back to the Soviet past. But the current situation has not been very conducive for making a fresh start.

Although the consequences of the East Asian crisis of the late 1990s, and the policies that were implemented to deal with it, were not as catastrophic as in Russia, they still hold out important lessons for developing countries. These are discussed in the next three papers, employing different analytical frameworks. The crisis ended the remarkable period of nearly three decades of rapid growth popularly known as the East Asian Miracle, with Korea as its exemplar. Thanks to the work of several scholars, the Korean 'miracle' is no longer seen as a paragon of market-guided growth, but rather as an example of state-led transformation of the production structure, with export-competitiveness as a benchmark of success. Common to both stories, however, is an acceptance of the idea that growth in Korea was facilitated by an authoritarian political system, and accompanied by an exceptionally equitable distribution of income. Chapter 2, 'National Choice of Industrial Structure, Financial Repression, and Credit Policy in Korea' by C.G. Yoo offers a revisionist account of these and other aspects of the 'miracle'. According to him, the strategy was backed by the 'common will of the people', who were willing to defer democratization and greater equity in favour of rapid growth and structural transformation.

Yoo's account of the high growth years focuses on the financial system, which was based on state-directed and subsidized credit to particular industries within a particular socio-economic system. Among the little-known facts that Yoo highlights are the government guarantees for most foreign commercial loans, the importance of the private property of industrialists as collateral for domestic loans, and the fact of labour being subjected to the longest working hours in the world, and to brutal competition in unprotected sectors. When pent-up demands for democracy and social justice were articulated in the mid to late 1980s, the Korean 'model' was abandoned, with both the state and the industrial conglomerates abdicating their social responsibilities. Yoo argues that some of the measures introduced in the wake of the 1997 crisis, such as greater shareholder control of banks and adoption of BIS standards, amount to discarding some of the vital ingredients that enabled the financial system to contribute to long-term lending and thereby to industrial transformation.

The next two papers are more theoretical in nature, although they employ very different macroeconomic models and come to rather different conclusions. It has been widely noted that Malaysia was exceptional in instituting controls on capital mobility in response to the 1997 crisis, and has made a smart recovery—although as Eu Chye Tan points out in Chapter 3, 'Exchange Rate Arrangements: Their Suitability to the Malaysian Economy', so have most of the other countries which did not impose capital controls. He presents an exceptionally clear exposition of the Mundell-Fleming model of macroeconomic adjustment in an open economy, and seeks to identify which of its several cases apply to Malaysia. Tan predicts that a combination of restrictions on capital mobility, a fixed exchange rate, and high growth will eventually deplete the country's foreign exchange reserves and make the exchange rate peg unsustainable, resulting in the kind of currency crisis which more recent theoretical models have tried to analyse. If not a dramatic 'speculative attack' on the currency as predicted by the 'first-generation' balance-of-payments crisis models, he expects the kind of problems dealt with in the 'second-generation' models. That is, the government may be unable to induce a capital inflow to shore up the currency by raising interest rates, because this may cause banks and firms to become insolvent and also raise the cost of government borrowing. Tan rules out either a crawling peg or a currency union with other South-East Asian countries, and argues for using the current period of financial tranquillity to move to a loosely managed float with capital mobility. He believes that any speculation will be stabilizing, and agents will learn to hedge against exchange rate risk.

Amit Bhaduri's paper in Chapter 4, 'The Dynamics of Balance of Payments under Capital Flows', in contrast, allows for destabilizing speculation. He develops a model of dynamic adjustment in the balance of payments in which a crucial role is played by a parameter that represents lenders' response to a change in a country's reserve position. If this is above a crucial level, the system becomes dynamically unstable in either the upward or downward direction. Bhaduri identifies several other behavioural parameters that make this possibility more likely, and argues that the analysis shows that the way forward lies in moving the debate beyond simply re-regulation versus deregulation. He suggests the deregulation of the exchange rate combined with greater regulation of short-term capital movements and a more cautious attitude to foreign borrowing.

Chapter 5, 'Increasing Returns, Trade, and Development', by Aditya Bhattacharjea critically surveys a relatively recent body of trade theory that attempts to formalize some ideas that date back to classical writings as well as 1950s development theory. Unlike traditional (Heckscher-Ohlin type) models, this literature allows for economies of scale and international transport costs. It shows how trade between countries at different levels of industrialization can induce a pattern of cumulative causation which leads to agglomeration of manufacturing activity in the leading countries and possible deindustrialization in the periphery. None the less, trade still appears to be mutually beneficial except in very special cases. Bhattacharjea argues that this is because the new models retain many features of the older neoclassical theory that predispose them to show such benign results. At the same time, they employ some new techniques in order to escape the problems that increasing returns creates for standard general equilibrium models, and these techniques also constrain their ability to explain economic divergence between nations. The limitations of these models are manifested in the way they deal with consumer choice, production technologies, competitive behaviour, and comparisons between equilibrium states of the economy. Bhattacharjea traces the origins of the new literature in the new industrial organization and trade theories of the late 1970s and 1980s, followed by their more recent incarnations in economic geography and development economics. He also critically examines neo-Keynesian alternatives, as well as the limited empirical evidence for the various approaches, and suggests directions for future research that draw on their strengths.

In Chapter 6, 'Wages, Labour Mobility, and International Trade', Sugata Marjit and Saibal Kar provide a comprehensive analysis of the economic issues involved in the international mobility of skilled and unskilled labour. The chapter surveys the conventional results and builds on them to consider labour as a heterogeneous factor. The impact of the mobility of labour, so heterogenized in terms of their skills, is then studied with respect to the socio-economically and politically most relevant and interesting issues of wage inequality, unemployment, and capital formation in the developing nations. The authors analyse the economic growth process in the poor nations as influenced by the specific pattern of emigration of labour and more precisely the way it works through the domestic expansion of physical and human capital.

Apart from categorizing the types of migration and the economic implications thereof, the authors also take note of the 'Classical' and 'Keynesian' explanations of the direction of factor (labour) flows and its impact on wage and rental gaps. The classical models have proposed that in the long-run, internal and international movement of factors unambiguously equalize the factor returns. The self-correcting migratory pattern thus predicted seems unrealistic when post-'Great Depression' empirical evidence from Britain shows that capital and labour moved in the same direction leading to a perpetual dis-equilibrium. The chapter also provides an account of all the other possible connections between labour migration, skill diversity, wage-gap and economic welfare. The common thread that binds all these interesting aspects together is obviously international trade in goods and services. This brings under consideration features such as the 'migration hump'—a result of the complementarity between trade and labour migration. No less important are references to the 'new economics of labour migration', where market imperfections mainly in the form of asymmetric information between potential migrants and their prospective employers abroad dictate the pattern of present and future migration. The complex nature of migratory patterns make it difficult for some of the economic models used so far to capture the true welfare characteristics. They use an application of a neoclassical general equilibrium model for a small open economy with two sectors to show that the distribution of income between the skilled and the unskilled may very well worsen by the export of unskilled labour. The construct of the model makes it clear that if technological differences across the globe are not so prominent, relative factor abundance becomes crucial in dictating the wage-differential and the consequent movement of labour. Although a rise in the unskilled wage, due to emigration of unskilled labour, is always welfare enhancing, it does not guarantee that emigration would lead to a decline in the wage-gap in a society.

The idea is extended to include the impact of remittances on overall economic growth. Citing examples drawn from some recent works, the authors argue that remittances can be an effective means to bypass the 'entry barrier' for the poorer section of the population in an economy with imperfect capital markets. Whether substantial remittances facilitate growth of local small business, investment and therefore employment is, however, an empirical question that needs more attention. The authors also suggest an idea for further research, namely as to what extent subsidized higher education in the local economy is related to 'net resource inflow' and the role of emigration in dictating the magnitude of such an impact. There is need for further critical analysis in this area, simply because it connects the earlier issue of 'brain drain' to more recently debated issues of education policy and emigration.

Chapter 7, 'Export Diversification, Market Shares, and Issues of North-South Terms of Trade', by Prabirjit Sarkar is more empirically oriented. It focuses on two important changes in the pattern of trade of the developing world in recent years and tries to check whether such changes have improved the terms of trade (TOT) for the South. The developing world's share in manufacturing exports has increased over time, and therefore the basic premise of the TOT debate that the South is an exporter of primary products does not hold. Also there has been an increasing degree of export diversification. Thus the problem of relying too much on volatile primary exports seems to have lost its significance over the years. Hence, a natural theoretical or empirical conjecture should be that these changes should have helped the Southern nations to arrest the decline in their TOT. Sarkar observes, however, that the declining trend in the commodity TOT continued for the South as a whole. The more diversified is the country's export share, the more is its share in world exports, but no less is the deterioration in its TOT. Sarkar has been careful in observing that the well-known TOT debate focuses on the relative gains from trade between the developed and the developing world, not on the absolute gains, as countries are likely to gain from trade relative to autarky. The virtue of the paper is a carefully constructed database from secondary sources, along with a clear statistical analysis, the methodology of which will be of help to similar exercises in the future.

Sarkar attributes the decline in TOT in the contemporary world to the well-known product cycle hypothesis. Since he does not do any econometric analysis, he leaves it as an open-ended question providing a good point to pick up for future research. Also he agrees that a large part of transactions today is carried out by the multinationals in terms of their intra-firm activities and one is not sure about the extent of the impact of transfer pricing on the price data available for statistical analyses. Hence, some of the movement in TOT might be fictitious. Here also lies the essence of a very important and challenging research topic. Sarkar's essay is a nice beginning for a productive and fruitful research agenda for the future.

Chapter 8, 'Changing Food Preferences, Nutritional Intake and Nutritional Status: Emerging Perspectives and Issues', by R. Radhakrishna, S. Inderkant and C. Ravi also undertakes statistical analysis of a vitally important contemporary issue, but moves to more domestic concerns. Over the last three decades, a disturbing trend has become manifest in India: the growth of incomes seems to bear no relationship—or possibly even a negative relationship—with per capita cereal and calorie consumption. The 1990s decade of reform, in fact, witnessed a clear decline in cereal consumption. There is also no obvious relationship between levels of income and nutritional status across Indian states. Radhakrishna and his co-authors examine a number of data sources to try to solve these puzzles. It is true that the relative price of cereals increased in the 1990s, but (following from Radhakrishna's earlier pioneering work on this subject) they also find evidence of a shift in consumer preferences from food to non-food consumption, from cereals to non-cereals, and from coarse to fine cereals across all income groups, including the very poor. This phenomenon seems to be exacerbated in rural areas with better infrastructure, which have easier access to the outside world.

The connection between food intake and nutritional status is also problematic. The authors present evidence of high levels of child malnutrition (although this has been declining in recent years) and chronic energy deficiency amongst rural adults. Thus, income growth does not necessarily translate into increased calorie intake, which in turn does not necessarily translate into better nutrition. This shifts the focus of concern from strategies oriented towards income growth to public interventions such as education (to encourage better nutritional and especially, weaning practices), health, and sanitation (to reduce the incidence of gastrointestinal diseases that are responsible for the failure of food intake to translate into better nutritional status).

In Chapter 9, Nirmala Banerjee provides a detailed overview of the literature on 'Socio-economic Analysis of Reproduction and the Family'. One of the most crucial questions faced by the poor countries in particular has to do with the issue of gender-gap in terms of socio-economic capabilities. It is now confirmed through several studies that such a gap has widened in many countries over the last few decades. It also goes without saying that increase in women's literacy, occupational mobility, access to ownership of assets, and social protection of women's rights go a long way in aiding the process of economic development desperately needed in the poor countries.

Banerjee starts with a microscopic analysis of the Beckerian approach towards modelling the economics of the family with gender as the analytical tool. She critically appraises the role of women in Becker's treatment of the family to the extent that outside work is compared and contrasted with the intra-household activities. She questions the basic assumption that women's work inside the household is not a cost to them but a source of pleasure. This in turn means that women's biology is their destiny and the costs they incur in carrying out too much intra-household work can be disregarded. In discussing policies for regulating fertility, she suggests that the relationship between education and fertility has behaved differently at different stages of development. An important point stressed by Banerjee is the independence of women in the decision-making process within a family. An alternative to the Beckerian approach towards modelling gender issues has to do with the more recent approach involving bargaining and cooperation within families. Banerjee argues that such models and their applications can explain some of the observed behaviour otherwise unexplained by more conventional treatments. She concludes that the formulation of bargaining problems within a family must incorporate society-specific traits beside the standard one of self-interest.

The transaction costs approach focuses on marriage and the family as institutions that somehow economize on the social transaction costs. Banerjee is of the opinion that although such models are difficult to implement empirically, they are useful for understanding the nature of intra-family gender relations, particularly in a patriarchal society such as in India. This tends to explain relatively stable marital relations, somewhat accommodating behaviour from the husbands when women are weak in terms of bargaining strength, and the role of social and familial sanctions in governing family relations. Banerjee concludes with a wide array of suggestions for future research in this area. In particular, the importance of market wage differential between men and women and career prospects are highlighted as factors that have a major impact on the overspecialization of women in household work. Wage rates and labour force participation levels dictate the pattern of fertility even in societies where most women get education and can participate in social activities at will. Yet, a disproportionate share of household activities is shared by them. This is possibly a fallout of the employment bias that exists in the market and hence calls for serious investigation as an interesting research topic.

The nine essays in this volume thus use different analytical approaches: historically-informed analytical case studies (Chapters 1 and 2); a mix of standard theory and application (Chapter 3); original models (Chapters 4 and 6); critical surveys of the theoretical literature from the perspective of developing countries (Chapters 5 and 9); and statistical analyses (Chapters 1, 7 and 8). The more theoretically-inclined contributions have different attitudes to mainstream theory: while Tan adopts an orthodox perspective, Bhaduri at the other extreme presents a very heterodox model, while the remaining authors fall somewhere in between. Most are sceptical of neoclassical orthodoxy, although they take care to give it a fair exposition, and draw several important insights from it even if they criticize it. The opportunities and threats of a deeper integration into global economic activities are a recurring theme in all the papers, as is the need to reorient teaching and research in developing countries so as to comprehend this process. We hope the book will be of help to researchers, teachers, and students in developing countries who are looking for alternatives to textbooks and journals emanating from the developed world.

1

# Can Russia Survive the IMF Medicine?

*Nirmal Kumar Chandra*

## INTRODUCTION

Russia today is a byword for political and economic disaster. It is a unique case of *katastroika*; the polity and the economy were restructured in such a manner that it led to catastrophe in practically every conceivable sphere—ethical, social, political, and economic. Few will doubt that the contemporary tragedy had its roots in the Soviet epoch though there are violent disagreements among analysts about its 'true' causes and the exact moment when the rot set in. The 1917 revolution, Stalin's forced collectivization, Khrushchev's de-Stalinization, the removal of Khrushchev by the Brezhnev group, Gorbachev's *glasnost* and *perestroika*—each of these major events in Soviet history has been identified as the turning point by different writers.

The question of the turning point may appear to be an esoteric issue that is better left to historians and other specialists, and has little relevance to 'what needs to be done now'. However, the dominant 'Washington consensus' on Russia is firmly rooted in Hayek's axiom that socialism is unworkable, and hence the Soviet planned economy was doomed to extinction. It follows that once such an economy is in the throes of death, any salvage operation comparable to the Marshall Plan that revived West Europe shattered by World War II, would be counter-productive. For, a similar aid to Russia might leave intact a large number of socialist institutions and thus impede any eventual restructuring. It is no wonder that the joint report of the International Monetary Fund (IMF), World Bank, Organization for Economic Cooperation and Development (OECD), and the European Bank for

Reconstruction and Development (EBRD) (IMF et al. 1991) prepared at the request of the Soviet authorities, categorically rejected the agenda of gradual reform in favour of the big bang. It was admitted that radical reforms might lead to a significant decline in output and consumption in the short-to-medium term, but ultimately the rejuvenated market economy would move on to a higher growth trajectory. The forecast, it has repeatedly been claimed, followed Schumpeter's famous theory of depression as a phase when 'the gale of creative destruction' clears the ground for many-sided progress during the boom that inevitably follows.

From the very outset of the transition from socialism, there were many critical voices. Among the more powerful ones was that of Alec Nove (1994). After two years of reform in Russia, he saw evidence of the destruction of productive forces, with no sign whatever of any new creativity along the Schumpeterian line. One year later, a group of leading West European economists with a social-democratic persuasion strongly criticized the IMF for its transition policy in Eastern Europe and the former Soviet Union (Eatwell et al. 1995, p. 6). They lamented that the 'policy debate over the past six years has been dominated by disagreement' over 'shock therapy' and 'gradualism', although that 'particular debate was now a piece of transition pre-history. . . . The question is what to do next.'

After the Korean crisis of 1997 the debate has taken a new turn. Many economists who formed part of the 'Washington consensus' sharply attacked the IMF conditionalities imposed on South Korea, a country hailed till then by all concerned as a miracle economy worthy of emulation by all developing nations. Most of these economists, such as J. Sachs, M. Feldstein, and J. Bhagwati, confined themselves to Korea, as they had earlier supported similar IMF conditionalities for countries such as Russia and India. An important exception was J.E. Stiglitz, then Vice-President of the World Bank, who castigated the IMF for the poverty of the underlying economic theory and the shoddy quality of the country reports that formed the basis of the IMF policy package for the indebted countries. He went on to reveal for the first time how the recommendations of a group of leading American economists such as Kenneth Arrow, himself, and others, for a gradual reform of the Soviet economy were jettisoned by the US Department of Treasury on grounds of *realpolitik* and shock therapy became the new *mantra* in Washington circles (*The Economist*, 18 September 1999; Stiglitz 2000b).

Back in 1993, I wrote a piece on Russia's 'sinking economy' (Chandra 1993), and followed it with another on the multiple dimensions of the crisis from which there appeared to be no issue so long as neoliberal reforms continued (Chandra 1996). Subsequent developments have amply confirmed the scepticism and the present essay is a continuation of the same argument with new data and analysis. Here I first look at the macroeconomic trends, focusing on the extent of the output fall and the changes in income distribution in Russia since 1992. Next I take up for separate discussion the magnitude and causes of capital flight, which has been crippling the economy. In the next section, a key institutional feature of new Russia, namely, the all-pervasive role of criminal groups reaching to the highest levels of the government, is highlighted. The following section briefly explores the unique demographic crisis confronting Russia. The final section examines the economic programme of President Putin announced in mid-2000, and a set of radical measures proposed by a group of distinguished Russian and American economists. I also argue that the systemic debate mentioned at the outset of this paper remains a live issue.

## MAIN ECONOMIC INDICATORS

We first look at the economy up to 1999 and then consider the situation in 2000 when there was apparently a significant improvement. Russia's gross domestic product (GDP) began its monotonic descent in 1989 and continued up to 1996, though at varying rates. The index (with 1991=100) went flat at about 60, and stayed there till 1999. Industrial output declined simultaneously though somewhat more steeply to a range of 46-50 during 1995-9. Agricultural crop output declined at a slower rate, but livestock output steadily went down to an index of 48 in 1999.

From the early 1990s, critics have claimed that the official estimates do not take into account the 'shadow' economy for which unofficial estimates were made in different quarters. A widely respected scholar, Kaser (1999) presented estimates showing that Russia's 1998 GDP exceeded that of 1991. He extrapolated to 1998 the share of the informal sector not included in the 1995 official GDP; the ratio was taken from *Transition Report, 1997* of the EBRD. Actually, current Russian official data do include the shadow economy. In the new methodology for national income estimates (Goskomstat 1998a, pp. 15-17), production covers 'productive activity' of households, whether

TABLE 1.1: RUSSIA'S GDP AND SELECTED COMPONENTS (INDICES 1990=100)

| | 1991 | 1992 | 1993 | 1994 | 1995 | 1996 | 1997 | 1998 | 1999 |
|---|---|---|---|---|---|---|---|---|---|
| GDP | 95 | 81 | 74 | 65 | 62 | 60 | 61 | 58 | 59 |
| Industrial product | 92 | 75 | 65 | 51 | 50 | 48 | 49 | 46 | 50 |
| Agricultural product | 96 | 87 | 83 | 73 | 67 | 64 | 65 | 56 | 57 |
| Crops | 100 | 95 | 92 | 83 | 79 | 79 | 85 | 66 | 72 |
| Livestock | 93 | 82 | 77 | 67 | 60 | 54 | 51 | 50 | 48 |
| Freight transport | 93 | 80 | 70 | 61 | 60 | 57 | 55 | 53 | 56 |
| Retail trade | 97 | 94 | 96 | 96 | 89 | 89 | 92 | 89 | 82 |

SOURCE: Goskomstat (1998b), Table (7.1). for the years to 1995, and Goskomstat (2000) for the rest.

for sale or not, and includes crops grown on individual plots, construction on own account, and different services performed as a side activity. In household services for own consumption is included notional rent from own houses. Production also covers 'hidden and informal' activities that would otherwise be subjected to taxes and other obligations. Measurement is indirect—by the application of the balance method, other sector-specific methods and expert evaluation. Gross domestic product, by both production and expenditure methods, is corrected upwards by 20-5 per cent. Illegal activities are, however, not captured in the GDP estimates. Non-market goods and services are valued at either the market prices for comparable items, or the costs incurred by the suppliers. These changes came about in response to the earlier criticisms. Goskomstat made an upward revision of the GDP for all the years since the late 1980s. In essence, to the shadow economy was attributed the difference between the 'aggregate demand' as revealed by the data on household expenditure, etc., and the 'reported output' of firms. The revisions show that the GDP had attained its peak in 1989, and not 1991 as was earlier believed (Broeck and Koen 2000, p. 9). With 1989=100, the GDP index for 1996 turns out to be 58, and that for 1998 is 56. In other words, in post-reform Russia, the GDP was nearly halved by 1998.

While noting that the GDP might ignore the informal sector, Stiglitz (1999, p. 46) felt that since barter is widespread, the reported value of the transactions might be inflated. Gaddy and Ickes (1999) observed that barter accounted for more than one-half of the payments among industrial enterprises, going up to 73 per cent for the large ones. While they paid 80 per cent of their tax dues to the federal government, only 8 per cent was in the form of cash. Further, the prices charged in barter transactions exceed the market prices by a factor of two or three, and up to five times in sales through promissory notes. 'Since the reported value of the nation's economic product is based on these inflated prices, Russia's GDP may be even smaller than official figures suggest, even after taking into account the underreporting of the hidden economy.'

I believe that Gaddy and Ickes have wrongly interpreted the current Goskomstat methodology. If 'reported outputs' were measured at inflated barter prices, their sum might exceed 'aggregate demand' obtained from household expenditure surveys, etc. Consequently, the shadow economy would make a negative contribution to the GDP. But that is nobody's case. The puzzle disappears if barter transactions are evaluated at prevailing market prices. I am not sure that the 'notional' or 'corrected' barter price ought to be lower than the market price because producers failed to find cash buyers for their products. That certainly is not the case with 'natural monopolies' like oil or gas suppliers who could easily export at a higher price. On the other hand, for non-market services like education and health provided by the government, the cost of supply might be overstated due to the wage arrears, implying that Russia's GDP is inflated. But the shadow economy may be larger than is shown in official data. Do these cancel each other?

Khanin and Suslov (1999) suggest a slightly sharper fall in GDP in 1993-6 by 48 per cent, as against 40 per cent in Table 1.1. For 1999, Khanin (2000, cited by Ellman 2000b) doubts if the GDP rose at all. From my perspective, the difference between the two sets of figures is hardly of any importance. I may add that in its country report on Russia, the IMF (2000a, p. 59) states: 'There is no hard evidence at hand to conclude that, on balance, there is a systematic bias in the official GDP estimates.'

According to many neoliberal writers, the welfare implications of the contraction in output are not clear-cut. A good part of the Soviet-era GDP had a negative welfare, such as the production of the military-industrial complex and the polluting industries in the civilian sectors, e.g. nuclear energy or plants belching hazardous smoke and spewing foul smell. Ericson (1998) takes an extreme position, claiming that for over 70 years resources were poured by the Soviets into unviable industries rotten to the core with obsolete technology. 'A large proportion of firms in any industry and all firms in some basic industries are non-viable in the most basic sense—they could never produce goods that could sell for more than the cost of production.'

The report on Russia by McKinsey (MGI 1999), the American consulting group, after an in-depth techno-economic survey over 12 months in 1998-9, flatly contradicts the stereotyped Western view that Soviet industry was hopelessly backward. It was found that despite 8-9 years of low capacity utilization and practically no fresh investments, three-fourths of the Soviet-era fixed assets could become competitive by international standards with additional investments amounting to just 5 per cent of value-added. In priority sectors favoured by the planners there was hardly any technological gap, and elsewhere the gap could be easily overcome with small outlays. As I have discussed the report at some length elsewhere (Chandra 2001), I shall not go further into the matter.

Returning to the contemporary Russian economy, one feature deserves special attention. From Table 1.2a it can be seen that domestic demand over time has fallen more rapidly than the GDP, the indices for the former being consistently lower. The percentage share of domestic demand in the GDP (Table 1.2b) took a nosedive in 1991-2 and again in 1997-9, reflecting the country's dependence on export. Thus the export-GDP ratio in those critical years jumped from 0.14 in 1991 to 0.64 in 1992 and from 0.23 in 1997 to 0.43 in 1999. I shall come back to the issue later.

From a long-term perspective, more ominous than the fall in GDP is the fact that fixed capital formation has witnessed a much more severe contraction; the volumes for 1998 and 1999 were well under one-fifth of that in 1990 (see Table 1.2a). Actually, very little investment took place in the last decade. Official data indicate that the percentage of end-year fixed assets at constant prices, excluding cattle, renewed each year broadly equalled the percentage written off during the same year (Goskomstat 1999, Table 3.9). Indeed, considering the old accounting norms and the gross underutilization of fixed assets, it is more than likely that either the renewals did not cover all 'unserviceable' assets or that future maintenance costs for equipment will be much higher than 'normal'. A recent estimate by a committee, including economists like Abalkin, Glaz'ev, and others (Anon. 2000), of the 'wear and tear' (*iznos*) of machinery in Russian industry puts the percentage at 68.3 for 1998. These estimates are on the high side compared to those of McKinsey cited above. In any case, considerable outlays on maintenance and replacement are needed to bring the Russian production capacity back to the pre-reform level.

TABLE 1.2a: GDP AND SELECTED EXPENDITURE GROUPS

*(Indices 1990=100)*

| | 1991 | 1992 | 1993 | 1994 | 1995 | 1996 | 1997 | 1998 | 1999 |
|---|---|---|---|---|---|---|---|---|---|
| GDP | 95.4 | 81.5 | 75.3 | 66.5 | 63.5 | 59.2 | 59.8 | 56.5 | 58.3 |
| Domestic demand | 96.0 | 79.7 | 69.4 | 61.4 | 58.3 | 53.9 | 54.6 | 49.6 | 48.9 |
| Total Consumption | 93.9 | 89.0 | 88.1 | 85.4 | 83.1 | 80.5 | 82.9 | 81.0 | 78.2 |
| Households | 95.4 | 92.5 | 93.6 | 94.8 | 92.1 | 87.8 | 92.5 | 89.2 | 84.5 |
| Capital Investment | 84.5 | 49.4 | 36.7 | 27.1 | 25.1 | 20.3 | 19.1 | 17.0 | 17.4 |

TABLE 1.2b: PERCENTAGE SHARE OF SELECTED EXPENDITURE GROUPS IN THE GDP

| | 1991 | 1992 | 1993 | 1994 | 1995 | 1996 | 1997 | 1998 | 1999 |
|---|---|---|---|---|---|---|---|---|---|
| Domestic demand | 100 | 85 | 92 | 95 | 97 | 96 | 97 | 93 | 84 |
| Total Consumption | 63 | 50 | 64 | 70 | 71 | 71 | 75 | 77 | 69 |
| Households | 41 | 34 | 41 | 44 | 49 | 49 | 50 | 54 | 50 |
| Capital Investment | 24 | 25 | 21 | 22 | 21 | 21 | 19 | 17 | 16 |
| Export of Goods & Services | 14 | 64 | 39 | 28 | 28 | 25 | 23 | 31 | 43 |

SOURCE: IMF (2000b), Table 2.

Another crucial variable, R & D outlays (see Table 1.3), points to an equally bleak future. Compared to 1990, expenditure in real terms fell to just 27 per cent in 1997. In terms of 'international dollars' or the purchasing power parity between the rouble and the dollar, total expenditure declined from 29.0 billion dollars to 7.6 billion dollars between 1990 and 1995. The amount should be considerably lower by now, and probably less than the sums spent by some of the largest global firms. The picture appears to be less bleak if one looks at the size of the R & D personnel that shrank from 1.5 to 0.9 million during 1992-7, or by 39 per cent. The number of researchers, however, dwindled faster by 44 per cent over the same period. Although data are not readily available, there is some evidence that R & D outlays on 'material' items like books, journals, laboratory inputs, equipment, etc., have been compressed to a far greater extent than total outlays. What do the remaining scientists do in this situation? Anecdotes suggest that low pay and meagre rewards compel them to seek second or third jobs, leaving little time for 'real' research. In other words, the statistical picture tends to underestimate the depth of crisis facing Russian science and technology.

With investments declining more rapidly than the GDP, household consumption was maintained at a relatively high level (see Table 1.2a). That is not at all unusual. During the Great Depression of the 1930s in USA, the percentage fall in personal disposable income amounted to 25 as against a 19 per cent fall in personal consumption between 1929 and the trough of 1933 (USA 1967, p. 319). What is rather 'strange' in the Russian case is that all through the 1990s barring 1999, household consumption stayed at around 90 per cent of the previous peak, while the GDP was almost halved. In 1999, consumption was still high at 85 per cent.

Just as abnormal is the trend in household savings. In the USA, personal net savings in relation to disposable personal income fell from 5.0 in 1929 to 2.0 per cent in 1933. In Russia, however, household savings rate as a percentage of their money income stood at an unusually high 24 per cent in 1992 when the income (as compared to 1991) dropped by as much 48 per cent in real terms. The high savings rates continued till 1997, but came down significantly in the wake of the 1998 crisis (Table 1.4). All through, the dominant part of savings went towards the acquisition of foreign currencies or assets, which will be further examined later. Clearly, all this reflects the worsening distribution of income in Russia.

While the overall consumption level was maintained, the real income of households, wages and pensions fell sharply (see Table 1.5). During the very first year of reform in 1992, the 'shock therapy' slashed income by 48 per cent, wages by 33 per cent, and pensions by 48 per cent. There was a partial recovery in later years, but the 1999 levels were 56-68 per cent below the benchmark year of 1991.

Alongside falling wages, the Russian workers have faced a rising rate of unemployment since 1992 (Table 1.6). The number (in million) of actual workers fell from a 1990 peak of 75.3 million to a low of

TABLE 1.3: DOMESTIC R & D EXPENDITURE (DRDE) AND PERSONNEL

| | 1990 | 1991 | 1992 | 1993 | 1994 | 1995 | 1996 | 1997 |
|---|---|---|---|---|---|---|---|---|
| DRDE as % of GDP | 2.03 | 1.43 | 0.74 | 0.77 | 0.84 | 0.77 | 0.88 | 0.94 |
| DRDE volume indices | 100 | 66.5 | 28.7 | 27.7 | 26.4 | 22.2 | 24.2 | 27.8 |
| DRDE in $ bn PPP | 28.99 | 19.85 | 9.41 | 9.15 | 9.08 | 7.63 | | |
| All R & D personnel | | | 1533 | 1315 | 1106 | 1061 | 991 | 935 |
| Researchers only | | | 804 | 645 | 525 | 519 | 485 | 455 |

SOURCES: OECD (1999), Table 1, and Goskomstat (1998 b), Table 21.4.

TABLE 1.4: HOUSEHOLD INCOME (HHI), SAVINGS (HHS), AND FOREIGN CURRENCY PURCHASES (FCP)

| | 1992 | 1993 | 1994 | 1995 | 1996 | 1997 | 1998 | 1999 | 2000 |
|---|---|---|---|---|---|---|---|---|---|
| Real HHI* | -47.5 | 16.4 | 12.9 | -15.1 | 0.1 | 5.3 | -16.3 | -14.8 | 7.2 |
| HHS/HHI# | 23.9 | 23.5 | 28.7 | 23.9 | 24.7 | 25.0 | 15.5 | 13.7 | 13.9 |
| FCP/HHI# | 0.5 | 8.0 | 17.7 | 14.8 | 18.8 | 21.2 | 12.6 | 8.2 | 7.1 |
| FCP $ bn | | 6.5 | 29.5 | 29.6 | 49.3 | 60.1 | 22.0 | 9.3 | 9.2 |

NOTES: * percentage change over the previous year.
# percentages.

SOURCES: Goskomstat (1999) and CBR (2000) for HHI, HHS, and FCP; *International Financial Statistics*, various issues, for average annual exchange rate.

TABLE 1.5: REAL INCOME, WAGE AND PENSION (INDICES 1991=100)

| | 1992 | 1993 | 1994 | 1995 | 1996 | 1997 | 1998 | 1999 |
|---|---|---|---|---|---|---|---|---|
| Income | 52.5 | 61.1 | 69.0 | 58.6 | 58.6 | 61.7 | 51.7 | 44.0 |
| Wage | 67.0 | 67.3 | 62.0 | 44.7 | 47.4 | 49.6 | 43.0 | 33.2 |
| Pension | 52.0 | 68.1 | 66.1 | 53.5 | 58.3 | 55.4 | 52.7 | 32.1 |

NOTE: Real wage in 1991 was 3 per cent below 1990.

SOURCES: Goskomstat (1998b), Tables 1.2, 8.1, and 8.3 till 1995, and Goskomstat (2000) for the rest.

TABLE 1.6: EMPLOYMENT AND UNEMPLOYMENT

*(in millions)*

| | 1991 | 1992 | 1993 | 1994 | 1995 | 1996 | 1997 | 1998 | 1999 |
|---|---|---|---|---|---|---|---|---|---|
| Employed | 73.80 | 72.07 | 70.85 | 68.48 | 66.44 | 65.95 | 64.64 | 63.64 | 64.50 |
| Unemployed | | 3.59 | 4.16 | 5.48 | 6.43 | 7.18 | 7.80 | 9.30 | 8.50 |
| Labour force | | 75.67 | 75.01 | 73.96 | 72.88 | 73.23 | 72.82 | 72.24 | 73.80 |
| Unemployment rate (%) | | 4.7 | 5.5 | 7.4 | 8.8 | 9.6 | 10.8 | 11.9 | 12.6 |
| Hidden unemployment | | | | | | | | | |
| No. on short work-day | | | 1.13 | 4.38 | 2.05 | 3.21 | 2.00 | 3.35 | 2.49 |
| Unemployed | | | 0.23 | 0.88 | 0.41 | 0.64 | 0.40 | 0.67 | 0.50 |
| No. on forced leave | | | 3.32 | 6.60 | 2.13 | 2.13 | 1.53 | 3.87 | 2.65 |
| Average leave (days) per quarter | | | 21.2 | 30.3 | 10.8 | 10.8 | 10.0 | 27.8 | 24.8 |
| Unemployed | | | 0.94 | 2.66 | 0.31 | 0.30 | 0.20 | 1.43 | 0.88 |
| Overall unemployment | | | 5.33 | 9.02 | 7.15 | 8.13 | 8.40 | 11.40 | 9.88 |
| Do as % of Labour force | | | 7.1 | 12.2 | 9.8 | 11.1 | 11.5 | 15.8 | 13.4 |

SOURCES: Goskomstat (1998b), Tables 1.1 and 7.1; IMF (2000b), Table 8.

63.6 million after the 1998 crisis, but rose by 0.9 million in 1999. However, not all those on the payroll of firms are actually engaged on a full-time basis. 'Hidden unemployment' is widespread; many work fewer days per year than usual, while others are forced to go on leave. These arrangements are often mutually beneficial. Employers save wholly or partially on the wage-bill, and workers prefer to be nominally employed rather than join the ranks of the unemployed at a time when jobs are scarce and the doles are meagre for those registered as unemployed.

Official data indicate the number of workers who are on short workdays, but not the extent of the shortfall. To be on the conservative side, I reckon the shortfall to be no more than 20 per cent of the workdays so that one-fifth of these workers are deemed to be unemployed. Further, while the data for 1994 cover the whole period, those for other years pertain to the end of each quarter. By averaging the quarterly data I obtain the annual figures. As for the workers on forced leave, I again use the quarterly average both for the number of workers and the average number of days of forced leave. I assume that the usual number of workdays is 75 per quarter and estimate the number unemployed on this count. One must add a caveat here. The figures on hidden unemployment do not cover all sectors, notably agriculture that employed about 14 per cent of the workforce (Goskomstat 1999, Table 7.3). Considering both unemployment according to the definition given by the International Labour Organization (ILO), and hidden unemployment, its percentage in the labour force shot up from 7.1 in 1993 to 12.2 in the next year, fell in 1995, but went on rising to a peak of 15.8 in the crisis year of 1998. Though the rate fell in 1999, it was significantly above the pre-crisis level. Two further points deserve attention. While the working-age population rose slowly from 84 to 85.6 million in 1991-8, actual employment shrank by over 9 million from 73.8 million to 63.6 million. Further, the labour force (the sum of the employed and the unemployed) dwindled by 3.5 million. These persons were neither at work nor seeking work. In times of general penury the withdrawal of so many persons from the labour market could hardly have been voluntary. If one adds this number, overall unemployment at the end of 1998 would go up to 14.5 million or 19 per cent of the augmented labour force. In 1999 the situation improved a little, the corresponding figures being 13.3 million and 17.5 per cent.

Rosefielde (2000) puts the 'missing' number of jobseekers in the civilian labour force even higher at 7.9 million. This is based on the US Bureau of Census forecast in 1988 for the USSR over the period 1985-98. As for Russia, the forecast for 1990 stood at 75.7 million and coincided with the actual Soviet figure; it was to rise to 81.4 million in 1998. Allowing for the decline in Russia's working age population not foreseen earlier, and the transfer of defence personnel to the civilian labour force, the size of the latter in 1998 should have been 81 million, but the number employed was only 63.4 million. Hence the jobless totalled 17.6 million, or 21.7 per cent of the augmented labour force.

Tikhomirov (2000) believes that the rate of unemployment is even higher; if employment fell in step with the GDP, only 43.4 million would be employed in 1998 as against the actual 64.1 million. This, however, is not a meaningful approach. Nowhere does employment vary directly with output; typically, the former expands (contracts) more slowly than output in the upswing (downswing).

Another post-Soviet curse is poverty. It is not that everyone was above the poverty threshold before the reform, but the picture is qualitatively different. Milanovich (1998, pp. 66-8) from the World Bank defined poverty as per capita daily income below 4 'international' dollars of 1990, and estimated that only 2 per cent of the Russians were poor in 1987-8, as against 50 per cent during 1993-5, the absolute numbers being 2.2 million and 74.2 million respectively. The threshold of poverty corresponds to the Russian official 'minimum subsistence level' of July 1993; the rouble value is converted into dollars at the current purchasing power parity. Using appropriate price deflators the dollar threshold is put at US$ 4 of 1990. Ellman (2000a) thinks that poverty in the late 1980s was somewhat higher, but agrees that it has risen dramatically since 1992.

Official estimates (see Table 1.7) are considerably lower than those of Milanovich and show that the poverty ratio or the percentage of the population with an income below the subsistence minimum stood at 33.5 per cent in 1992, gradually fell to 20.8 per cent in 1997, and then rose again to 29.9 per cent in 1999; in this case, the minimum is determined by the government as a fixed basket of goods and services. But the official data may not be reliable. The Russian Longitudinal Monitoring Survey (RLMS) utilized the official poverty threshold, and adjusted the raw family-wise data for regional price differences, household types, and 'equivalent scales'. These are also given in Table 1.7. Instead of declining as in the official estimate, the poverty ratio went up sharply from 11 to 36 per cent between 1992 and 1996. The percentage for 'extreme' poverty, defined as one-half the poverty-level income, also went up steeply over the same period from 3 to 20.

As a corollary to low wages and high unemployment, income distribution has become much more skewed. The decile ratio for household incomes, i.e. the ratio of the top to the bottom 10 per cent of households, rose dramatically from 4.3 in 1991 to 15.6 in 1993, but fell to 10.4 in 1997. The Gini coefficient over the same years also rose steeply from 0.26 to 0.40 and 0.38 respectively. The coefficient in 1999 was marginally higher at 0.39.

On the latest post-crisis period, the IMF (2000a, p. 36) finds that Russia's 'macroeconomic performance has been impressive, with a strong output recovery and a notable measure of financial stability'. This appears to be confirmed by Table 1.8. GDP, output in basic sectors (industry, construction, agriculture, transport and retail trade), fixed investment and foreign trade—all went up markedly. The retail trade index also went up. Real wages and real income of households rose significantly, but the number unemployed (by the ILO definition) fell by just 9 per cent. Exports registered a dramatic increase while imports showed a modest rise.

A good part of the GDP growth in 2000 is due to the export sector. The weakness of domestic demand is reflected in the much slower rise in import. This underlines the vulnerability of the economy to external factors. A closer look at export performance brings out its limitations (see Table 1.9). Export growth was mainly propelled by the spurt in oil prices. Oil, oil products, and natural gas contributed

TABLE 1.7: INCOME DISTRIBUTION AND POVERTY RATIOS

| | 1991 | 1992 | 1993 | 1994 | 1995 | 1996 | 1997 | 1998 | 1999 |
|---|---|---|---|---|---|---|---|---|---|
| Gini coeff. | 0.26 | 0.289 | 0.398 | 0.409 | 0.381 | 0.375 | 0.381 | 0.398 | 0.394 |
| Decile ratio* | 4.28 | 8.17 | 15.55 | 9.41 | 9.96 | 9.6 | 10.4 | | |
| Poverty ratios** | | | | | | | | | |
| Official | | 33.50 | 31.5 | 22.4 | 24.7 | 22.1 | 20.8 | 23.4 | 29.9 |
| RLMS-I@ | | 11.10 | 13.1 | 17.2 | 29.5 | 36.1 | | | |
| RLMS-II# | | 3.00 | 5.6 | 6.9 | 11.5 | 20 | | | |

NOTES: * Ratio of the income of the top to the bottom decile of the population.
** Percentage below the subsistence minimum.
@ Using the official poverty line.
# At one-half of subsistence income.

SOURCES: IMF (2000a), Table 16; Goskomstat (1998b), Table 8.24; Goskomstat (2000); Zohoori (1998).

TABLE 1.8: PERCENTAGE CHANGES 1999-2000

| | | | |
|---|---|---|---|
| GDP[1*] | 7.1 | Real wage[1*] | 20.5 |
| Basic industries[1*] | 8.4 | Household real income[2@] | 9.1 |
| Industry[3] | 9.6 | No. unemployed[4] | -18.5 |
| Fixed investment[1*] | 17.7 | No. of poor[2##] | 36.8 |
| Retail trade[2] | 7.1 | | |
| Export[1#] | 37.5 | Import[1#] | 11.0 |

NOTES: * Forecast for year ** Jan.-Nov. # Jan.-Sept.
## Q3 2000/1999 @ End-June 2000/end-1999

SOURCES: 1. EEG (2001)
2. Goskomstat (2000)
3. *Russia: Daily Business Brief*, 1 March 2001, <www.russiatoday.com>;
4. CBR (2000).

TABLE 1.9: EXPORT AND IMPORT (*$ billion*)

| | 1992 | 1993 | 1994 | 1995 | 1996 | 1997 | 1998 | 1999 |
|---|---|---|---|---|---|---|---|---|
| Export | 53.6 | 59.6 | 67.8 | 82.7 | 90.6 | 89 | 74.9 | 75.3 |
| Oil & gas | | | 25.2 | 30.4 | 38.1 | 38.4 | 27.5 | 30.2 |
| Others | | | 42.6 | 52.3 | 52.5 | 50.6 | 47.4 | 45.1 |
| Import | 43.0 | 44.3 | 48.5 | 64.0 | 72.8 | 71.6 | 57.8 | 39.5 |

SOURCES: Goskomstat (1998b), Table 25.2; IMF (2000b), Table 37.

as much as 75 per cent of the incremental export of goods and services in January-September 2000 (EEG 2001, p. 33). However, overall export in 2000 was only 15 per cent higher than in 1996, which gives a compound growth rate of just 3.5 per cent per year. Other commodities did register a significant 19 per cent rise in export, but the expected level in 2000 should not exceed the 1996 peak by more than 2.3 per cent, implying an annual 0.5 per cent growth. As for domestic output, the GDP remains below the 1994 level, and industrial production is just above that. Retail trade volume, real wages, and real income of households have yet to recapture the pre-crisis (1997) threshold, while the number of unemployed stands above the 1996 or earlier figures. Interestingly, although employment expanded by 1.1 million, as many as 0.4 million persons dropped out of the labour force altogether during the year. The official poverty ratio shot up from 29.9 per cent to 41.2 per cent during 1999-2000. Thus, in practically all respects the Russian economy continues to operate at way below the Soviet era levels, and there is no sign of it getting out of the transformational tunnel.

The IMF has been particularly happy over the recent improvement in government finances. Thus total revenue as a percentage of the GDP rose from 11.0 in 1998 (against 12.3 in 1997) to 13.4 in 1999, and 17.3 in January-June 2000. Moreover, the cash component (non-barter) of total revenue rose from 41.5 per cent to 46.6 per cent in 1998-9. Simultaneously, total expenditure as a percentage of the GDP fell from 19.0 in 1997 to 14.8 in 1999 and 13.8 (projected) in 2000 (IMF 2000a, Table 7).

From a Keynesian perspective though, the same figures tell a different story. Starting with the pre-crisis year of 1997, the percentage of direct taxes (on profits of firm and personal incomes) to the GDP rose from 1.4 to 2.7 (projected) in 1997-2000, while that of indirect taxes rose much faster from 10.9 per cent to 13.6 per cent; or, three-fourths of the incremental revenue came from the latter source, accentuating the inequality in the distribution of income. Further, government expenditure on heads other than the servicing of loans shrank in 1997-2000, from 14.3 per cent to 10.8 (projected) per cent of the GDP. The budget surplus was used to meet the demands of creditors (domestic and foreign), leaving little scope for the government to spend on social sectors or on investment.

## CAPITAL FLIGHT

A malignant development in post-reform Russia is the enormous capital flight. Barely one year after the reforms started, the Opposition drew attention to it, but the measures taken so far by the government to check it have been rather haphazard and cosmetic. Loungani and Mauro (2000) have succinctly summarized the measures, and conclude that some outflows may have been halted, but when powerful interests were involved the restrictions were of no avail. Loungani and Mauro proceeded to give their own estimate of capital flight amounting to an annual $15 billion in 1994-8, which they believe is close to the estimates of Tikhomirov (1997) and of Loukine.

Loungani and Mauro prefer two measures of capital flight—'hot money' (HM) 1 and 2. The first consists of 'errors and omissions' in Russia's balance of payments plus increase in net assets held abroad by Russians other than the government and the banks. The second includes the incremental assets of Russian banks. Information on both counts are obtained from the IMF's *International Financial Statistics.* It is not clear if the figure of $15 billion refers to HM-1 or to HM-2. If it refers to both, then there would be no incremental net assets held abroad by Russian banks. Is that plausible?

In describing the modes of capital flight, Loungani and Mauro repeat all the points made by the Russian Opposition as well as earlier scholars. The fuel sector is a major source for capital flight. Quantities exported may be fudged, the unit-values understated, and there may be plain smuggling—all because of the collapse of the Russian state and corruption creeping up to the top of the administrative pyramid. Similarly, fake imports and inflated imported bills are quite common. As regards financial transactions, many Russian firms and banks had offshore links in tax havens, while several banks were 'correspondents' of established Western banks. As a result, regulations could be bypassed. Loungani and Mauro mention anecdotal evidence that a significant part of 'foreign' investments in GKO (Russian Treasury bonds) and the domestic equity market actually came from Russian residents.

In this complex situation it is strange that Loungani and Mauro rely on the figures of Russia's official balance of payments. One needs a heroic assumption that all the transactions just noted are covered by 'errors and omissions'. This last is actually in the nature of statistical discrepancy between inflows and outflows as recorded. If there are no records, and that is true in most cases for Russia, the measure of capital flight by Loungani and Mauro should understate the 'true' volume.

Tikhomirov examined the trade flows including barter trade, trade with CIS countries, and unregistered import in 1992-5, focusing on underpricing of exports and overpricing of imports in respect of specific commodities. His own estimate came to nearly $63 billion over the four years. It is not clear if export smuggling was taken into account. In any case, capital flight through primarily financial transactions was not analysed.

More comprehensive than this is the joint study over a period of two years by the Institute of Economics, Moscow and the University of Western Ontario, summarized by Abalkin and Whalley (1999). They estimated that since 1994, Russian residents had amassed abroad assets worth $68 billion at end-September 1997. The corresponding estimates for 1992 and 1993 were in the range of $56-70 billion. Thus the total stock in 1997 was $125-40 billion. In addition, there was internal capital flight or dollarization of the Russian economy. Foreign currency deposits in Russian banks and other financial institution rose from $3.7 billion at end-1992 to $79.4 at end-

September 1997; holdings of foreign currency in cash simultaneously went up from 2.1 to 171.7 billion dollars. Thus internal capital flight in 1992-7 totalled $245.3 billion and total leakage covering both types of capital flight ranged from 370 to 385 billion dollars. The authors also cite some estimates by Russian authorities, e.g. $200 billion in 1992-6 by the Duma's Committee on National Security and $230 billion in 1992-7 by the Ministry of Finance. For the period 1990-5 Tikhomirov also cited a range of estimates varying from 35 to 400 billion dollars.

All these estimates contain a large degree of error, which no amount of hard work can remove altogether. On the whole, the estimates of Abalkin and Whalley are nearer the mark from an economic point of view. Further, although illegal and semi-legal activities generated 70 per cent of the 1997 stock abroad, the remaining 30 per cent was probably legal.

Ordinary law-abiding Russians have seen their accumulated savings evaporate into thin air as a result of the hyperinflation after the price reform of early 1992 and hence tend to convert savings into dollars as a hedge against inflation and devaluation. The purchases (in $ billion) peaked at 60 in 1997, and then fell sharply to 22, 9.3, and 9.2 respectively during 1998-2000. Whether legal or not, all purchases of foreign currency constitute a leakage from the circular flow of income in Russia, amounting to about one-fifth of household incomes in 1996-7 and 7-8 per cent in 1999-2000. (CBR 2000-1) From 1993 to 2000 dollar savings by households (see Table 4) totalled $215 billion. In the absence of dollarization, these savings could be channelled into productive investments in the economy.

What makes the Russian case unique is the sheer size of the outflow, exceeding by far that from the Latin American countries in the 1980s. What is its relation to the GDP? Due to the volatility of the exchange rate, the latter measured at the nominal exchange rate fluctuated wildly, amounting (in $ billion) to 421, 435, 278 and 185 respectively during 1996-9. For 2000, the projected rouble value in IMF (2000a, Table 5) converted at 28.1 roubles per dollar comes to $228 billion. If one takes a 'reference' GDP of, say, $300 billion, the assets held abroad (in the estimate of Abalkin and Whalley) in 1997 amount to 42-7 per cent of the GDP, to which may be added 82 per cent on account of the internal flight. The overall leakage exceeds by far the 'reference' or the actual values of the GDP since 1998.

## CRIME AND THE STATE

The Russian state, as many writers from within and outside Russia have pointed out, has in effect been captured by vested interests—the oligarchs with strong criminal connections (Ellman 2000a). Trumpeting the success of capitalism in Russia, Aslund (1994, p. 69) wrote sometime ago that 'crime syndicates have benefited from the excessively slow transition to capitalism, but *now capitalism has basically taken hold, making it possible to defeat the mafia*' (Emphasis added). That turned about to be another false prophecy. Six years later Aslund (2000) blamed the mafia and the Russian politicians for the travails of the reform process. Stiglitz (2000a) argues that privatization became a fetish, and the IMF pushed for it at the fastest possible pace even before the institutional prerequisites of a functioning market economy were established. In the process, privatization inevitably led to the creation of financial oligarchs who were close to the authorities and who went on to milch the state.

Unlike most other countries, in Russia 'crime is not at the margin of society; it is at its very centre', as *The Economist* (28 August 1999) put it. The mechanism is described by Jensen (1998) in the following words:

> Many FIG [financial industrial groups] leaders got rich from the privatisation process of 1992–94, when state-owned enterprises were auctioned off. Most [of these] were bought by consortia of managers and workers, though in effect the managers controlled the enterprises. Many managers then sold to or went into partnership with outside interests, including criminal organisations, or sold their interest to FIGs. During this period the government also handed out tax breaks, import-export licenses and other privileges to raw materials exporters, trade and financial interests in order to secure their support in the face of increasing political opposition. In the absence of a strong treasury system, the government ensured large profits for many banks with close ties to the regime by 'authorising' them to manage state funds for a wide variety of government agencies.

For financing Yeltsin's re-election in 1996, Oneksimbank obtained direct representation in the government. Grigoriev (2000) estimated that the proceeds from privatization in $ billion amounted to 3.14 in 1992–6, 4.53 in 1997, and 1.76 in 1998. The total was a small fraction of the actual value of assets running into scores of billions of dollars. It goes without saying that the beneficiaries had the blessings of President Yeltsin. And it is by no means a coincidence that the latter obtained from his successor, President Putin, complete immunity from prosecution for any act committed during his tenure as President.

A few examples of how the state was robbed may suffice. According to Jensen (1998) again,

> the Audit Chamber, the non-partisan, independent state auditor analogous to the US General Accounting Office, has extensively chronicled the pervasiveness of the problem [of corruption]. The chamber recently found that at least one-sixth of Russia's budget in 1997 was misspent due to mismanagement and corruption—a loss of more than $10 billion. The Chamber's head, Venyamin Sokolov . . . surmised that the real amount may have been twice that sum. In 1995 and 1996, he added, 'not a single article of the federal budget law was observed'.

Another report states that of $3 billion earmarked for the reconstruction of Chechnya, only $150 million was actually sent to the war-devastated region, while the rest disappeared mysteriously (Fabre 1999, p. 159). In 1998 the Bank of New York was involved in a scam estimated at $10–15 billion (including $10 billion of IMF credit to Russia), in which a son-in-law of Yeltsin was implicated. As the Russian Procurator Skuratov started investigation, the President forced him to go on vacation, and that was the end of investigations. The Russian Federation Council rejected Yeltsin's demand to sack Skuratov, on three occasions in 1999 but ultimately agreed to Putin's request in April 2000. The US Congress demanded an explanation from President Clinton on the IMF loan, a couple of officers of the Bank of New York were dismissed, but nothing much came of the probe in the USA (Bonnet 1999; Radio Free Europe/Radio Liberty, 6 September 1999 and 20 April 2000). In July 1999, Price Waterhouse confirmed that in 1996, Russia's Central Bank moved $1 billion to its affiliate, Fimaco in the Channel Islands, without informing the IMF. Even then the IMF gave a loan (to service past loans) to Russia of $4.5 billion in mid-1999. IMF officials privately stated that Russia was a special case, and loans were politically motivated, e.g. to help re-elect Yeltsin in 1996 (*The Economist*, 28 August 1999). In the autumn of 2000, George Bush, then presidential candidate, made a similar charge, and Boldyrev, Deputy Chairman of the Russian Audit Chamber, confirmed it over the Moscow Echo Radio. The latter further observed that President Yeltsin rebuffed attempts by Primakov, who became Prime Minister shortly after the August 1998 crisis, to probe corruption in the Kremlin (Radyuhin 2000).

The business environment is described in these words:

> The weakness of the state requires that businesses have a *krysha*—protection—to be able to operate. . . . Often the *krysha* provided by a crime group include other services such as protection of property, debt collection, customs assistance, legal and business advice, and banking privileges at crime-controlled banks. A *krysha* can also include forms of corrupt government, protection involving the militia, tax, police, military, and customs authorities and border guards. (Jensen 1998)

To most neoliberal reformers, the bad guys from Russia were the only ones responsible for the mess. The contribution of Western governments to this state of affairs has been swept under the carpet by the media and most Western scholars. But as Fabre (1999, pp. 155-7) tells us, since the 1988 UN convention on money laundering at Vienna, and the 1989 G-7 Summit where an Action Group on the subject was constituted, there is apparently a general agreement on the need to regulate these activities. The European Union in 1990 resolved to have laws and regulations that would cover all transactions of a criminal nature. But none of the member-states passed enabling laws at the national level. In 1996, 500 European magistrates met at Geneva and called for co-operation among the national judiciaries, and repealing banking secrecy laws to combat money laundering. But the governments lacked the political will and so far no effective steps have been taken.

The manner in which the interests of the Russian mafia–oligarchs and Western governments are intertwined, is spelled out with great clarity by two columnists of *The Times*, Maddox and Kaletsky (1998). Writing just after the August crisis, they argued that the task for Clinton was not to support Yeltsin, but to

> ensure that the inevitably authoritarian and corrupt regime that will replace Yeltsin is more or less responsible, pro-Western and benign. The oligarchs . . . have profited mightily from the political chaos of the Yeltsin years, which allowed them free rein to plunder Russia's natural and financial wealth. . . . Like feudal barons, they will be more than happy to show allegiance to the sovereign with the power and prestige to help them to stabilise their newly acquired financial and political domains. And when they look around the world, there is only one conceivable contender for this sovereign role: the US President.

But the oligarchs remain insecure. Public opinion polls indicate that about one-half of the voting population would support measures to 'seize' the wealth of the 'new' Russians (Shlapentokh 1999, p. 1176). Indeed, the redistribution of wealth was one of the main campaign issues in the presidential election of 2000 (Radvanyi 2000). It is no wonder that the *nouveaux riches* prefer to stash away their wealth outside the country rather than make domestic investments.

## DEMOGRAPHIC CRISIS

There is another time bomb clicking away at the very foundation of Russian society, namely the catastrophic changes in the nation's demographic profile. Thus population fell by 2 million from 148.3 million in 1992 to 146.3 million in 1998 (Goskomstat 1999). It declined further by 0.8 million in 1999. The birth rate per thousand population fell continuously from 13.4 to 8.4 during 1990-9; the mortality rate jumped from 11.2 in 1990 to a peak of 15.7 in 1994, fell to 13.6 in 1998, and rose again to 14.7 in 1999 (Ellman 2000b). Average life expectancy for men and women similarly dropped from 67.9 to 64.0 years during 1992-4, but improved to 67.2 years in 1998 (Goskomstat 1999). Feshbach (1999), a leading American demographer, believes that if the current trends continue, the Russian population around 2050 could come down to nearly one-half or 80 million. 'All experts agree', writes Traynor (2000), 'that [the current trends] cannot be reversed in the short term, and Russian's population will shrink by one-third to 100 million in 2025.'

The term 'genocide' is often used by Russians like the well-known economist, Glaz'ev (cited by Ellman 2000a), a Duma member and social policy expert, A. Aparina, and the former Moscow Mayor Popov who calls it a 'Russian holocaust' (cited by Traynor 2000). The contention cannot be dismissed on the semantic ground that one cannot identify any group of persons that have a stake in the depopulation of Russia comparable to the Nazis in the extermination of the Jews. For Russia the 'culprit' is the invisible 'system', the set of economic policies pursued by the government at the behest of the Washington consensus. The long-run effects are just as crippling.

Contradicting Glaz'ev, Ellman rightly notes that the fall in Russia's birth rate is by no means unprecedented; many industrially mature countries have also experienced it. What is unique about Russia is the *combination* of a falling birth rate (per thousand population) from 15 to 10 in 1970-98, and a rise in death rate over the same years from 9 to 14. For the industrial countries as a whole the corresponding changes were from 17 to 10 in the birth rate, and 10 to 9 in mortality (UNICEF 2000, Table 5). In the familiar demographic transition of developing countries, both the rates fall at different speeds until the population approaches a stable level. But a combination like that of the rates in Russia over the past decade is *unique*. The magnitudes of birth and death rates given above for Russia are somewhat different from the Russian official sources cited earlier, as I felt that for inter-country comparisons the UNICEF data might be more appropriate.

On both birth and death rates, the changes cannot be attributed solely to the neoliberal reforms of the last decade. A recent publication by Goskomstat (1998c) provides long time series on a number of demographic variables, which suggest that there was no 'smooth' trend over the past few decades. This is a complex subject that cannot be examined here in depth.

It is widely acknowledged that though it was free, the Soviet health system was increasingly unable to cope with 'modern' diseases associated with the circulatory or respiratory system, not to speak of cancer. *Ceteris paribus*, the mortality rate should have climbed upward as the median age of the population went up unless the health system was thoroughly revamped. That would require much larger budgetary outlays and/or the creation of an alternative private system. Since the population has been pauperized in the 1990s, the private system can only cater to a tiny minority of the affluent. And the Russian government in the past decade has severely curtailed health expenditure, aggravating the crisis.

A closer look at some of the causes of mortality in the recent past lends further substance to this view. Traynor (2000) makes four points. (*a*) According to the medical journal, *Meditsinskaya gazeta* of May 2000, only one baby out of 10 was born healthy. (*b*) For women, pregnancy and child bearing are about 10 times more dangerous in Russia than in Germany, according to Dr Venonen, head of the WHO in Russia; (*c*) Goskomstat figures indicate that in 1999 poisoning from alcohol caused 7 per cent of all deaths among males aged 20-55 years. In the first 4 months of 2000, death from drinks has soared by 43 per cent year on year. Further, a three-year study by the International Family Research Institute in Moscow found for the same age group that in two-thirds of cases the men had died drunk. Moreover, alcohol plays a big role in suicide (now the third largest killer of middle-aged men), in road accidents, heart disease, and violent deaths. (*d*) A bottle of vodka costs the same as a kilo of apples, milk is more expensive than beer, and a packet of cigarettes is cheaper than a bottle of mineral water—a direct consequence of the cynical tax policy of the government.

Furthermore, what is very striking about the recent past is the sharp rise in the mortality rate of working-age men. Among the plausible explanations are the high rate of open or hidden unemployment, the low wages, and the constant search by the employed for an additional part-time job to make both ends meet, and so on. The psychological strain is both a cause and effect of alcoholism, and has also an adverse effect on the desire of both women and men to have babies.

In short, the roots of the demographic crisis must be traced to the Soviet past. Instead of overcoming the shortcomings, the post-reform state in Russia has made the situation much worse, and the country is heading towards massive depopulation.

## CONCLUSION

Let me first summarize the earlier sections. First, the Russian economy is in a state of unparalleled depression, and the end of the tunnel is not in sight. Second, there is a massive capital flight from the country, though at varying rates over the years. Third, the reins of government are in the hands of a vicious circle of politicians, financial oligarchs and outright criminals who have been merrily subverting the rule of law with impurity. Moreover, these elements are dependent on Western powers, especially the USA as the sole superpower. Lastly, the country faces a demographic disaster with no parallels except during the worst phases of colonial rule and slave trade in Africa and Latin America.

In July 2000, the Russian government adopted what IMF (2000a, p. 29) calls a 'far reaching plan' for development of the Russian economy. It proposed among other things to:

(*a*) improve protection of socially vulnerable households;
(*b*) raise consumption levels of workers;
(*c*) increase public spending on (i) education and (ii) health to ensure free health care for all;
(*d*) reform labour laws to facilitate greater labour mobility through a simpler retrenchment procedure and 'continue to raise the minimum wage';
(*e*) create a favourable business climate through reduction in tax burden, stimulation of structural changes in the economy, and

reform of the infrastructural monopolies and property rights, with less interference from the state;

(*f*) reduce the average customs duty and their diversity;

(*g*) privatize a significant number of state-owned enterprises;

(*h*) provide state funding of R & D and venture investments; and

(*i*) restructure the military–industrial complex to raise efficiency and encourage conversion into civilian use.

The IMF (2000a, pp. 30, 38) broadly endorsed the programme and thought that the objectives were 'generally ambitious.' It added that 'most of the policies in the long term programme have been part of Fund and World Bank supported programmes in the past, and that previous governments have failed to implement these policies because of fierce resistance from vested interests'.

If the recent programme has very little that is new, and if successive governments under Yeltsin failed to implement previous programmes, there is no reason why Putin's administration would fare any better. The government as well as the IMF ignore the inner contradictions, and are merely content to put the onus on the 'vested interests'. First, the reform of labour laws will mean in effect that a good part of the 'hidden' unemployed will now become openly unemployed. In view of the already huge backlog of the unemployed, there is likely to be a downward pressure on wages. The intention to raise the minimum wage is hardly credible; for, in real terms it went down every year in the last decade, excepting 1996, and by 1999 shrank to one-twentieth of the 1990 level (IMF 2000b, Table 17). The theory behind the move toward flexibility is the Say's Law that posits that more jobs would be created as a result of wage reduction. A whole decade of Russian experience is not enough to shake the neoliberals' faith in the Law. But long ago, Keynes was confident that in a situation of severe output contraction a wage-cut would only aggravate the crisis.

Secondly, how can the state spend more on education, health care, and R & D, while it reduces customs duties on imports, and introduces one the world's most regressive regimes of personal income tax at a flat rate of 13 per cent? A main source of higher government revenue in 2000 was the export tax on minerals, especially oil, the price of which went up sharply. Commodity prices cannot remain indefinitely at the present plateau. Besides, the government decided in early 2001 to fulfil the demands of external creditors rather than utilize the extra revenues to enhance outlays on social sectors.

Third, through various tax and other concessions, the government can successfully raise the share of profits in total income, but may not induce a higher rate of investment in the absence of an expanding home market. The market is not only restricted by the greatly reduced household incomes, but also by the flood of imports, especially of consumer goods for the affluent sections. The four-fold devaluation of the rouble after the 1998 crisis provided some relief to domestic producers, but no lasting improvement can be expected. If the tariffs remain low, and the profit share in total income rises as a result of tax concessions for the business sector, the inequalities will increase, and there will be even fewer incentives for private investment geared to the home market.

Fourth, the government proposes further privatization without institutional changes that would oblige large firms to operate in a competitive environment. It can only enhance the power of entrenched interests, as Stiglitz pointed out forcefully. More generally, there is nothing to suggest that there is a serious attempt to sever the umbilical chord between crime and the Russian state. In short, the new programme of the Russian government will contribute to the further underdevelopment of Russia like all previous Fund–Bank packages.

Quite refreshing in this context is the joint statement of June 2000 by a group of 18 distinguished economists, including L.A. Abalkin, O.T. Bogomalov, D.S. Lvov, etc., from Russia, and M.I. Goldman, L.R. Klein, F. Modigliani, D. North, L. Taylor et al. from the USA. They suggested five broad measures (*Transition*, vol. 11, nos. 3-4, May-July 2000):

1. *Institutional infrastructure*: The government should eliminate the deep distortions in the market mechanism and reorient large and medium enterprises from asset stripping to net worth maximization.
2. *Fight against crime*: Extortion and bribery should be rigorously prosecuted irrespective of the position or political views of the officials involved.
3. *Growth-oriented policy*: 'Growth of production and investment should be the primary goal of the government rather bringing inflation to near zero levels. . . . Concerted action should be taken against illegal capital flight.' The purchasing power should be bolstered within economically justified limits through higher pensions and restoration of a portion of the savings that were lost as a result of sustained inflation and the financial collapse of 1998.

4. *Restructuring and competition*: The government should not unduly interfere with the market discipline. However, 'government leadership is needed for Russia to realize its potential in the information economy, biotechnology and some other high-tech spheres due to its scientists, research institutes and some productive capacities. This implies careful elaboration and firm implementation of a realistic industrial policy. Until steady growth resumes selected temporary import tariffs conditional on output performance could be introduced.' Further, 'privatisations that have been carried out in violation of the law should be reconsidered'.
5. *Social contract*: Only the government can ensure that the benefits of the new economic order are shared. To this end, there should be a law on minimum subsistence pensions indexed to the inflation rate, and to reduce inequalities a well-enforced system of progressive taxation is needed. High taxes on extractive industries would ensure that the Russian people are the main beneficiaries of the export of natural resources.

The joint statement (JS), it appears to me, amounts to a repudiation of the fundamentals of the IMF-type reforms in Russia:

1. Growth of production and investment, rather than macroeconomic stabilization and inflation control, should be the main policy objective. Hence the JS proposes much larger budgetary outlays on a number of fronts like the social sectors, infrastructure, R&D, and venture capital.
2. The JS puts accent on distributive justice and wants the higher expenditure to be financed by a progressive tax on income, protective import tariffs, and high export taxes on commodities with a low production cost compared to the world market prices. It follows that domestic prices of these commodities would diverge significantly from world prices, contradicting the neoliberal dogma (not followed by the USA in respect of fuels) of 'one global price for each good'.
3. Following Keynes, the JS rejects wage flexibility as a cure. The Russian government should raise the purchasing power of the common people, and pensions in particular, both on distributional grounds and as a means to strengthen effective demand.
4. The JS advocates an active industrial policy considering the *dynamics* of comparative advantage—something that is anathema to all shades of neoliberals, including occasional critics such as J. Bhagwati, J. Sachs, M. Feldstein mentioned earlier. As a corollary, the JS espouses

temporary protection of selected industries until steady growth is achieved.

5. The JS calls for resolute action by the state against capital flight, which would imply strict control over capital mobility. The IMF does not appreciate such 'draconian' controls.
6. The JS goes well beyond a ritualistic call for an end to the mafia *raj*. It wants the earlier privatizations to be reconsidered, which might lead to the present owners being dispossessed.

While endorsing the JS, I want to make two points. First, if the illegal privatizations are to be annulled, who could buy the big state-owned firms? Once the oligarchs are dispossessed, only Western firms would remain as potential private-sector buyers. That would face stiff opposition from the Russian public on both nationalist *and* economic grounds. In view of the global overcapacity in a large number of sectors, oligopolistic firms from the West may buy up factories at bargain basement prices and keep them idle. It is for this reason that Korean workers have been struggling to prevent foreign takeover of their firms in distress. If foreigners are kept at bay, most of the Russian firms would revert back to state ownership. A return to the over-centralized system of planning introduced in the early 1930s is unlikely. The Russians would have to find ways to foster competition among the state-owned firms, taking a leaf out of China's post-1978 experiment or that of post-War Japan, described variously as a 'plan-oriented market economy system' (Johnson 1982, pp. 9-10) or 'a kind of democratic "planned" economy' (Morishima 1982, p. 197).

Second, will the West, notably the USA, acquiesce in such transformation? One may recall what Stiglitz (2000a) wrote about the role of the US Treasury in the choice of Russia's transition strategy. There is nothing to indicate that the American perspective has changed.

The lesson is clear. Either Russia must forsake its dependence on the IMF and the US Treasury, or go on suffering indefinitely.

## REFERENCES

Abalkin, A. and J. Whalley (eds) (1999), 'The Problem of Capital Flight from Russia', *The World Economy*, vol. 22, no. 3.

Anon. (2000), 'Strategiya sotsial'no-ekonomicheskogo razvitiya Rossii—innovatsionnyi put', *Rossiiskii ekonomicheskii zhurnal*, no. 4.

Aslund, A. (1994), 'Russia's Success Story', *Foreign Affairs*, vol. 73, no. 5, September-October, pp. 58-71.

Aslund, A. (2000), 'Why Has Russia's Economic Transition Been So Arduous?', *Annual World Bank Conference on Development Economics 1999*, World Bank, Washington, D.C.

Bonnet, F. (1999), 'Qui gouverne la Russie? Une affaire de "famille"', *Le Monde*, 15 December.

Broeck, M. de and V. Koen (2000), 'The Great Contraction in Russia, the Baltics and Other Countries of the Former Soviet Union: A View from the Supply Side', IMF, WP/00/32, Washington, D.C.

CBR (2000-1), 'Main Macroeconomic Indicators', Central Bank of Russia, <www.cbr.ru>.

Chandra, N.K. (1993), 'Russia's Sinking Economy: External Dimensions', *Economic and Political Weekly*, 15 May, vol. 28, no. 20, pp. 1139-50.

——— (1996), 'Dimensions of Social and Economic Crisis in Russia Today', *Economic and Political Weekly*, 11 May, vol. 31, no. 9, pp. 995-1003.

——— (2001), 'McKinsey's Plan for Russia: Unlocking Growth or Bottling the Genie?', *Economic and Political Weekly*, 10 November, vol. 36, no. 45, pp. 4300-7.

Eatwell, J., M. Ellman, M. Kartsson, D.M. Nuti and J. Shapiro (1995), *Transformation and Integration: Shaping the Future of Central and Eastern Europe*, Institute for Public Policy, London.

EEG (2001), *Obzor ekonomicheskikh pokazetelei*, Ekonomicheskaya ekspertnaya gruppa, Ministerstvo Finansov Rossiiskoi Federatsii, 15 January, www.eeg.ru.

Ellman, M. (2000a), 'Social Costs and Consequences of the Transformation Process', Economic Commission for Europe, *Economic Survey of Europe 2000*, no. 3, United Nations, New York.

——— (2000b), 'The Real Economy under El'tsin', *Europe-Asia Studies*, vol. 52, no. 8.

Ericson, R.E. (1998), 'Economics and the Russian Transition', *Slavic Review*, vol. 57, no. 3, Fall, pp. 609-25.

Fabre, G. (1999), *Les prosperités du crime: Trafic de stupéfiants, blanchissement et crises financières dans l'après-guerre froide*, L'editions de l'Aube, Paris.

Fesbach, M. (1999), 'Interview with A.F. Tully', *Radio Free Europe–Radio Liberty*, 25 October <www.rferl.org>.

Gaddy, C.G. and B.W. Ickes (1998), 'Russia's Virtual Economy', *Foreign Affairs*, September-October, vol. 77, no. 5, pp. 53-67.

Goskomstat (1998a), *Natsional'nye scheta Rossii v 1989-1996 godakh*, Moscow.

——— (1998b), *Rossiiskii ezhegodnik ststistiki* 1998, Moscow.

——— (1998c), *Population of Russia: 1897-1997: Statistical Abstract*, Moscow.

——— (1999), *Rossiya v tsifrakh: Offitsial'noe izdanie 1999*, Moscow.

——— (2000), 'Osnovnye sotsial'no-ekonomicheskie pokazateli po Rossiiskoi federatsii za 1996-2000 gg.', *Voprosy statistiki*, no. 8.

Grigoriev, L. (2000), 'Comments on "Why Has Russia's Economic Transition Been So Arduous?" by Anders Aslund', *Annual World Bank Conference on Development Economics 1999*, World Bank, Washington, D.C.

IMF (2000a), *The Russian Federation*, etc., Staff Country Report No. 00/145, September.

——— (2000b), *The Russian Federation*, etc., Staff Country Report No. 00/150, November.

IMF et al. (1991), *The Economy of the USSR: Summary and Recommendations*, International Monetary Fund, World Bank, Organization for Economic Cooperative and Development and European Bank for Reconstruction and Development, Washington, D.C.

Jensen, D.N. (1998), 'How Russia is Ruled—1998', <www.rfl.org>.

Johnson, C. (1982), *MITI and the Japanese Miracle: The Growth of Industrial Policy*, Stanford University Press, Stanford.

Kaser, M. (1999), 'Escape Routes from Post-Soviet Inflation and Recession', *Finance and Development*, June, vol. 36, no. 2, pp. 24-7.

Khanin, G. (2000), 'Stabilizatsiya krizisa', *EKO*, no. 3.

Khanin, G. and N. Suslov (1999), 'The Real Sector of the Russian Economy', *Europe-Asia Studies*, vol. 51, no. 8, December.

Loungani, P. and P. Mauro (2000), *Capital Flight from Russia*, IMF Policy Discussion Paper No. PDP/00/6, June.

Maddox, B. and A. Kaletsky (1998), 'When Lame Duck Meets a Dead Duck', *The Times*, 29 August.

MGI (1999), *Unlocking Economic Growth in Russia*, McKinsey Global Institute, October, available on <www.mckinsey.com>.

Milanovich, B. (1998), *Income, Inequality and Poverty During the Transition from Planned to Market Economy*, World Bank, Washington, D.C.

Morishima, M. (1982), *Why Has Japan 'Succeeded'? Western Technology and the Japanese Ethos*, Cambridge University Press, Cambridge.

Nove, A. (1994), 'A Gap in Transition Models? A Comment on Gomulka', *Europe-Asia Studies* (formerly, *Soviet Studies*), vol. 46, no. 5.

OECD (1999), *Science and Technology Main Indicators and Basic Statistics of the Russian Federation, 1992–97*, OECD Centre for Co-operation with Non-members, CCNM/DSTI/EAS(99)23, 30 June.

Radvanyi, J. (2000), 'Elections to the Sound of War: Russia Seeks a New Deal', *Le Monde Diplomatique*, English edition, March.

Radyuhin, V. (2000), 'Russian Auditor Confirms Graft in Government', *The Hindu*, Chennai, 15 October.

Rosefielde, S. (2000), 'The Civilian Labour Force and Unemployment in the Russian Federation', *Europe-Asia Studies*, vol. 52, no. 8, pp. 1433-47, December.

Shlapentokh, V. (1999), 'Social Inequality in Post-communist Russia: The Attitudes of the Political Elite and the Masses (1991-1998)', *Europe-Asia Studies*, vol. 51, no. 7.

Stiglitz, J.E. (1999), 'Knowledge for Development: Economic Science, Economic Policy and Economic Advice', *Annual World Bank Conference on Development Economics 1998*, World Bank, Washington, D.C.

Stiglitz, J.E. (2000a), 'Whither Reforms? Ten Years of the Transition', *Annual World Bank Conference on Development Economics 1999*, World Bank, Washington, D.C.

——— (2000b), 'The Insider: What I Learned at the World Economic Crisis', *The New Republic*, 17 April.

Tikhomirov, V. (1997), 'Capital Flight from post-Soviet Russia', *Europe Asia Studies*, vol. 49, no. 4, pp. 591-616.

——— (2000), 'The Second Collapse of the Soviet Economy: Myths and Realities of the Russian Federation', *Europe-Asia Studies*, vol. 52, no. 2, pp. 207-36, March.

Traynor, I. (2000), 'Russia Dying of Drink and Despair', *The Guardian*, 30 June.

UNICEF (2000), *The State of World's Children 2000*, Geneva.

USA (1967), *Statistical Abstract of the United States 1967*, US Department of Commerce, Bureau of the Census, Washington, D.C.

Zohoori, N. et al. (1998), 'Monitoring the Economic Transition in the Russian Federation and its Implications for the Demographic Crisis—the Russian Longitudinal Monitoring Survey', *World Development*, November, vol. 26, no. 11, pp. 1977-93.

# 2

# National Choice of Industrial Structure, Financial Repression, and Credit Policy in Korea: Socio-political Conditions for Valid Credit Policy

*Chul Gyue Yoo*

## INTRODUCTION

The dominant ideology of an unfettered market may be said to negate the possibility that an economy can choose its fortune by changing its industrial structure, establishing its institutions, and mobilizing or creating its resources. According to this ieology, the existing social and international order and hierarchy, including the prevalence of inequality and poverty, should be regarded as the result of the natural laws of market forces. From the viewpoint of this blind faith, the experiences of the East Asian countries, especially Japan and Korea, can be disconcerting because they have shown an ability in improving their social and economic situation through the collective intention of their members and political intervention in market. To deliberate on the potential advantages of political control over financial markets is one

*An earlier version of this paper was presented at the UNESCO Participation Programme at the Centre for Studies in Social Sciences, Calcutta (CSSSC), held on 1-3 December 1999. The author wishes to thank Amiya Kumar Bagchi at CSSSC for inviting him to the conference. Many scholars at the conference provided useful criticism. In particular, thanks are due to Sushil Khanna, of the Indian Institute of Management, Calcutta and Aditya Bhattacharjea of the Delhi School of Economics for their useful comments.

thing and to consider the fact that some of these countries have suffered or are suffering from a political dictatorship and corruption is another thing.

The ongoing development experience of Korea can be regarded as a case in which the common will of the people and the government's industrial policy along with its credit policy determined the country's industrial structure and institutional settings under the specific international conditions that prevailed commonly in many countries. Korea has established itself as an industrialized country that is characterized by highly concentrated investment in the manufacturing sectors, since its economic development experience began around thirty years ago from the almost complete destruction of its industrial base, which was a result of the Japanese colonial occupation (1910-45), the rule of the US military authorities (1945-8), and the Korean Civil War (1950-3). Through rapid changes in industrial structure, right up until the recent 1997 East Asian financial crisis, its production shares of semi-conductor, automobile, shipbuilding, electrical appliances, and steel industry ranged widely from 5 per cent up to 30 per cent each in the World markets.

Even in the industrially advanced countries that have a long history of capitalist development and relatively solid social class structures, the common will of the individuals of a certain nation, as embodied in state or government policy, can affect their industrial structure. The literature on industrial restructuring in Europe has pointed out the different ideological approaches of privatization under the Thatcher government in the UK and the quasi-nationalization in the Mitterand government in France. During the industrial restructuring period from the late 1970s to the early 1990s, the state-owned British Leyland was divided into component parts and a few private auto manufacturing firms like Jaguar and Rover, which were later merged with foreign firms (it is also known that Rover's Longbridge auto plant was already abandoned by BMW, its parent). Peugeot was rebuilt as one of the leading private car makers in Europe during a similar upheaval as that in Leyland (Marklew 1995).

This chapter aims to provide a brief institutional profile in order to set out some of the controversial key factors behind the rapid growth of the Korean economy and in order to tentatively gain an understanding of the socio-political background of the manner in which Korea's economic and social resources are mobilized, managed, and created for development as well as how much 'the manner' has affected the recent economic crisis. In terms of credit policy, relying on the theoretical discussions of the imperfection of financial market and the merits of government intervention in markets, the essay focuses on picking up the policy spirit rather than the more concrete institutional mechanisms and their functions.

## INSTITUTIONAL SETTING OF THE ECONOMIC MIRACLE

The question for developing countries is whether there is scope for changing their industrial structure other than that forced on to them by pretended natural laws of market rules under the specific international conditions.

The case of South Korea, which suffered from the lack of reliable data and empirical works, can be interpreted as an ongoing experiment on whether the 'common will' of the people of a certain nation, as embodied in the state or government policy, can affect their industrial structure. Therefore, of importance is how the 'will' can be formed and organized, how the collective 'will' constrains, implicitly or explicitly, the government to minimize government failure, and how far the common will of the society can be directed toward increasing the inducement to invest. This idea may be helpful in understanding the fact that it is difficult to identify clear or significant differences in the individual credit programmes and interest rate policies in the African, Latin American, and East Asian countries.

## A BRIEF OVERVIEW OF KOREAN INDUSTRIALIZATION

South Korea's economic history can be divided into a few phases as the Korean developmental institutions have continuously and rapidly changed since industrialization began under the regime of development dictatorship. Appropriately speaking, the so called Korean Model recognized by Westerners should be applied to the period of the Heavy and Chemical Industrialization (HCI) Programme, declared in January 1973 and completed in the great boom of the mid to late 1980s.

### *A Background to the Development Dictatorship*

Before examining the establishment of the development dictatorship in Korea, it is useful to review very briefly the historical background preceding it. During the period of its colonial rule by Japan, which lasted for 36 years, a very progressive (or revolutionary) and nationalistic resistance movement had developed. With the impending defeat of

Japan in the summer of 1945, socialistic liberation committees were organized and took over the actual political power in many local villages. The colonial experience gave rise to drastic demands by the Korean people for radical social change in the old feudal social structure, which was acknowledged to be responsible for and used by Japanese colonialism. For example, the basic popular demands included the expropriation of the big landowners who had heavily supported the colonial system. However, with the invasion of the US army in Korea, this progressive movement and will was eliminated by force. The American military government prevented and removed any local self-administration, as well as trade unions and peasant associations. To the Korean people it meant just another form of colonialism, against which was required another resistance.

It was the Korean War, as a surrogate of the Cold War, that led to 'ideological cleansing' and termination of the idea of an alternative to the capitalist development required by the US. Nevertheless, the strong nationalist and socialist ideas could not be completely removed and have remained in the fabric of development institutions in the form sometimes of communitarianism ('get rich together' or the priority given to 'shared growth') and at other times in the campaigns of the strong nation-state and so on. The recent episode of the 'Gold Collection Movement' in late 1997 and early 1998, which seemed like a ridiculous and extremely irrational self-sacrifice to most Western observers (*Financial Times*, 6 June 1998), can be interpreted as such. It can be easily agreed that the other side of the miraculous system was its members' self-sacrifice.

Last but not least, emphasis should be placed on the bitter experience of corrupt nepotism of the state administration, 'bureaucracy capital' of the early form of 'the State—private large enterprise complex', and the chronic drain on public finance under the first president Sung-Man Rhee, whose government was supported by the US. With a severe economic depression and electoral forgery, the unfulfilled popular demands for the construction of a democratic national state burst out in bloody revolts by students and civilians.

### *Development of the Development Dictatorship (1961-79 and the late 1980s)*

When the armed forces under Chung-Hee Park established a 'development dictatorship' with the coup in 1960 amidst the virtual chaos that afflicted the country, they in some way supported these popular demands and included the new ruling elite as their important partners in accomplishing the development plans, which gave them a degree of legitimacy. This means that their ideological orientation included the nationalistic and communitarian aspects as remnants of the liberation movements and students–civilian revolts, and provided as well as the justification of an emerging new capitalistic ruling class. At least temporarily, the former 'bureaucracy capital' could establish itself as the means or servants for the construction of a new country. Any political row or scandal over corruption was also avoided or at least hidden, because of the possibility that such a row of scandal could provoke people and ruin the regime's legitimacy.

Because a regime of oppression does not automatically produce successful capitalist industrialization, the underlying popular demands and the constraints on policy the common will of the people provided should be regarded as important factors in understanding the uniqueness of Korea's experience. However, as dictatorship cannot coexist with demands for democracy, implicit or explicit compromise or distortion of the common will may be necessary. This has resulted in an artificially sequential separation of political matters from economic activities. In other words, 'growth first, distribution later', 'concentration of political and economic power first to get what we need, decentralization of them later', 'the economy first, democracy later'. This political promise needed a guarantee to redistribute the national wealth sometime in the future, which required and justified keeping political control over the fruits of economic growth. The guarantee functions to reinforce the political dictatorship and its intervention in the economy.

Contrary to the impression held by many observers, the secret of rapid, shared growth was rather simple, namely the organization and concentration of the people's common will, and their participation. A distorted view of democracy thus found its way through the only allowed open door of frenetic economic expansion.

During the relatively long investment period (1975-9) required for HCIs (Heavy and Chemical Industries), the forced high investment into heavy industries could not prevent a growing trade deficit and a widening gap between the rich and the poor. At the same time, external conditions turned adverse especially through the second oil crisis. The political–economic crisis culminated in the assassination of Park in 1979, which was followed by General Doo-Whan Chun's coup after a short interim 2-year period of relative democratization. The priority of the Chun Government, also supported by Washington institutions and the US, was basically a tight containment policy with regard to social demands for equality and democracy in order to let industry continue its investment and export. Despite several policy changes towards liberalization, Park's regime extended to the late 1980s.

### *Dismantling of the Development Regime (the late 1980s to 1997) and the 1997 Crisis*

When, with its overwhelming shares in gross domestic product (GDP) and exports, the capital-intensive HCI programme of the 1970s fully showed its potential in one of the greatest booms the country has ever seen, from 1986 to 1988, at least to the Korean people, it seemed that Korea had become an industrialized country.

Even though the 'compressed' capital accumulation[1] was accompanied by structural vulnerability such as extreme dependence on external borrowing and unequal development between the domestic and export industries, the realization of an industrialized country meant economic feasibility for the realization of the delayed part of the vision, i.e. substantial democracy and institutional reforms for more equal distribution.

As a matter of fact, the national tragedy began after a political betrayal against the other part of the ongoing promise for 'ex-post distribution'. While, accompanying a very fierce labour movement, the real wage rate increased rapidly during 1986-9 (yearly average being more than 15-20 per cent), the ruling class represented by large conglomerates had been preparing a very lethal weapon of importing or 'creatively' imitating a new ideology and replacing substantive democracy with a procedural democracy acting against the interests of working population. The so-called neo-liberalism has two functions in this context: one is the retiring of government from the position in which, according to the old political agreement, it is responsible for the promotion of the interests of ordinary people, i.e. social welfare and more equal distribution; the other is unburdening the social responsibility of private enterprises which it has historically formed.[2] In fact, the American-style transparent property rights has naturally meant ignoring all historical background such as the historical experiences of using people's pocket money and taxes to support and 'breed' the industrial conglomerates (just imagine the national football champion) in the development period. It is not merely by chance that the hottest political issue about systemic reform since the late 1980s, the period of the beginning of the dismantling of the old system, has been the limits of private property rights. The large conglomerates have argued that their property rights should be divine and any socio-political obstacles or responsibility cannot be accepted. Of course this argument had been supported by neo-liberalism ideologically, the USA's pressure in real political terms.

These two opposite ideologies and demands clashed head-on with each other on the eve of the crisis, paralyzing any kind of possible policy response to the imminent crisis. From this point of view, the concordance between the 'IMF-imposed structural reform programme' and earlier Korean reform initiatives may have an important implication. The first official Korean reform initiatives were announced in the Korea-US Financial Talk of 1993. Chang, Park and Yoo (1998) argued that the financial liberalization implemented in Korea has been most responsible for the concrete form (foreign exchange crisis) of the recent crisis. In that paper, a more fundamental and internal reason has been referred why a certain type of financial liberalization could have been left without appropriate supervision.

With regard to the question of whether there is a Korean Model and whether the crisis is causing it to break down or whether it needs to break down, a brief answer can be provided: there 'had been' a Korean Model. The crisis cannot cause it to break down simply because it did not exist at that time and, if anything, there existed institutional remnants or inertia without their institutional spirit.

## Institutional Background of High Exploitation and Delayed Democratization

If at all, the so-called Korean Model might apply to the period from the early 1970s to the late 1980s, i.e. the period from the beginning of the Heavy and Chemical Industrialization programme to its completion as the manufacturing sector's share of the economy's GDP reached its peak.[3]

In the macroeconomic view, the Korean Model could be identified with a system to accelerate investment as much as possible. To use Keynes' terminology, it is a good match with the concept of 'Socialization of investment' in the sense that the state or government was able to determine the aggregate volume of resources to be devoted to augmenting the instrument of production and the basic rate of reward to those who own them (Keynes 1949).

For accelerating investment usually beyond any private economic agents' ability, the financial system must have supplied the required financial resources. It has been known as a 'repressed system' following Shaw (1973), which means that interest rates are artificially fixed below the market clearing level and credit allocation is directed by the government. But more important aspects have tended to be very often ignored, such as how the huge investment projects in Korea could persuade the Western and international financial markets to lend their money. One of the main reasons was the 'Combined Guarantee of the State–Banks–Large Enterprises'. In fact, the national economy itself became collateral.[4] From the beginning the investment and credit programmes could not avoid the task of providing political legitimacy to the military regime.

Secondly, in regard to domestic aspects, the 'Combined Credit System of the State–Banks–Large Enterprises' could provide a certain level of fulfilment of commercial contracts and wide confidence in financial savings or financial institutions.[5] Thirdly, it also provided a kind of social insurance for entrepreneurial ventures. Actually, in the early stages of development, almost all kind of investment in the HCI programme could be called venture investment.

The Banking system was structured to support the required investment and to suit the industrial structure. Heavy Industries are

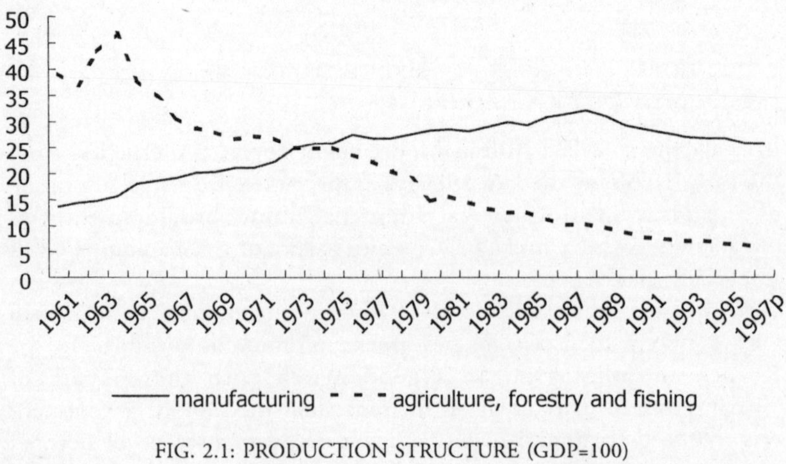


FIG. 2.1: PRODUCTION STRUCTURE (GDP=100)

SOURCE: Major Statistics of Korean Economy, National Statistical Office, various years.

characterized by a long generative period over which stable supply of fund is required.

> It seems unlikely that the influence of banking policy on the rate of interest will be sufficient by itself to determine an optimum rate of investment. I conceive, therefore, that a somewhat comprehensive socialization of investment will prove the only means of securing an approximation to full employment; though this need not exclude all manner of compromise and of devices by which public authority will co-operate with private initiative. (Keynes 1949, p. 378)

To borrow Keynes' expression again, the repressed financial system was a repression against the rentier aspect of capitalism or rentier classes:

> We have shown that the extent of effective saving is necessarily determined by the scale of investment and that the scale of investment is promoted by a low rate of interest, provided that we do not attempt to stimulate it in this way beyond the point which corresponds to full employment. Thus it is to our best advantage to reduce the rate of interest to that point relatively to the schedule of the marginal efficiency of capital at which there is full employment. (Keynes, 1949, p. 375)

As to the criteria of investment, parts of the basic story have been already mentioned. In the earlier stage of development planning, the selection criteria for strategic industries had less to do with business logic than with social necessity: essentially, what kind of industries were needed for an industrialized country and self-defence—steel, chemical, energy industries as major national industries, as well as social infrastructure and education institutions and so on. Another important principle was the sustainability of the development projects. Essentially, the financial resources had to be recycled or replenished in order to keep continuing to invest. A result of this principle was the promotion of export, economies of scale, and high pressure for keeping profitability. At the present moment, even after the crisis, the Po-Hang Steel Company, one of the biggest public enterprises in Korea, is known as one of the most profitable companies in the world. Contrary to Latin American countries in the early stages of industrialization, the constraints of foreign exchange were very hard: there was simply nothing to sell in the world market. The practical workings of the 'foreign exchange concentration system' in Korea should be regarded as the most important institution for development.

Meanwhile, the most basic element of the success of the Korean Model has been probably the longest working hours in the world.[6]

Long working hours combined with capital-intensive investment produced a huge amount of economic surplus in the sense of the classical political economy theories. In reality, by contrast with already matured countries, Korea's economy has had to bear the enormous surplus-outflow in the form of interest for borrowing, rents for technology, consultancy fee and commissions for selling, etc. It may be unnecessary to search for more clear evidence than the fact of the highest growth with only residual surplus.

This level of exploitation of labour probably relied on the people's political commitment in the absence of real alternatives, once they accepted the political decision of development. This phenomenon cannot be explained only by the absolute physical repression that prevailed in many developing countries. Partly, it might have been possible due to the 'ideological cleansing' following the Korean War. With the tabooed ideological disputes, economic growth and material improvement of everyday life themselves had become located in the centre of an ideological vacuum.[7] Subordinate ideologies at different levels are important to compare countries that are classified under the same category in terms of a higher level of ideology such as capitalism. In this sense, the sharp contrast between market and plan or state may be a misleading way to approach the difference between capitalist countries.

It seems to be generally accepted that the foundations on which the Korean Model was built are: an efficient and autonomous state bureaucracy, a tight central planning apparatus, and systematic planning to change the economic structure; a preference for big conglomerates in the big development projects and a financial system that channelled capital to them; an education system with the object of ideological and professional qualities, etc. (World Bank 1993). In addition to these elements, what is emphasized in this chapter is the implicit social agreement supported by the socio-political background that has been formed through historical experiences. This made the apparent state autonomy possible with people's identification with conglomerates and the state. This identification played a role in giving high flexibility and pragmatic behaviour to policy decision-making procedures.

The cohesion structure of politics with economy has been criticized for aggravating 'corruption' or 'moral hazard' problems. However, as recognized by World Bank (1993), the problems seem to have been restrained for quite a long time. Helpful though not wholly satisfying clues for further research can be found in some institutional behaviours as to the relationship between the government and large conglomerates.

In the period of concentrated investment, of chief shareholders of beneficiary firms or groups targeted by the industrial and credit policy had to offer their personal properties as a collateral.[8] If they failed with the national resources, they could lose everything including their private wealth. It was very risky for the entrepreneurs to accept policy-based credit for long-term investment other than short-term working capital. But it was also dangerous not to accept the government's offer, because they knew that if government asked another entrepreneur to accept the project, they could lose in the competition when the other competitors succeeded in the project. Worse they could be disqualified for the next project. Therefore, government's risk sharing for HCI projects was not for individual entrepreneurs (though by no means all), but for the systemic continuity of the national projects.

Figure 2.2 indicates two possible ways to relate a state (or government) with vested interests. In the former (Type A), every member of the pool of conglomerates cannot assert his right to special consideration or treatment for his monetary contribution for political activities, including quasi-tax for cost of oppressing the anti-establishment movements and staying in power, because every member of the pool pays his contribution through their representative organizations and they know very often how much the others contributed. The political power can be free to choose who will be entrusted with national big businesses, without regard to how much and by whom the political money was paid. The state autonomy referred to often as Korean industrial policy may mean this situation.

In Type B, the situation is quite different. Every conglomerate lobbies individually not for the common interests of the group but for its own interests and it does not know how much the others have contributed. The decision-making process can be affected much more severely by the amount of money paid for political activities.

It was the political burden on the government imposed by the people

FIGURE 2.2: WAYS TO RELATE POLITICAL POWER WITH VESTED INTERESTS

that prevented the transition from the first type to the second type government–big industrial interests, even though we witnessed the appearance of the second type after the early 1990s in earnest. It was the rise of neo-liberal ideas that allowed a wrong solution to the inevitable reform of the traditional relationship between government and industrial conglomerates. As Chang et al. (1998) reported, for the first time in the Korean development history, a few particular conglomerates had been systemically close to the political power since the early 1990s, which could be interpreted as a sign of the transition to the American style lobby system as well as of the substantial demise of coordinated investments in major industries.

Recently some researchers have stressed the effectiveness of internal organization and internal capital market among government, banks, and big businesses as the main source of the successful government intervention in Japan and Korea (Cho and Hellman 1994; Lee 1994). This concept is useful to emphasize the role of communication, coordination, and cooperation among the participants as well as being more coincident with the historical reality than others. However, implicating a supposed smooth cooperation in the same organization, it missed out the unrestrained competition among the industrial conglomerates and conflicts between government, who should gain political support by voters, and large industrial groups. Industrial firms were not in a relationship of cooperation but in rivalry. It should be also pointed out that 'over-competition' which would destroy their common basis and waste the national financial resource was restrained by political reasons and means.

While things such as the implementation of an overall strategy could be seen in the socialist states, it seems to be necessary to mention an aspect different from the realistic socialist authoritarian states. One of the outstanding differences of Korea from these states was that its government did not control all the economic processes in a bureaucratic way. Development planning was concentrated on a few selected strategic sectors. The remaining sectors were left open to unrestrained competition and market rules, a situation similar to that of the early stage of industrialization in the UK in the early to mid nineteenth century. The pressure through the markets was so threatening that the extremely aggressive competition and rivalry towards higher productivity and reduction of wage costs were often justified as a struggle for existence or survival. Therefore, the sectors that were excluded from the state planning were not demotivated, but provided buffers in times of depressions or failures of large conglomerates. Once again, we can see who bore the expenses of the Miracle.

The organization of common will and its distortion were established by the extension of the education system and summarized well by the following propaganda prevailing during the HCI programme period: 'All individuals are on their own in the competition struggle', which means 'Struggle of all against all, by any means they have or create'. 'Certainly win in the economic competition against the rest of the world' aimed to promote competitions among individuals and business groups.

These ideological social demands were accepted successfully so much so that suicide cases arising from the fear of dropping out of the line were not a rarity, e.g. in middle and high school students. In addition, a certain amount of material incentives for promoting the credibility of the propaganda had to be provided. The tangible improvement of life standards, even though tiny, strengthened the commitment to the previous way. This justified the over-exploitation of labour and produced new sources of giving more material incentives. The 'shared growth' (World Bank 1993), which has been evaluated by a considerable amount of existing literature, could be partly achieved in this way, with the help of repeated political resistance, self-sacrificing high savings, and investment.

The sinews of the Model mentioned above have been dismantled by destroying the major components of state governing, through misguided market liberalization from the late 1980s to the mid 1990s (Chang et al. 1998). Its result can be called 'accelerated investment alone without governing'. Under the different socio-political configuration, the government could not have substantial intention to counteract the crisis of confidence any more except to watch it in 1997, contrary to the previous periods.

## THE KOREAN FINANCIAL SYSTEM DURING THE RAPID INDUSTRIALIZATION PERIOD

### Features of the Financial System and the Politics of Financial Repression[9]

It is well recognized that during the rapid industrialization period, the Korean government had intervened deeply in financial resource allocation in order to promote 'priority industrial sectors' by credit rationing and ceilings on interest rates. Financial policy was run as an accessory to industrial policy. Various directed credit programmes were implemented and the loans from the government-controlled (or state-led) 'bank-based' financial system were the most important instrument in the industrial policy regime.[10] This process required tight capital control on both outflows and inflows.[11]

To summarize, the prominent feature of the Korean economy that lasted until the late 1980s was the 'repressive' nature of its financial system. Although it is often called the repression of financial development, it can also mean that the interests of the financial rentier class were repressed, as indicated in the previous section. Such regime of 'financial repression' was based on the view that the financial rentier class was a 'necessary evil' or a parasitic group damaging the industrial enterprises. Such view is well reflected in the following commentary on the pre-1961 financial system made by the official Summary of the First Five-Year Plan published in 1962:

> [O]nly the privileged few who had access to bank credits were able to enjoy profit from production activities. . . . Instead of making creative and honest efforts to improve management and techniques of production, many entrepreneurs went into unsavory league with politicians and bureaucrats seeking to amass easy fortunes. . . . Industries were compelled to resort to high interest private loans, and, consequently, usurious lending activities flourished. . . . The degradation of banking not only discouraged development but also distorted or corrupted the ideals underlying national institutions and distorted the sense of social justice. (pp. 11-12; translation by Kim 1995)

These views eventually gave way to monetarist thinking, which puts the interest of the financial sector before that of the industrial sector, but it will be difficult to make sense of Korea's financial system before the early 1990s without recognizing that finance was seen as a servant to industry. It may be worth mentioning that the financial repression policy had an ideological function of justifying government intervention and motivating people to participate in the development programmes because at least a part of the economic ruling class seemed to share the cost of industrial development against their own interests.

A political character of financial repression, i.e. the repression of financial rentiers, can be understood best through several extraordinary measures aiming to alleviate the financial burdens of manufacturing sectors at the cost of the financial rentiers and the working population. Among them, it was the government-declared moratorium on curb market loans in 1972 in which the repression of the financial rentier's interests can be dramatically exemplified. The President's Emergency Decree on Economic Stability and Growth was announced on 3 August 1972 (the 3 August decree) to counteract the near financial crisis which developed since the introduction of a McKinnon–Shaw-style financial reform in 1965. The reform created a huge interest gap between the domestic loans and foreign loans, generating an investment boom through contracting foreign loans. However, the high interest rates that prevailed after the 1965 liberalization, the current account deficits, and rapid rise in foreign loans resulted in a sharp fall in the profitability of non-financial firms and a rapid piling-up of non-performance loans in the banking sector. By 1972, the consequent increase in corporate bankruptcy pushed the country closer to a full-blown foreign debt crisis, as many of the bankrupt firms had foreign debts, and prompted the Korean government into implementing a series of extraordinary measures. The 3 August decree, which was the most important one, bailed out debt-ridden manufacturing firms by declaring a moratorium on the payments of all corporate debt to the curb market lenders for 3 years—probably one of the most extreme examples of 'financial repression' in recent world capitalist development history. It was declared that, after the end of the moratorium, all curb market loans were to be converted into 5-year loans at the annual interest rate of 16.2 per cent.[12]

### Credit Allocation Control: A Micro-level

Under the economic situation prevailing in Korea three decades ago, the most important task for realizing the development plans was how to provide long-term financing to companies that did not have adequate access to private funds due to lack of adequate credit rating or the fixed costs involved. Actually, from the view point of the lending criteria of any private financiers, almost all-private firms must not have got what they needed.

When the government decided to launch development programmes with nearly state-owned banking system and state-guarantee system for foreign loans, it had to cope with crucial problems: how to ensure the delivery of funds to the selected industries and projects and how to restrain the diversion of the funds to other than planned uses. Government control of foreign and domestic borrowing above a certain degree meant that the government could not only control it at the macro-level but also control the flows of investment at the micro-level, if it had the will. With the earmarked policy loan system, nearly firm-level credit controls had been designed and introduced to cope with these problems. By nature, the policy loan system requires suitable pipelines for the funds, which was met by the government's substantial control of the banking system and special HCI funds such as the 'National Investment Fund',[13] and exercising foreign credit allocation backed on the state guarantee system for foreign loans as indicated above. Even the commercial banks were urged to earmark a certain share of new credits to targeted priority sectors and projects, and to monitor the diversion of funds to other uses such as real estate speculations. Even though several previous measures can be found (Kim 1995), it was following the 3 August decree that *ex ante* credit control tools using banks as monitors and information collectors were introduced in earnest. As a matter of fact, out of fear that the rescued firms would become lax in management, believing in continued government support, the Korean policy makers introduced a series of policy measures intended to improve corporate governance more systemically in the aftermath of the 3 August decree.[14] It should be also noted that political resistance to the one-sided benefits to a group of private firms and 'wasteful' use of scarce public financial resources contributed partly to force the government to implement the measures.[15]

## THE EFFECTIVENESS OF THE KOREAN CREDIT POLICY

### The Size of Policy-based Loans: A Mild Repression?

While credit policy in Japan does not appear to have provided large subsidies but to have given much more weight in accessibility to credit facilities for priority borrowers, in Korea interest rate subsidies were quite large and accompanied by preferential availability of funds (Vittas and Wang 1991; Kato et al. 1994; Cho and Kim 1997). On occasion, the rates for export and investment finance were lower than the market rates by between 5 and 24 percentage points in the 1960s and the 1970s (Cole and Park 1983).

Responding to the selectiveness, the cost of capital in the preferential sectors was reduced. During 1973-81, HCI and the export sectors had a lower cost of capital than the light industries and domestic sectors by 2.8 per cent and 1.4 per cent respectively.

On the other hand, it is not so completely simple to measure the size of policy-base loans because of the basic problem of defining it,

TABLE 2.1: INTEREST RATES

*(annual average, per cent)*

| | Time deposit (1 year, at bank) | Bank loans | | Curb markets | CPI |
|---|---|---|---|---|---|
| | | General | Export | | |
| 1966-70 | 26.56 | 25.04 | 6.0 | 54.6 | 12.22 |
| 1971-5 | 15.92 | 16.8 | 7.4 | 41.42 | 15.58 |
| 1976-80 | 16.44 | 18.4 | 9.8 | 41.52 | 17.36 |
| 1981-5 | 10.44 | 12.0 | 11.0 | 28.6 | 7.34 |
| 1986-90 | 10.0 | 12.2 | 10.0 | 21.16 | 5.44 |

SOURCE: Bank of Korea, *Economic Statistics Yearbook*, various years.

TABLE 2.2: BORROWING COST* GAP BETWEEN SECTORS

*(percentage)*

| | 1973-81 | 1982-6 | 1987-90 |
|---|---|---|---|
| Domestic sector-Export sector | 1.4 | 2.1 | 0.6 |
| Light industries –HCIs | 2.8 | 1.4 | 0.8 |

NOTE: *average borrowing cost: the ratio of financial cost to the total of corporate bond, foreign loans and loans supplied by the financial institutions.
SOURCE: Bank of Korea, Financial Statements Analysis.

even though we can understand that the size was substantial, whichever definition we use. For example, considering that the government substantially owned the major banks and the interest rates ceilings for bank loans was set below the market rates, all bank loans could be regarded as policy loans.

Lee (1994), confining his attention to only Korean Won funds, estimates preferential funds in terms of interest rates and availability at above half of the total loans from the deposit money banks and development institutions during 1962-92. Cho and Kim (1997) focus on the explicit credit programmes and show that policy loans constituted about half of the total credit by domestic financial institutions in the 1970s and fell to about 30 per cent of total credit in the 1980s. The portion of policy loans in total loans from deposit money banks averaged annually 61.2 per cent between 1973 and 1991. Export loans accounted for 21.3 per cent of total policy loans supplied by deposit money banks during 1973-81 and 5.2 per cent during 1987-91.

As often noted, unlike in Japan and Taiwan, one of the salient features in Korea's selective credit policy is that the sources of policy loans depended heavily on the central bank credits and the deposits mobilized by deposit money banks, and much less on fiscal funds or government-mobilized funds. This difference may be explained by the fact that Korea suffered from a chronic foreign exchange shortage all through the development investment periods unlike Japan and Taiwan, setting aside the political fear caused by historical experience. The export credits supported by central bank amounted to 51.1 per cent of the total Central Bank lending during 1973-81, 26.1 per cent during 1982-6 and 7.2 per cent during 1987-91. In the mid 1980s, the special loans for restructuring of firms in distress increased sharply and the export support fell dramatically. The rediscount system of the central bank also functioned as a dominant instrument for directing commercial bank loans toward strategic sectors, as the ratio of the central bank's rediscount on commercial bills to deposit money banks' discount on commercial bills was almost 50 per cent during 1973-91.[16] Therefore, we agree that the directed credit has relied heavily on high-powered money in Korea (Cho and Kim, 1997, p. 54).

These facts imply that it may be not easy to accept without reservation the argument that 'a mild repression' is a condition of successful credit and industrial policy.[17] It is noteworthy once again that substantial uses of private sector-mobilized funds and central bank credits to support private investment by policy direction should require much more justification than otherwise. What is believed to be of central importance, but is often not paid much attention, is that the success or failure of credit policies is strongly influenced by how they can acquire political justification in order to organize collective social intention by getting the cooperation of those who eventually bear the expense of those policies. In a last dimension, the problem is about who should share (and how to share) the costs and distribute the fruits. Even complete free-market oriented policy benefits some participants who can often exploit the market itself better. The only difference is that they tend to quibble over the results as an unavoidable natural law.

### THE EFFECTIVENESS OF CREDIT POLICY

On government intervention in the financial resource allocation, it has been found that almost all developing countries have similar institutions for supporting targeted industries. However, it has also been found that most developing countries did not experience much success for promoting the industries.

In Korea, however, HCIs promotion had resulted in a dramatic substitution in the composition of those industrial sectors in GDP, with a big change in export composition.[18] In this sense, it is reasonable to assume that there must be a link between directed credit and the changes in industrial structure, notwithstanding the contradictory results of existing empirical works. Given the nature of credit policy as part of government funding activities carried out to realize national policy objectives (Kato et al. 1994), the effectiveness of credit policy cannot be separated from that of industrial policy. This section confines the discussion to the policy impact on HCI investment. To assess sufficiently the costs and benefits of credit policy in Korea's industrialization is beyond the scope of this paper.[19]

With corporate profitability restored through the 3 August decree, the Korean government reverted to a lower interest rates policy.[20] In 1973, the government announced the Heavy and Chemical Industrialization programme, with an emphasis on six strategic industries—steel, non-ferrous metal, shipbuilding, chemical, electronics, and machinery. The credit policies became literally 'selective'. The government provided support to the HCI industries through preferential bank loans, government investment and loan programmes, tax exemptions, accelerated depreciation allowances, cuts in import tariffs for capital and intermediate goods, the establishment of industrial estates by state expenditure, and so on. The five-year development plans, pursuing an investment-led development strategy, combined with export-led strategy were required to match investment plans with funding plans for it. It was to support the HCI programme that the government established the National Investment Fund in December 1973, and reorganized the rediscount system of the central bank.[21]

After experiencing a minor decline in growth during 1974 and 1975 in the aftermath of the first oil shock—the GDP growth rate slowed down from 12.8 per cent in 1973 to 8.1 per cent and 6.6 per cent in 1974 and 1975 respectively—a major investment and growth spurt started. Gross fixed capital formation grew in real terms by 21 per cent in 1976, 28.7 per cent in 1977, and an astonishing 34.4. per cent in 1978. GDP grew at 11.8 per cent, 10.3 per cent and 9.4 per cent in 1976, 1977, and 1978 respectively.

Unless the intended investments were reduced, such a large amount of term financing for HCI investment could be met only with government involvement. The involvement of the government was critical to mobilize and provide loans at low interest rates with long maturity to meet the long gestation period of HCI investment.

It seems clear that a discrete jump in the level of industrial development that Korea experienced would have been impossible without government intervention through credit and industrial policies. From the viewpoint of mainstream economics, however, what is most puzzling in the Korean experience arises here. Many researchers have tried to ascertain either qualitatively or quantitatively, or both, the effects of a financial repression policy on economic growth and development on economic efficiency grounds. However, the results do not lead to any clear solution due to their contradictory findings according to periods and countries. Nevertheless, considering the features of finance that may result in financial market failures such as the volatility of financial variables, short-term business horizons, coordination or information problems, and especially its externalities, it is very difficult to believe that a market-oriented financial regime could have endorsed Korea's investment programmes as well as export–driven policy (Park 1994). It is also obvious, as addressed above, that a repressed financial regime cannot always encourage social investment and export. That is why more fundamental aspects of intervention in the allocation of credit should be found. We do not have, and are not likely to have, a completely satisfying theory of the Korean industrialization experience as long as there is a blind faith in the efficiency of free capital markets.

## CRISIS MANAGEMENT AND ITS IMPLICATION FOR THE NEW MODEL

Korea's development regime introduced by Park's government (1961-79) was strongly restricted by the failure of the governments preceding it and by people's demands. However, once they decided to get what they needed by a concentrated investment and by people's participatory mobilization, whatever its form, the contingent events including institutional schemes, could easily be set in motion as long as the government retained strong pragmatism and flexibility. One of the most important pillars has been the participation of the people, at least in economic activities, although there has been strong resistance in political matters. This kind of participation under dictatorship was very incomplete and unsustainable because it was, in fact, accompanied by self-sacrifice. The original Korean Model had a critical flaw, that is, a separation of economic growth from democracy and hence a possible revocation of the fundamental commitment to dictatorship once industrialization has been established. To combine sustainable economic growth with substantial democracy will require another social challenge.

At the present moment, however, it is too soon to make any prediction about a new model. What can be said is that insofar as the people's unfulfilled will or demands can be organized to induce them to participate in economic activities, a dynamic development can also be expected. We can also expect the worst case, i.e. a transformation of 'self-sacrifice' into 'self-destruction of society'. In any case, what the Korean experience has shown is that even forced and incomplete participation of the working population could produce sufficient resources for industrialization to take place.

The fundamental reason why the IMF reform after the recent crisis should be criticized is that it is designed to contain the possibility of democratic participation of the working population in economic activities at the cost of Western style private property rights. Contrary to the popular Western evaluation of the Miracle or the shared growth (of course, before the crisis), ordinary Koreans have long been complaining about Korea's economic performance and have been worried about unequal income distribution. The reason why the Korean people cannot be satisfied with a relatively good level of income sharing can be found in the fear that their historically virtual communal property might be stolen without appropriate compensation.

## Institutional Changes after the 1997 Crisis

The policy package that was adopted to manage the (still unresolved) 1997 crisis was not entirely in the mould of the standard IMF package and still showed some traditional Korean streaks. For example, the Korean government pushed the *chaebols* into a 'voluntary' industrial restructuring programme involving mergers and business swaps in eight industries (semiconductor, automobile, power-generating equipment, naval diesel engine, aircraft, petrochemical, petroleum refining, and railway carriage). Although this programme is not part of a coherent long-term industrial policy as in the case of previous industrial restructuring programmes, it looks similar to its earlier counterparts in its appearance.

However, in general, the crisis management package implemented since 1997 has resulted in institutional changes that are likely to significantly transform the nature of the Korean economy. Important changes were also made in other areas such as labour market institutions, bureaucratic recruitment, and appointments. If the discussion is confined to institutional changes concerning the financial system, the following changes are worth receiving attention.

Firstly, the move to 'pro-finance' policy stance, which characterized the macroeconomic policy in the early days of the crisis, was subsequently institutionalized through a series of legal changes in the financial system. To begin with, the role of the central bank was redefined into a fundamentally monetarist mould. In the old central bank act, the Bank of Korea was supposed to maintain the 'soundness of the banking and the financial system', which means many things in practice, as well as price stability. The new Act that took effect from April 1999 specifies that price stability should be the sole aim of the Bank of Korea. This change may have profound implications for the Korean financial system, as it de-legitimizes the kind of pro-investment, pro-growth monetary policy that characterized the Korean financial system. The banking law and other financial laws were also revised in a way that strengthened the shareholder interest in the running of the banks, thus making it possible and legitimate to protect openly financial interests at the cost of industrial interests.

The second important institutional change in the Korean financial system after the crisis was the introduction of the BIS standard on capital adequacy ratio into the financial system. The BIS standard has certain merits like simplicity and transparency, but an important problem with it is its pro-cyclical nature as proven by the recent Korean experience; in recession, increased bankruptcy and fall in asset prices will shrink banks' asset bases, which requires that the banks withdraw their loans in order to meet the standard, thereby making the recession even worse.[22] Moreover, the manner in which the BIS standard is defined encourages the holding of liquid assets and therefore a strict enforcement of the standard, to which the Korean government claims to be committed, will make the banks reluctant to lend to industrial projects that involve large sunk costs.

Thirdly, the asserted overhaul of the Korean financial market aimed at the American style market-based financial market. It can restrain the bank-based financial system from developing its strong points for encouraging investment in large-scale industries. The deregulation of the stock market is expected to lead to a greater reliance on direct financing, but given the well-known short-term orientation of the stock market, it is unlikely that the Korean firms are going to be able to mobilize through the stock market enough 'patient' funds needed for the investments in their major industries in the long run.

The fourth institutional change after the crisis was a full-scale capital account opening. Especially notable are the full-scale liberalization of corporate borrowings from abroad, which makes government regulation of foreign debts much more difficult, and the complete opening of the stock and bond markets to foreigners. These changes have increased the volatility in the financial market, which is not conducive to long-term investments. This will have negative effects on the country's investment–growth dynamics.

## CONCLUDING REMARKS

Very often, even advocates of government intervention in financial markets tend to interpret what happened in Japan and Korea after their rapid industrialization period as evidence for the argument that the merits of credit policies would diminish as the private industrial sector becomes more sophisticated (Cho and Hellman 1994). At least in the case of Korea, however, it cannot be true, simply when we consider the big industrial development gap between Japan and Korea. Also, there must be a big space for the other developing countries. What is required is not merely unilateral withdrawal of government intervention, but a rearrangement of the social and political control including the role of government, as otherwise transferring control to the private market merely means market control by the monopolized market forces. I argue that Korea has got what it wanted in terms of industrial structure through an organization of collective public's intention. But it can raise a subsequent question. What if every country want to have the same industries? The only solution we have may be coordination and negotiation unless a catastrophe is welcome.

We consider below whether it is possible to describe different models of capitalism and whether there is any pressure for convergence towards one model. Globalization and its neo-liberalism ideology, whose actual influence has been exercised less by anonymous market forces than by political intervention through institutions like the US government and international organizations, acts certainly as a pressure towards homogenization among capitalist national economies.

Still, the present globalization processes do not mean that all national

TABLE 2.3: CHANGES IN THE CONTENTS OF THE IMF PROGRAMME DURING THE 1997 CRISIS*

| | Macroeconomic targets for 1998 | Monetary policies | Measures for promoting domestic demand |
|---|---|---|---|
| First Memorandum (3 December 1997, revised 24 December 1997) | - Growth rate (GDP): 3%<br>- Inflation: 5%<br>- Trade Surplus: $4.3 billion<br>- Central Government Deficit: Balance or Surplus<br>- Unemployment Rate: 3.9% | - Tight monetary policy<br>- High interest rate policy<br>- Financial sector restructuring<br>- Interest rate over 30%<br>- Elimination of upper limit in interest rate | - Emphasis on tight fiscal policy rather than promotion of domestic demand |
| 7 January1998 Agreement | - Growth rate: 1~2%<br>- Inflation: 9%<br>- Trade surplus: $3 billion<br>- Usable reserves: $24 billion (1st Qtr.)<br>- Unemployment Rate: 5% | - Establishing foundation for interest rate stabilization<br>- Monetary base: 14.9% (1st Qtr.) | - Inevitable Fiscal deficits allowed |
| 7 Februray 1998 Agreement | - Growth rate: 1%<br>- Inflation: 9%<br>- Trade Surplus: over USD 8 billion<br>- Usable reserves: $20 billion (1st Qtr.), $30 billion (2nd Qtr.)<br>- Unemployment Rate: 6-7% | - Cautiously permit lowering inter-bank call rate conditional on the market situation<br>- Increase in money growth rate target monetary base: 13.5% (1st Qtr.), 14.1% (2nd Qtr.) | - Allow fiscal deficit up to 0.8% of GDP<br>- Reduction in luxury goods tax |

| | | | |
|---|---|---|---|
| 2 May 1998 Agreement | - Growth rate: -1% or less<br>- Inflation: less than 10%<br>- Trade Surplus: \$21–23 billion<br>- Usable reserves: \$32 billion (2nd Qtr.) | - Pursue a continuous fall in inter-bank call rate<br>- Increase in support for small and medium sized companies | - Fiscal deficit allowed up to 1.7% of GDP |
| 24 July 1998 Agreement | - Growth rate: -4%<br>- Inflation: 9%<br>- Trade surplus: \$33–35 billion | - Lower interest rate by flexible monetary control | - Fiscal deficit allowed up to 5 % of GDP |
| 29 October 1998 Agreement | - Growth rate: -4%<br>- Inflation: 8%<br>- Trade Surplus: \$37 billion | - Eliminate the limit on the growth rate of reserve money | |
| 13 November 1998 Agreement | - Growth rate for 1999: positive<br>- Inflation: 5%<br>- Current accounts surplus: about \$20 billion (7% of GDP)<br>- Usable reserves (targeted to reach \$41 billion at end-1998): already reached \$45 billion at end-October and are expected to rise moderately in 1999 | - Maintain the easy monetary stance, consistent with achievement of the inflation target and stability of the exchange rate<br>- BOK intervention in exchange rate: limited to smoothing operations<br>- Public works programmes: W2 trillion<br>- Outlays for job training: W0.8 trillion in 1999 | - Fiscal deficit: around 5% of GDP in 1998<br>- Direct social safety net outlays: to increase from W5.7 trillion in 1998 to W8.2 trillion (about 2% of GDP) in 1999 |

(contd.)

TABLE 2.3 (contd.)

| | Macroeconomic targets for 1998 | Monetary policies | Measures for promoting domestic demand |
|---|---|---|---|
| 31 March 1999 Agreement | - Growth rate for 1999: over 2%<br>- Inflation: around 3%<br>- Current account surplus to narrow significantly but remain substantial.<br>- Usable reserves (which reached $48.5 billion at end-1998): to rise further in 1999 | - Continuing a flexible Interest rate policy<br>- Broad money (M3) growth expected at 13–14% in 1999.<br>- BOK intervention in exchange rate will be limited to smoothing operations.<br>for small- and medium-sized enterprises: $0.3 billion | - Fiscal deficit allowed up to 5% of GDP for 1999<br>- Import financing for small- and medium-sized enterprises: at least $1 billion<br>- BOK rediscount of exports (rediscounts of export) bills |

NOTE: * Cited from Chang and Yoo (1999).

SOURCES: Korea Institute for Economic Policy (1998), *Adjustment Reforms in Korea since the Financial Crisis (Dec. 1997-June 1998);*
Ministry of Finance and Economy (1998), *The Agreement between Korea and the IMF for Fourth Quarter;*
Ministry of Finance and Economy (1999), *The First Letter of Intent Agreed between Korean Government and IMF in 1999;*
Samsung Economic Research Institute (1998), *One Year after the IMF Bailout: A Review of Economic and Social Changes in Korea.*

economies will have the same industrial structure. In fact, the homogenization processes have been more significant among Western Europe, North America, and Japan (and parts of South-East Asia at least before the recent crisis) than between these regions and the other developing economies. This has meant a systemic exclusion of the remaining countries, regions, and individuals. The more unrestrained the competitions are, the more severe is the exclusion of losers.

At the same time, the division of labour in the world economy has deepened and will deepen. Therefore, the pressure for convergence is accompanied by its counter-tendencies. Different kinds of capitalism may well reflect their different industrial structures and positions in the worldwide division of labour. The literature which describes the diversity of capitalism tends to point out the differences in the banking and financial systems. At least from the Korean experience, it can be said that their determinants are the nature, amount, and composition of the investment of a country, along the way with to mobilize and create the financial resources. Korea's industrialization has been pursued at the general public's expense and with the repression of the financial rentiers' interests. Actually, it can be said that the repression of rentier interests has contributed to a political justification of the industrialization being at the public's expense. In the sense that every political intervention to change an industrial structure produces necessarily benefactors and cost payers, political as well as economical justifications and a vision of compensation are required. Successful political justification may be necessary to operate directed credit programmes for quite a long time. The next requirement is to implement institutional instruments to assure the channelling of the limited available funds to targeted strategic sectors. In retrospect, from the Korea example of financial repression has a function of governing large industrial conglomerates supported by public money as well as of repression of financial rentiers' interest.

It should also not be overlooked that the effects of the neo-liberal regime on individual countries, despite strong pressure for convergence towards one model of capitalism, will always be mediated by the distinctive institutions and practices specific to each country. This points to the presence of certain distortions as the external pressure passes through a sieve of internal social structures. As is well known, Japan, Germany, and Korea have a common experience in regard to their formation of the national institutional framework. In Korea, the basic framework of financial institutions, including the Law of the Central

Bank, was created with the assistance of the US scholars and officers under the US military authorities' rule. Where will the present difference come from? An institutional approach, which is implicitly suggested in this presentation, is to try to pick up the spirits reflected in the institutional settings. It may be different from the functional approaches to the mechanisms of the individual institutions.

## NOTES

1. To give a brief perspective on Korea's economic achievement, the UK took nearly 60 years to quadruple per capita income in their early capitalistic development (1860-1920) while Korea took around 10 years only to do so (1966 to mid 1970s). See World Bank (1993) for details on the difference of growth rates between the East Asian and industrial economies.
2. A characteristic of the weak Korean social safety nets was that private firms took substantial charge of them.
3. The Heavy Industry's share of manufacturing has grown continuously even after the manufacturing sector's share of GDP reached its peak. But it has not been under the regime of selective industrial policy any more since the late 1980s.

   Heavy Industry's Share of Manufacturing Production

   *(manufacturing production=100)*

| 1962 | 1967 | 1972 | 1977 | 1982 | 1987 | 1991 |
|---|---|---|---|---|---|---|
| 28.6 | 34.7 | 36.1 | 49.2 | 52.8 | 57.0 | 64.9 |

   SOURCE: National Statistical Office.

4. As a matter of fact, the government-owned or government–controlled domestic banks provided repayment guarantees for 88 per cent of the total foreign commercial loans in 1975. Therefore, the government provided *ex ante* payment guarantees to almost all foreign debts.

   Repayment Guarantee of Commercial Loans *(end of 1975)*

| | Amount (million US$) |
|---|---|
| Korea Exchange Bank | 1,786.070 |
| Commercial Bank* | 92.491 |
| Local Bank** | 12.093 |
| Korea Development Bank | 302.550 |
| Total repayment guarantee (A) | 2,193.204 |
| Total commercial loan (B) | 2491 |
| A/B (per cent) | 88.0 |

   NOTES: * Commercial bank includes four national-wide commercial banks.
   ** Local bank includes two local banks.

   SOURCE: C.-J. Kim (1976).

5. The virtual 'Combined Guarantee System of the State-Banks-Large Enterprises' in Korea may have a very important implication for the question of how transaction trust can grow in developing countries or post-communist societies. As to the role of credit policy in developing countries, an ever-ignored aspect is its role in ensuring enforcement of contract for commercial transactions. An orthodox idea might be that the recurrent acts of trade themselves can build up quickly a level of 'trust' required for prevailing capitalist economic transactions. However, the experiences in most developing countries and post-communist countries have told a different story (see Humphrey and Schmitz 1996). It is obvious that in the absence of a certain level of trust there will exist only spot markets, let alone the case of commercial credit. In the case of Taiwan, Amsden (1991) devotes passing attention to the possibility that big businesses may have been intermediaries to provide smaller-size firms with trade credit.
6. Working Hours per Week in Manufacturing Sector *(as of 1996) (hours)*

| Korea | Japan | UK | USA | Portugal | Belgium (94) | Denmark (93) |
|---|---|---|---|---|---|---|
| 48.4 | 43.3 | 41.9 | 41.6 | 39.6 | 33.0 | 31.5 |

SOURCE: *International Key Statistics*, BOK.

7. This implies that a subordinate ideology could replace the major ideologies such as socialism and capitalism. Without alternatives and opposite ideologies, in fact there cannot exist any ideology alone. It was not until the 1980s that the endogenous social democracy or socialist movements began to make their appearance.
8. Even in the 1990s, it was not a rarity that banks required the borrower firms to offer the chief shareholders' private properties as a collateral, even though the largest conglomerates were relieved of this sort of custom earlier than the other firms.
9. This section draws from Chang and Yoo (1999).
10. The banks were run like public enterprises, regardless of their ownership status. A substantial proportion of the banks were 100 per cent owned by the government. In the other banks, where the government did not have the majority stake, the government maintained its absolute control through the 'temporary' law introduced in 1961, which limited private shareholders' voting rights, and subsequently the 1981 provision in the Banking Act that replaced the 'temporary' law, which set an 8 per cent ceiling on bank share ownership for any individual or a group of related shareholders. In the 1962 revision of the Central Bank Act, the Bank of Korea Act, the Minister of Finance was made the head of the Monetary Board (later renamed the Monetary Policy Committee of the Bank of Korea), thus depriving the Central Bank of its independence. The regime of policy loans was perfected when the Korean-style 'main bank' system was introduced in May 1974, following the 1970–2 debt crisis, on the recognition that tight monitoring is necessary in order to ensure efficient use of policy loans and of foreign debts that usually accompanied policy loans.
11. Central to the regime of tight control on capital outflow was the Foreign Exchange Concentration System, under which all foreign exchange had to be surrendered to the central bank, and the Foreign Exchange Management Act, which put severe restrictions on the use of foreign exchange. This system of foreign exchange control began to be relaxed from the late 1980s.
12. At the time, the curb market interest rate was more than 40 per cent. The total amount of curb market loans reported by debtors and creditors was equivalent to

around 42 per cent of total bank loans. An extensive rescheduling of bank loans at a preferential rate was also implemented, with the central bank supporting the rescheduling by accepting the special debentures issued by the commercial banks.

13. The National Investment Fund Act was enacted in 1973 for the purpose of financing HCI projects. One of the important characteristics of the fund was its sources: it has been raised from financial savings and the government funds not from the central bank's money creation, which means the National Investment Fund (NIF) was intended not to mobilize new savings but to reallocate the existing resources. The share of the NIF in total policy loans was not large (around 5 per cent of total bank loans in the 1970s), but its influence over the direction of HCI investment was crucial because it headed directly by the Economic Planning Board. See Cho and Kim (1997), pp. 107–17 for a detailed discussion on the NIF.
14. These measures were mainly based on the Presidential Directives on the Inducement of Public Listing and the Sound Management of Private Enterprises announced on 29 May 1974. The Directives were also accompanied by a few more implemental measures to provide the Office of Bank Supervision with the authority to extensively scrutinize the financial state of the business conglomerates (the *chaebols*), which were the main beneficiaries of policy loans and foreign borrowing (see Cho and Kim 1997 for details).
15. The World Bank (1993, p. 287) concluded that continual and pragmatic review and adjustment of policy implementation reduced the moral hazard costs of government intervention.
16. See BOK (1996).
17. The last sentence of a bulky study (Kato et al. 1994) on policy-based finance in Japan, published by the World Bank and commissioned by the Japan Development Bank and the Japan Economic Research Institute, concludes that 'as also recognised by the World Bank, low interest rate can indeed work effectively, under three assumptions—that a financial institution does not bend to political pressure to fund non-viable projects, that it makes financing decisions independently, based on sufficient appraisal capabilities, and that it implements a strict ex-post-facto audit. In this sense, it is not an exaggeration to say that the Japan Development Bank has been this type of institution.' Surprisingly, we cannot find a name-matched independence from political pressure and sufficient appraisal capabilities of a financial institution in the Korean development experiences.
18. In 1991, the share of HCI products in Korean exports reached 60 per cent. 35 per cent comprised light manufactured products, and 5 per cent primary products.
19. In the literature on Korea's case, it is very rare to find a purist position arguing either that the industrial and credit policy was very successful or that they retarded growth and caused negative results (Vittas and Wang 1991).
20. The measures taken to resolve Korea's first debt crisis, while very unconventional, set the stage for renewed growth in the following years. The profitability and the financial health of industrial corporations were restored through a brutal confiscation of the financial rentier class as well as through a government-mediated corporate restructuring. In addition, the corporate governance system was improved by strengthening the banking system as a monitoring agent over the *chaebols*.
21. See BOK (1996) for the detailed operation and the development of the rediscount system in Korea.
22. Many studies reported that the BIS standard, introduced in the middle of the deepest recession, brought a vicious circle between a credit crunch and increasing bankruptcy.

## REFERENCES


Amsden, Alice H. (1991), 'Big Business and Urban Congestion in Taiwan: The Origins of Small Enterprise and Regionally Decentralized Industry (Respectively)', *World Development,* vol. 19, no. 9, pp. 1121-35.

BOK (1996), 'Rediscount System in Korea', Research Department, The Bank of Korea, Seoul.

Chang, H.J., H.J. Park and C.G. Yoo (1998), 'Interpreting the Korean Crisis', *Cambridge Journal of Economics,* vol. 22, no. 6, pp. 735-46.

Chang, H.J. and C.G. Yoo (1999), 'The Triumph of the Rentiers?: The 1997 Korean Crisis in a Historical Perspective', Workshop on The Third World Financial Authority, CEPA, New School for Social Research, New York.

Cho, Yoon Je and Joon Kyung Kim (1997), *Credit Policies and the Industrialization of Korea,* Korea Development Institute, Seoul.

Cho, Yoon Je and Thomas Hellmann (1994), 'The Government's Role in Japanese and Korean Credit Markets: A New Institutional Economic Perspective', *Seoul Journal of Economics,* vol. 7, no. 4, pp. 383-415.

Cho, Yoon Je (1986), 'Inefficiencies from Financial Liberalization in the Absence of Well-Functioning Equity Markets', *Journal of Money, Credit, and Banking,* vol. 18, no. 2, pp. 191-9.

Cole, D. and Y.C. Park (1983), *Financial Development in Korea, 1945–1978,* Harvard University Press, Cambridge, MA.

Hellmann, Thomas, Kevin Murdock, and Joseph Stiglitz (1996), 'Financial Restraints: Toward a New Paradigm', in Masahiko Aoki, Hyung-Ki Kim, and Masahiro Okuno-Fujiwara, *The Role of Government in East Asian Economic Development,* Clarendon Press, Oxford, pp. 163-207.

Humphrey, J. and H. Schmitz (1996), 'Trust and Economic Development', Discussion Paper, no. 355, Institute of Development Studies, Sussex.

Kato K. and T. Shibata (1994), 'Policy-Based Finance: The Experience of Postwar Japan', World Bank Discussion Paper, no. 221, The World Bank, Washington, D.C.

Keynes, J.M. (1936, 1949), *The General Theory of Employment, Interest and Money,* MacMillan, London.

Kim, C.J. (1976), *Theory of Foreign Capital: Introduction* (in Korean), ILJoKak, Seoul.

Kim, P.J. (1995), *Financial System and Policy (1961-79),* Paper no. 95-02, Korea Institute of Finance, Seoul.

Lee, Chung H. (1992), 'The Government, Financial System, and Large Private Enterprises in the Economic Development of South Korea', *World Development,* vol. 20, no. 2, pp. 187-97.

Lee, K.Y. (1994), 'Institutions of Policy Loan: History, Effects and Improvement Measures', Korea Tax Institute, Seoul.

Marklew, V. (1995), *Cash, Crisis, and Corporate Governance,* The University of Michigan Press, Ann Arbor.

Park, Y.C. (1994), 'Korea: Development and Structural Change of the Financial System', in H.T. Patrick and Y.C. Park, (eds), *The Financial Development of Japan, Korea and Taiwan*, Oxford University Press, New York, pp. 129-87.

Shaw, E.S. (1973), *Financial Deepening in Economic Development*, Oxford University Press, London.

Sobhan, R. (ed.) (1998), *Towards a Theory of Governance and Development: Learning from East Asia,* Center for Policy Dialogue, The University Press, Dhaka.

Vittas, Dimitri and Yoon Je Cho (1995), 'Credit Policies: Lessons From East Asia', Working Paper 95-04, World Bank Reference, The World Bank, Washington, D.C.

Vittas, Dimitri and Bo Wang (1991), 'Credit Policies in Japan and Korea: A Review of the Literature', Working Paper WPS 747, The World Bank, Washington, D.C.

World Bank (1993), *The East Asian Miracle: Economic Growth and Public Policy*, Oxford University Press, New York.

# 3

# Exchange Rate Arrangements: Their Suitability to the Malaysian Economy

*Eu Chye Tan*

## OVERVIEW

This chapter discusses the implications of the macroeconomic policy measures undertaken by Malaysia in response to the 1997 East Asian financial market crisis, and alludes to the relevance of the Mundell-Fleming model to a developing country such as Malaysia. The primary objective of the paper is to assess the suitability of the fixed and flexible foreign exchange regimes to Malaysia. The Malaysian government has fixed the exchange rate of the ringgit at RM 3.80 to the US dollar and imposed capital controls since September 1998 to gain the breathing space for resuscitating the economy following the East Asian financial crisis triggered by the run on the Thai baht in July 1997 after adhering to the IMF prescription for about a year. The capital controls were subsequently relaxed by the imposition of a graduated exit levy on short-term capital. Malaysia has in fact bucked the trend amongst developing and transition economies to move to regimes of greater exchange rate variability amid high international capital mobility. It is calling for a speedy reform of the international financial architecture to redress the volatility of capital flows by regulating hedge funds and highly-leveraged institutions.

The suitability of the different exchange rate arrangements will be evaluated against the backdrop of the policy preference of the Malaysian government to maintain high economic growth with relatively less emphasis placed on maintaining a current account balance and low inflation. Malaysia is accustomed to a very high growth environment as the annual economic growth rate during the pre-crisis years always exceeded 8 per cent. Currently, the policy configuration of the Malaysian government involves expansionary monetary and fiscal policies, imperfect capital mobility, and a peg to the US dollar. Hence, it would be interesting to consider the macroeconomic implications of such policies from a theoretical perspective. It is generally believed that the macroeconomic policies pursued by the government in response to the economic crisis have aided in the turnaround of the economy. The Malaysian economy staged an impressive growth of 4.8 per cent by the second quarter of 1999, 8.5 per cent by the third quarter and 10.8 per cent by the fourth quarter (see Table 3.1). Private sector sentiments about the economy also recovered by the first quarter of 1999 with sales of passenger cars and commercial vehicles recording a positive growth throughout 1999 (see Table 3.2).

However, Table 3.1 also suggests that the economic recovery witnessed in the aftermath of the financial crisis was not an experience unique to Malaysia. Countries such as South Korea, Indonesia, Thailand, and the Philippines were also recovering around the same time as Malaysia, or in fact one quarter earlier with the exception of Indonesia. South Korea's economic recovery was even more dramatic as it recorded higher rates of economic growth throughout 1999. Notwithstanding this similarity in the growth experience, Malaysia's policy mode of economic recovery may be more socially acceptable as growth was achieved without any significant socio-economic

TABLE 3.1: GDP GROWTH OF SELECTED EAST ASIAN COUNTRIES

*(annual % change)*

| Year/Qtr | Malaysia | South Korea | Indonesia | Thailand | Philippines |
|---|---|---|---|---|---|
| 1996 | 10.0 | 6.8 | 7.8 | 5.9 | 5.8 |
| 1997 | 7.3 | 5.0 | 4.7 | -1.8 | 5.2 |
| 1998/Q1 | -1.6 | -3.6 | -7.9 | -8.2 | 1.7 |
| 1998/Q2 | -5.9 | -7.2 | -16.5 | -12.3 | -0.8 |
| 1998/Q3 | -10.1 | -7.1 | -17.4 | -13.6 | -0.1 |
| 1998/Q4 | -11.2 | -5.9 | -19.5 | -5.8 | -1.9 |
| 1999/Q1 | -1.5 | 4.4 | -10.3 | 0.8 | 1.2 |
| 1999/Q2 | 4.8 | 9.9 | 1.8 | 3.3 | 3.6 |
| 1999/Q3 | 8.5 | 12.8 | 0.5 | 7.4 | 3.1 |
| 1999/Q4 | 10.8 | 13.0 | 5.8 | 6.5 | 4.6 |

SOURCE: Bank Negara Malaysia, *Monthly Statistical Bulletin*, April 2000.

TABLE 3.2: SELECTED INDICATORS OF PRIVATE SECTOR SENTIMENTS

*(annual % change)*

| Year/Qtr | Sales of Passenger Cars | Sales of Commercial Vehicles |
|---|---|---|
| 1996 | 22.8 | 48.7 |
| 1997 | 12.3 | 8.4 |
| 1998/Q1 | -67.6 | -77.9 |
| 1998/Q2 | -60.6 | -83.3 |
| 1998/Q3 | -57.7 | -81.2 |
| 1998/Q4 | -33.9 | -54.3 |
| 1999/Q1 | 141.3 | 35.9 |
| 1999/Q2 | 105.4 | 78.4 |
| 1999/Q3 | 76.7 | 77.6 |
| 1999/Q4 | 40.1 | 27.4 |

SOURCE: Bank Negara Malaysia, *Monthly Statistical Bulletin*, April 2000.

dislocations as witnessed in these other crisis-hit countries. This speaks much about the policy ingenuity of Malaysia. However, the economic growth attained can essentially be viewed as a short-run phenomenon imparted by expansionary fiscal and monetary policies as predicted by the Mundell-Fleming model and its variants augmented by favourable developments on the export front. The depreciated ringgit has boosted the competitiveness of Malaysian exports abroad.

The rest of this chapter is configured as follows. The next section presents a discussion of the macroeconomic implications of fixed and flexible exchange rate regimes. Their intermediate variants such as the managed float, adjustable peg, crawling peg, and monetary union are also dwelt upon. The following section then assesses the appropriateness of the fixed and flexible exchange rate systems to Malaysia, the last section concludes with remarks.

## MACROECONOMIC IMPLICATIONS OF EXCHANGE RATE REGIMES[1]

In a fixed exchange rate regime, there is government intervention in the foreign exchange market via its monetary authority in order to maintain the exchange rate at a certain prescribed level. There will be buying and selling of currencies to stem the variation of the exchange rate, which makes it necessary for the monetary authority to hold international reserves. The monetary authority would lose its controllability over money supply. Monetary policy actions have to be subordinated to the goals of maintaining the parity exchange rate. The monetary authority must relinquish control over the domestic money supply to hold the exchange rate fixed.

There are two variants of the fixed rate regime, namely the crawling peg and the adjustable peg regimes. In the case of the crawling peg, the government makes frequent but small adjustments to the pegged rate while in the case of the adjustable peg, the adjustments are infrequent. A crawling peg would permit the monetary authorities to hold a smaller volume of international reserves as a buffer to finance balance of payments deficit, by virtue of a greater reliance on exchange rate changes as a device for restoring external balance. However, if future exchange rate movements are not predetermined, speculation of exchange rate changes based on inflationary expectations might arise and this could generate instability. Hence, it may be desirable to pre-announce the path of exchange rate movements, as practised by Chile by means of its '*tablita*' (a table of pre-set exchange rate changes) in the late 1970s and by Argentina from 1978 to 1991. This could alleviate instability brought about by speculative forces and hence the possibility of a foreign exchange crisis, provided governments strictly abide by the exchange rate rules.

On the other hand, a freely flexible exchange rate regime exists when exchange rates are freely determined by market forces, i.e. by the demand for and supply of currencies by private agents. Monetary authorities do not have to contend with balance of payments problems as they are under no obligation to intervene in the foreign exchange market. Thus they need not be concerned with movements in the international reserves and could exercise a more effective control over the domestic money supply.

A variant of the flexible exchange rate regime is the managed float regime. The regime involves government intervention in the foreign exchange market in order to influence the exchange rate movement though it involves no commitment to maintain a certain fixed rate or some narrow band around it.

Another international monetary arrangement is the monetary union such as the European Monetary System (EMS). The EMS was established in March 1979 with the primary aim of promoting European monetary cooperation. A monetary union such as the EMS could involve member countries floating their currencies *vis-à-vis* those of non-member countries while pegging their currencies to each other.

Member countries have to abdicate their active use of monetary policy in favour of a central organization or fund that coordinates their monetary actions. The extreme case of a monetary union is a common currency area within which countries utilize a common currency. A well-functioning monetary union could contribute to price and income stability and facilitate payments adjustment among member countries. Mundell (1961) has stressed on substantial factor (capital and labour) mobility as a prerequisite for a successful monetary union. Mundell maintains that regions or countries with high factor mobility should form a single currency or a multi-currency area with fixed exchange rates, referring to it as an optimum currency area. Factor mobility would serve as a substitute for exchange rate changes in achieving equilibrium and improving welfare amongst member countries or regions. Flexible exchange rates would be more suited to countries whose factors are relatively immobile.

However, factor mobility is neither a necessary nor sufficient condition for a successful monetary union. McKinnon (1963) maintains that small open economies will not be able to benefit from exchange rate flexibility since in such economies the domestic prices would react swiftly to exchange rate changes. The quick reaction would nullify any impact the exchange rate changes would otherwise have on the relative price of domestic and foreign goods. Exchange rate changes may not alter the relative prices of traded and non-traded goods in the case of countries with a relatively large traded goods sector. Thus, for such countries, it may be more appropriate for them to peg to each other's currency.

Under a fixed exchange rate system with no capital mobility, expansionary monetary policy can only sustain income at a higher level temporarily and is not effective in the long run. Suppose a government is experiencing a recessionary threat and its policy response is to maintain an expansionary monetary policy. Such a policy reaction would lead to a reduction in the domestic interest rate, which in turn would stimulate investment and aggregate demand and thus domestic income. However, the increased income that will be observed is only a short run phenomenon unless there is sterilization as rising income would lead to a deterioration in the balance of payments, thus eroding the monetary base, which in turn would result in a contraction of the domestic economy.

Neither will fiscal policy be effective in the long run. If the government were to prop up the economy via increasing its expenditure on domestic goods and services instead, the impact on income and employment will be positive in the short run. However, the increased income tends to raise the transactionary demand for money, thus exerting an upward pressure on the domestic interest rate. Concurrently, the rising domestic income would cause a surge in imports, thus contributing to a deficit in the balance of payments. All this would finally push the economy back to its initial income level. Moreover, the increased government spending could crowd out private sector investment, and given that the private sector has a higher productivity compared to the public sector, the overall productivity of the economy will be jeopardized.

Thus, in order to achieve internal and external balance, both monetary and fiscal policies will have to be complemented by some exchange rate policy. In this instance, the government may be forced to devalue ultimately.

However, in view of the higher priority attached by governments to employment rather than current account imbalances, the automatic adjustment mechanism is usually denied the opportunity to operate via sterilization operations. The breakdown of the automatic adjustment mechanism induced by governments in the world has been referred to by Mundell (1968a) as the international disequilibrium system. For instance, to offset the negative impact of a balance of payments deficit on the monetary base in the quest for employment stability, governments may sterilize by increasing domestic credit creation. However, sterilization operations cannot continue for an indefinite period of time when there is a persistent external payments deficit as ultimately the international reserves will be fully depleted.

When a fixed exchange rate system is accompanied by capital mobility, monetary policy would still be ineffective. Suppose a monetary authority wishes to boost its domestic economy by increasing money supply. While domestic interest rates would decline and investment and output be stimulated, low domestic rates *vis-à-vis* the foreign rates could result in massive capital outflows, thus precipitating a balance of payments deficit and a contraction in domestic money supply. That monetary policy is ineffective is true irrespective of the degree of capital mobility.

However, an expansionary fiscal policy will be quite effective if accompanied by fixed exchange rates and capital mobility. If instead of increasing the money supply, the government increases spending to fuel the economy, the immediate impact is an increase in the aggregate demand for domestic goods and hence the domestic income. This could bring about a tight credit situation with a surge in the domestic interest rate above the world rate. This in turn could generate capital inflows, and the positive impact on the capital account can be expected to outweigh the negative impact of rising incomes on the current account. Capital inflows would persist until the domestic interest rate tends to the foreign interest rate. This is true even if capital is not perfectly mobile. Nevertheless, this may not be a desirable situation as it implies a protracted financing of the current account deficit by foreign funds.

However, if policy-makers have a short run horizon, monetary and fiscal policies may be optimally mixed to influence the capital account and hence the balance of payments without any need for an expenditure-switching policy in a fixed exchange rate regime with capital mobility. Assuming that initially an economy is experiencing a balance of payments deficit and unemployment, both problems may be resolved by adopting an expansionary fiscal policy and a contractionary monetary policy. Both the internal and the external imbalances can be eliminated by an appropriate combination of fiscal and monetary policies. However, the use of a monetary-fiscal policy mix has its shortcomings. It may be inadvisable for an economy to continue relying on a capital account surplus to finance the trade deficit as it would constitute a negative burden on the economy, particularly when capital inflows need servicing in the future. The funds that flow in may not be optimally mobilized to enhance the productive capacity of the economy which could enhance the future ability to repay but instead be used to finance conspicuous consumption. Moreover, a central bank may have to be concerned with the need to maintain a balance of payments surplus as large as possible from a surplus in the merchandise trade account to defend a currency peg.

If, however, the aim of policy-makers is to maintain balanced trade and full employment, the monetary-fiscal policy mix alternative becomes unworkable. For an economy that is experiencing a trade deficit, an expenditure switching policy is still required to promote greater consumption of domestically-produced goods rather than foreign goods.

In a flexible exchange rate system with perfect capital mobility, the equilibrium of an economy is characterized by a simultaneous equilibrium in the goods and asset markets at the given world interest rate. Under such arrangements, fiscal policy will be impotent in terms of stimulating output growth (Mundell 1968b; Fleming 1962). This follows from the fact that an increased government spending could raise domestic interest rates and result in incipient capital inflows, thus inducing an appreciation of the domestic currency. Both the higher domestic interest rate and the appreciated domestic currency could dampen the aggregate demand for goods. This contractionary effect will operate until the domestic interest rate is re-aligned with the world rate. Output will consequently revert to the level that prevailed when the increased government spending was first introduced. The increase in government spending could also contribute to a decline in the nation's average productivity given that the public sector productivity is normally lower than that of the private sector.

In contrast to fiscal policy, monetary policy is highly potent in influencing national output in a flexible exchange rate and capital mobility environment. If money supply is being expanded in the quest for a higher output level, domestic interest rates would fall as a result of an excess supply of money. This could cause massive capital outflows and hence a depreciation of the domestic currency. The depreciation in turn would enhance exports and stimulate the demand for domestically produced goods. This may help eliminate any trade deficit that may exist. As domestic income rises in tandem with the aggregate demand, domestic interest rates would be partially relieved of the downward pressure. This exchange rate depreciation will persist until the wedge between the domestic interest rate and the world rate is eliminated.

Monetary policy would remain potent even in the case of flexible exchange rates with imperfect capital mobility, though the potency would vary directly with the degree of capital mobility. If the degree of mobility is low, a decline in the domestic interest rates would induce smaller capital outflows, with correspondingly smaller effects on the exchange rate and output. Nevertheless, fiscal policy would also be effective in enhancing national output when capital is imperfectly mobile, though its tendency to raise domestic interest rates and thus to appreciate the domestic currency could thwart investment and exports from the country. However, the net impact is still expansionary. Unlike monetary policy, the net expansionary effect of fiscal policy would vary inversely with the degree of capital mobility.

## APPROPRIATENESS OF THE DIFFERENT EXCHANGE RATE ARRANGEMENTS

This section deliberates on the suitability of the different exchange rate arrangements to Malaysia. As mentioned earlier, the government's prime concern is with economic growth, with a relatively less regard for the current account position and price stability. Malaysia is currently maintaining a comfortable current account surplus without any significant inflationary pressure. However given the fact that it has pegged its ringgit to the US dollar, it is imperative that vast external reserves be maintained. In fact, the government is targeting its reserves up to 12 months of the country's retained imports.

If Malaysia decides to maintain a fixed exchange rate with short-term capital mobility totally prohibited and at the same time pursuing a high growth strategy, it will face the prospect of dwindling external reserves and abandoning its exchange rate peg ultimately. While boosting money supply could stimulate aggregate demand, it could lead to a rise in imports and hence to a deterioration in the balance of payments. Hence, while the Malaysian economy may experience a growth in income in the short run, income could decline over time via the loss of international reserves.

The problem will be exacerbated by an increase in government expenditure on goods and services. Though fiscal policy will be reinforcing monetary policy in generating growth for the Malaysian economy in the short run, it will augment the negative impact of the latter on the balance of payments and thwart economic growth in the long run. Unless external borrowing is feasible, all this may force a devaluation of the ringgit eventually.

However, if fixed exchange rates and perfect capital mobility are favoured by Malaysia, it may not be a suitable arrangement either given that it is striving for a low interest rate environment even though it is increasing its spending at the same time. Low interest rates could discourage capital inflows while the trade balance would turn unfavourable in tandem with the rising income brought forth by expansionary monetary and fiscal policies. Consequently, the monetary base would be eroded and economic growth could falter.

Fixed exchange rates and perfect capital mobility is a more suitable arrangement if Malaysia allows its increased government spending to exert an upward pressure on interest rates. This could attract massive capital inflows, thus broadening the monetary base if capital inflows more than compensate for the worsening trade balance. Domestic income could be sustained at a higher level though there would be a persistent trade deficit financed by capital inflows. In fact, output could still be enhanced by an expansionary fiscal policy even if capital is not perfectly mobile. However, the country could incur a loss in productivity and become less competitive as private investment is dampened by rising interest rates, given that the productivity level is higher in the private sector than in the public sector.

If a monetary-fiscal policy mix is favoured instead, a suitable mix would entail the adoption of a contractionary monetary policy alongside an expansionary fiscal policy instead of both being expansionary. This could enable Malaysia to strike both external and internal balance amid a system of fixed exchange rates and capital mobility. However, the wisdom of maintaining an expansionary fiscal policy alone or adopting a monetary-fiscal policy mix is premised on the assumption that Malaysia disregards the origin of a balance of payments surplus, i.e. whether it is in the capital account or the current account. If the balance of payments surplus is sustained via a capital account instead of a current account surplus, Malaysia should ensure that capital flows are put to productive uses and not to support conspicuous consumption and investment as witnessed during the pre-crisis years.

In fact, an ideal situation can be created if Malaysia chooses to maintain a flexible exchange rate with at least some degree of capital mobility. Indeed, the pre-crisis exchange rate regime of Malaysia had served it well until the crisis struck. Despite the non-absolute peg to the US dollar, there were no complaints about any negative effect of exchange rate uncertainty on trade. While the increase in exchange rate variability witnessed since 1973 has led some economists to believe that the flexible exchange rate system has been counterproductive, international trade has actually not broken down (McCallum 1989). On the contrary, world trade in financial assets as well as goods and services has grown even more rapidly than during the fixed exchange rate era.

Economic growth can be boosted by maintaining an expansionary monetary policy which would keep the domestic interest rate depressed and the exchange rate competitive. This could facilitate national output growth. It is needless and in fact inadvisable to observe an expansionary fiscal policy at the same time. An expansionary fiscal policy would tend to raise domestic interest rates and precipitate an appreciation of the ringgit with a consequent deterioration of the current account and jeopardize economic growth. Moreover, increased government expenditure could crowd out private sector initiatives which may not augur well for the long term competitiveness of Malaysia, given that private sector productivity exceeds that of the public sector.

By observing a fixed exchange rate system and imperfect capital mobility, Malaysia in general needs to be cautious about the size of its fiscal deficit, current account position, and international reserves to avoid the crisis as predicted by the first generation models of balance of payments crises (Krugman 1979; Flood and Garber 1984). Capital controls are needed to maintain the peg but capital controls have its own vices. Speculative crises may also be triggered off by low growth, high unemployment, weak banking systems, and high ratios of public debt to gross domestic product as emphasized in 'second-generation models' of currency crises (Eichengreen et al. 1999). Speculative attacks need not be due to low official reserves but could also be due to domestic economic conditions that render the pursuit of policies necessary to defend the exchange rate peg. For instance, in times of unemployment and low economic growth, raising interest rates is not a feasible option without risking further declines in economic activity. Interest rate hikes could also make banks and borrowers insolvent especially with a weak banking system. The debt servicing cost would also increase with interest rates if there is a large public debt. Second-generation models do not count on the exhaustion of international reserves as an explanation for a speculative attack because in a world of high capital mobility, governments and central banks are able to borrow abroad (Buiter 1987; Ozkan and Sutherland 1994; Eichengreen et al. 1999).

Neither is a crawling peg nor an adjustable peg arrangement suitable for Malaysia. Such arrangements could create a self-destructive inducement toward speculative activities (Friedman 1953) as there would be a lot of one-way speculation by speculators with self-fulfilling prophecy. There will seldom be any doubt about the direction in which the exchange rate will be altered, if it is altered. While speculation is also bound to be present when exchange rates are flexible, such speculation is not the destabilizing type. The activity of speculators buying currencies when values are low and disposing of them when values are high is actually an activity that smoothens and dampens any fluctuations that do occur.

Experience has shown that an adjustable peg or a tightly managed float with occasional large adjustments is hard to sustain under high capital mobility (Eichengreen 1994; Obstfeld 1995; Obstfeld and Rogoff 1995; Collins 1996; and Leiderman and Bufman, 1996). In fact, a more loosely managed float that allows the exchange rate to move regularly in response to market forces, albeit with intervention and other policy adjustments to curb from time to time destabilizing speculation which is unwarranted by economic fundamentals, is still preferable.

A monetary union is not an institution that is easily realizable as the need to surrender monetary and fiscal autonomy to a supranational monetary authority might discourage countries in the region from establishing a monetary union (Kenen 1969). It would also require countries to share common political and economic interests and decide on some sort of convergence criteria. It would be unthinkable that countries with long-standing socio-political conflicts would align with one another in a monetary union. Regional cooperation needs to be enhanced before the arrangement can be successfully realized. There exists diversities amongst Asian countries, particularly in terms of the stage of economic development that each has attained. Table 3.3 shows that Singapore is far more developed in terms of gross national product (GNP) per capita than its neighbouring Asian countries. Malaysia's stage of economic development is comparable with that of Thailand while Indonesia's is comparable with that of the Philippines. Thus these countries are at three different stages of economic development. Combined with other political factors, a monetary union between Malaysia and its neighbouring countries may hence not be foreseen in the immediate future.

TABLE 3.3: GNP PER CAPITA AT CURRENT MARKET PRICES

*(US $)*

| Year | Malaysia | Indonesia | Philippines | Singapore | Thailand |
|---|---|---|---|---|---|
| 1993 | 2970 | 835 | 812 | 17,355 | 2159 |
| 1994 | 3515 | 920 | 934 | 20,472 | 2459 |
| 1995 | 3960 | 1035 | 1055 | 23,663 | 2831 |
| 1996 | 4543 | 1146 | 1152 | 25,150 | 3025 |
| 1997 | 4377 | 1066 | 1118 | 23,625 | 1501 |
| 1998 | 3093 | - | - | - | - |
| 1999 | 3255 | - | - | - | - |

SOURCE: Malaysia, *Economic Report,* various issues.

## CONCLUDING REMARKS

It is thus desirable for Malaysia to abandon the peg at this time of relative tranquillity in the foreign exchange market, unless it chooses to strictly adhere to the requirements for sustaining a pegged exchange rate regime. In fact, countries with lasting pegs have adhered to the need to maintain their inflation and money growth at rates consistent with those prevailing in the industrial countries to which they peg (Eichengreen et al. 1999). Most developing country pegs are short-lived. For example, Klein and Marion (1997) find that for 87 episodes of pegged regimes amongst Latin American and Caribbean countries for the 1957-90 period, the average duration of a peg was about 10 months. One-third of these were abandoned by the seventh month, and more than half abandoned by the end of the first year. As the fixed exchange rate was introduced in an environment of exchange rate instability or volatility, the peg should be removed now since calm has returned in the foreign exchange market. Moreover, Malaysia has benefited from the short run impact of expansionary money and fiscal policy with improved export performance. In fact, the ringgit was relatively stable prior to the crisis even without the fixed exchange rate and trade and economic growth was very impressive. It was only during the brief crisis period that the ringgit turned volatile, otherwise it was on a downward trend.

At this juncture, there will be no basis for market participants to infer that the change is forced on the authorities. Otherwise, the next appropriate time for Malaysia to phase out the fixed exchange rate will be when there is pressure for the ringgit to appreciate from large capital inflows. Under such circumstances, the switch could imply that the ringgit would begin with its more flexible position by appreciating. Although an appreciation could dampen its export performance, this will not undermine confidence as much as a depreciation, that typically accompanies a switch to a more flexible regime would. Moreover, measures could be adopted to limit the extent of the appreciation to mitigate the unfavourable effects on exports. For instance, a fiscal retrenchment could ease domestic monetary conditions and lessen the incentives for inflows. This could inspire greater investor confidence that fiscal policy will not involve large fiscal deficits and the need for inflationary finance and too much pressure on the current account. A more flexible exchange rate system would compel financial institutions, business enterprises and households to manage their foreign exchange liabilities by hedging. This is in fact consistent with Malaysia's objective to further modernize its financial system. Any failure of Malaysia to revert to a more flexible exchange rate regime during a period of financial tranquillity or encouraging capital inflows could imply that a transition would have to be made at other times when the need to do so is pressing and that could involve a great deal of misery. By then, businesses, banks, and enterprises, and perhaps the government would have accumulated significant huge sums of unhedged foreign currency liabilities. Under such circumstances, the credibility of the macroeconomic policies of the government will be suspect.

## POSTSCRIPT (MAY, 2003)

Since September 1998, Malaysia has been liberalizing its capital controls and is presently more receptive to foreign portfolio capital inflows though it continues to maintain its dollar peg. However, the peg seems sustainable until this time but only due to some 'fortuitous' external events such as the return to *de facto* peg to the US dollar amongst the other Asian countries since the 1997 financial meltdown, the slow-down of the U.S. economy and hence the global economy in 2001, the 11 September attack, the generally weak trend of the dollar particularly against the Euro and the Japanese yen and more recently the outbreak of SARS (Severe Acute Respiratory Syndrome) epidemic that have prevented any major misalignment of the ringgit exchange rate.

## NOTE

1. This section draws heavily from Batiz and Batiz (1989).

## REFERENCES

Batiz, F.L.R. and L.R. Batiz (1989), *International Finance and Open Economy Macroeconomics,* Macmillan, New York.

Buiter, W. (1987), 'Borrowing to Defend the Exchange Rate and the Timing and Magnitude of Speculative Attacks', *Journal of International Economics,* vol. 23, nos. 3-4, November, pp. 221-39.

Collins, S.M. (1996), 'On Becoming More Flexible: Exchange Rate Regimes in Latin America and the Caribbean', *Journal of Development Economics,* vol. 51, no. 1, October, pp. 119-38.

Eichengreen, B. (1994), *International Monetary Arrangements for the 21st Century,* Brookings Institution, Washington, D.C.

Eichengreen, B. et al. (1999), 'Transition Strategies and Nominal Anchors on the Road to Greater Exchange Rate Flexibility', *Essays in International Finance,* no. 213, April, Princeton University, Princeton, New Jersey.

Fleming, J.M. (1962), 'Domestic Financial Policies under Fixed and Floating Exchange Rates', *IMF Staff Papers,* vol. 3, November, pp. 369-79.

Flood, R. and P. Garber (1984), 'Collapsing Exchange Rate Regimes: Some Linear Examples', *Journal of International Economics,* vol. 17, nos. 1-2, August, pp. 1-13.

Friedman, M. (1953), 'The Case for Flexible Exchange Rates', in Milton Friedman, *Essays in Positive Economics,* pp. 157-203, University of Chicago Press.

Kenen, P.B. (1969), 'The Theory of Optimum Currency Areas: An Eclectic View', in R.A. Mundell and A.K. Swoboda (eds.), *Monetary Problems of the International Economy,* Ch. 2, pp. 41-60, University of Chicago Press.

Klein, M.W. and N.P. Marion (1997), 'Explaining the Duration of Exchange Rate Pegs', *Journal of Development Economics,* vol. 54, no. 2, December, pp. 387-404.

Krugman, P.R. (1979) 'A Model of Balance of Payments Crises', *Journal of Money, Credit and Banking,* vol. 11, no. 3, August, pp. 311-25.

Leiderman, L. and G. Bufman (1996), 'Searching for Nominal Anchors in Shock-Prone Economies in the 1990s: Inflation Targets and Exchange Rate Bands', in Ricardo Hausmann and Helmut Reisen (eds.), *Securing Stability and Growth in Latin America,* Organization for Economic Cooperation and Development, Paris, pp. 79-126.

McCallum, B.T. (1989), *Monetary Economics: Theory and Policy,* Macmillan, New York.

McKinnon, R.I. (1963), 'Optimum Currency Areas', *American Economic Review,* vol. 53, no. 4, September, pp. 717-25.

Mundell, R.A. (1961), 'A Theory of Optimum Currency Areas', *American Economic Review,* vol. 5, no. 4, September, pp. 657-65.

———(1968a), 'The International Disequilibrium System', in Robert Mundell, Chapter 15, pp. 217-32, *International Economics,* Macmillan, New York.

———(1968b) 'Capital Mobility and Stabilization Policy under Fixed and Flexible Exchange Rates', in Robert Mundell, Ch. 18, pp. 250-71, *International Economics,* Macmillan, New York.

Obstfeld, M. (1995), 'International Currency Experience: New Lessons and Lessons Relearned', *Brookings Papers on Economic Activity,* no. 1, pp. 197-211.

Obstfeld, M. and K. Rogoff (1995), 'The Mirage of Fixed Exchange Rates', *Journal of Economic Perspectives,* vol. 9, no. 4, Fall, pp. 73-96.

Ozkan, F.G. and A. Sutherland (1994) 'A Model of the ERM Crisis', *CEPR Discussion Paper,* no. 879, Center for Economic Policy Research, London, January.

# HIGH BLOOD PRESSURE

In 1992, Dr. Isabelle Abbott, a [illegible] botanist [illegible], noted that the most common uses of noni in Hawaii included the following: high blood pressure. [illegible] I searched the literature to find out which foods with healing properties, called phytonutrients, were in noni that could help to lower high blood pressure. Scopoletin, a phytonutrient constituent of noni, dilates previously constricted blood vessels. This means that the heart does not have to work so hard pumping blood through constricted blood vessels. As a result, a normalization of the blood pressure takes place, which results in less wear and tear on the heart.

Scopoletin was first isolated from noni in 1993 by researchers at the University of Hawaii. It is believed that besides dilating blood vessels, scopoletin also binds to serotonin. Animal studies have shown that scopoletin can lower normal and high blood pressures to hypotensive levels (abnormally low blood pressure). However, in noni, scopoletin synergistically interacts with other nutraceuticals (foods acting as medicinals) to bring high blood pressure to normal, but not lower than normal. It has not been found to bring normal blood pressure to hypotensive levels.

More recently, noni has been studied in the United States at Stanford University, the University of California at Los Angeles (UCLA), and the University of Hawaii; in England at the Union College of London; and in France at the University of Metz. Those who have studied it agree that in most cases noni can play a role in lowering high blood pressure.

I interviewed New York physician Scott Gerson, M.D., who completed a placebo-controlled clinical trial to evaluate whether noni juice lowered elevated blood pressure. For 14 weeks, Dr. Gerson studied nine patients—six males and three females. The high blood pressure patients were randomly selected and did not know that they were taking noni. They stayed on the same diet and did the same amount of exercise as before they started taking noni. Eight of the nine patients showed a decrease in blood pres-

# 4

# The Dynamics of the Balance of Payments under Capital Flows

*Amit Bhaduri*

## INTRODUCTION

Massive cross-border capital flows, usually of a footloose nature, present perhaps the most dramatic face of the current era of globalization. This has two contradictory aspects for movements in the exchange rate of a developing country subject to such capital flows. On the one hand, by supporting the current account deficit of the balance of payments, capital inflows may tend to slow down if not reverse, at least temporarily, the pressure on the exchange rate to depreciate. On the other hand, however, continuing current account deficit coupled with capital inflows build up the net international liability position of the country over time. Normally, this encourages expectations in the foreign exchange market about future devaluation, and market sentiments gather momentum about an exchange rate crisis, as the gap between the actual and the expected exchange rate widens. Thus, in any crisis driven by capital flows, international capital first flows in to sustain a current account deficit without adequate adjustment between the expected and the actual exchange rate; but then it flows out to close the gap between the two, leaving behind the country in the grip of an exchange rate crisis. While these are almost invariably the broad outlines of a typical exchange rate crisis in any developing country in recent years, it leaves unanswered two important, interrelated questions. First, why does capital continue to flow in, and international lending go on, despite current account deficits? Second, what change in circumstances leads to the withdrawal of lending? Or, to use more picturesque phrases, how and why does the 'mania' of lendings turn into a 'panic' of withdrawals precipitating the exchange rate crisis? (Kindleberger 1978).

These questions have been addressed repeatedly in the literature, both through historical research (e.g. Eichengreen 1991; Fishlow 1985; Strange 1998), and in terms of a variety of analytical and empirically oriented models (e.g. Batiz and Batiz 1989; Flood and Garber 1984; Krugman 1979; Froot and Thaler 1990; Frankel and Rose 1995). They try to capture this vast and complex problem in terms of either particular historical episodes, or by emphasizing specific analytical aspects. The purpose of the present paper is somewhat different. It attempts to provide an 'analytical description' in terms of a starkly schematized model of how the exchange rate and the balance of payment interact to generate both stability and instability in a regime of massive cross-border capital flows. The model focuses on the general aspects of this problem along the lines outlined above. However, each particular episode of crisis has its particular features, and how they might be incorporated in this general model is commented upon, only after the general model is outlined.

## THE 'GENERAL' MODEL

We follow the convention prevailing nowadays in most developing countries to represent by the exchange rate ($r$) the amount of 'domestic' currency per unit of 'foreign' currency (e.g. US dollar). Thus, a higher $r$ implies a weaker domestic currency. Moreover, using 'dollar' as the numeraire, we measure all the relevant magnitudes in the model in dollars. This avoids some unnecessary complications due to revaluation of the stocks of external debt and reserves through changes in the exchange rate. The following notations are used:

$r$, $\hat{r}$ = actual and expected rate of exchange of domestic currency respectively, per unit of foreign currency (dollar),

$B$ = the (absolute) magnitude of current account deficit, i.e. a larger $B$ implies a bigger deficit,

$F$ = gross inflow of foreign capital,

$M$ = import,

$E$ = export,

$Z$ = net factor payment,

$i$ = (constant) rate of interest on external debt,
$D$ = external debt.

Note moreover that,

$$\frac{dD}{dt} \equiv D \equiv F \text{ and } \frac{d}{dr}[M-E] = -b,\ b > 0. \tag{4.1}$$

$b > 0$ implies that the Marshall-Lerner condition is satisfied.

Assuming for simplicity that the net factor payment equals interest payment on debt (i.e. reserve earns no interest), the definition of the current account deficit is as follows:

$$B = [M-E] + Z = [M-E] + iD. \tag{4.2}$$

Differentiating equation (4.2) with respect to time, we obtain from equation (4.1)

$$B = -b\dot{r} + iF. \tag{4.3}$$

The adjustments in the current exchange rate is assumed to be governed by demand and supply in the foreign exchange market, i.e.

$$\dot{r} = \theta[B-F], \quad \theta > 0, \tag{4.4}$$

where, $\theta$ is some arbitrary speed of adjustment.

Using equation (4.4) in equation (4.3) we obtain

$$\dot{B} = -b\theta B + (i + b\theta)F. \tag{4.5}$$

We focus on the influence of exchange rate movements on capital flows by abstracting from 'Other' factors (e.g. interest or tax rate differentials across borders, see especially Dornbusch 1976). Thus, the 'long-term' capital flow, mostly in the form of direct foreign investment is assumed be a constant given by $L$, while the short-term flow depends entirely on the difference perceived by the lenders between the current and the expected exchange rate, i.e.

$$F = L + a(r - \hat{r}),\ a > 0. \tag{4.6}$$

Note that $a > 0$ implies that an expected appreciation, i.e. $(r - \hat{r}) > 0$, stimulates, while an expected depreciation of the domestic currency, i.e. $(r - \hat{r}) < 0$, depresses short-term capital inflows.

The expected exchange rate depends, in turn, on the external asset and liability position of the economy. Other things being equal, an increase in external debt (liability) strengthens market sentiments about the future devaluation of the currency. Obviously, an increase in reserves, $R$ (assets), encourages sentiments in the foreign exchange market towards an appreciation of the domestic currency. Formally,

$$\hat{r} = H(D, R) \tag{4.7}$$

or,

$$\dot{\hat{r}} = \frac{\partial H}{\partial D}\dot{D} + \frac{\partial H}{\partial R}\dot{R}. \tag{4.8}$$

To keep the algebra manageable, we shall make the assumption of linearity (to start with), and treat the partial derivatives in equation (4.8) as constant to yield,

$$\dot{\hat{r}} = (m-n)F + nB, \tag{4.9}$$

where,

$$\frac{\partial H}{\partial D} = m > 0, \quad \frac{\partial H}{\partial R} = -n, \quad n > 0,$$

and, definitionally, the change in reserve is,

$$\dot{R} \equiv F - B. \tag{4.10}$$

Differentiating equation (4.6) with respect to time and using equations (4.4) and (4.9) we obtain,

$$\dot{F} = a(\theta - n)B - a[\theta + (m-n)]F \tag{4.11}$$

Note that equations (4.5) and (4.11) define the basic dynamical system, depicting the interaction between the current account ($B$) and capital inflow ($F$) over time, So long as the relevant coefficients are considered constant within some relevant range, the (local) stability property of the system around its equilibrium at the origin ($B = 0$, $F = 0$) can be ascertained by routine calculation.

From equations (4.5) and (4.11), the (local) asymptotic stability of the system is guaranteed if the trace $\tau$ is negative and the determinant $\Delta$ is positive, i.e.

$$\tau < 0 \text{ implying } \theta[1 + (b/a)] + m > n \tag{4.12}$$

and,

$$\Delta > 0 \text{ implying } a[\theta(bm - i) + in] > 0. \tag{4.13}$$

Equations (4.12) and (4.13) together restrict the value of $n$ for stability in the interval $I(P, Q)$ where,

$$P = \theta[1 - (bm/i)] < n < \theta[1 + (b/a)] + m = Q. \tag{4.14}$$

Since $Q > P$ implies $(b\theta + am) > -(abm\theta/i)$ which is always satisfied, the interval $I$ is not empty, and if $n$ lies in this open interval, the system is asymptotically stable. Moreover, the length of the interval is given by,

$$I = (Q - P) = m + b[(\theta / a) + (m / i)] \quad (4.15)$$

From equation (4.15), by partial differentiation with respect to the relevant variable, it follows that the length of the interval increases with $b$, $m$, and $\theta$, but decreases as $i$ and $a$ increase. Therefore, other things being equal, for a given value of a stronger response of trade balance to the variation in the exchange rate (i.e. $b$), a stronger expectation of the devaluation of the exchange rate to increases in external debt (i.e. $m$) and a higher speed of adjustment in the market for foreign exchange (i.e. $\theta$) would tend to increase the (measure-theoretic) probability of the system being stable. On the other hand, larger short-term capital flows driven by expectation of variation in the exchange rate (i.e. $a$) and a higher rate of interest on external debt (i.e. $i$) would decrease the probability of the system being stable.

However, if we take the values of all the other parameters except $n$ as given, it can be seen from inequalities (4.12), (4.13), and (4.14) that the dynamic behaviour of the system might change qualitatively as different parametric values of $n$ are considered. For $n$ relatively small violating the extreme left hand inequality in inequality (4.14), which also implies violating inequality (4.13), the determinant $\Delta$ is negative, so that the system has saddle point instability. As $n$ is increased parametrically sufficiently to satisfy both inequalities in inequality (4.14), the system transits from saddle point instability to asymptotic, nodal stability. However, as $n$ is increased even more to violate the extreme right hand inequality in inequality (4.14), which also implies violating inequality (4.12), the trace becomes positive to give rise to nodal instability. Note moreover that the trace, $\tau$, changes sign at some critical value of $n$ given by inequality (4.12) as:

$$\tau = 0 \text{ implying } n = n_c = \theta[1 + (b / a)] + m \quad (4.16)$$

Therefore, by the negative criterion of Benedixon, the possibility of a limit cycle occurring, as $n$ is parametrically varied through this critical value, cannot be ruled out. However, the existence of a limit cycle cannot be ascertained from the linear (approximate) representation of the system depicted by equations (4.5) and (4.11). Nevertheless, the possibility of the existence of a limit cycle through Hopf bifurcation appears to be strong, from a closer examination of even this linear system whose characteristic roots are:

$$\lambda_1, \lambda_2 = \frac{1}{2}\{[an - am - \theta(a+b) \pm \sqrt{\tau^2 - 4\Delta}\} \qquad (4.17)$$

Thus, at $n = n_c$: (i) the roots are purely imaginary from equation (4.16); (ii) The real part of the characteristic roots, $[Re\lambda_1(n)]$ $\{Re\lambda_2(n)\}$, increase with $n$, satisfying $\frac{d}{dn}\{Re\lambda_1(n)\}|_{n=n_c} > 0$ ; (iii) The origin ($B = 0$, $F = 0$) is a fixed point for all values of the real parameter $n$ of the system depicted by equations (4.5) and (4.11). Also note that at $n = n_c$, the determinant $\Delta = (abm\theta + aim + bi\theta) > 0$.

Thus, most of the conditions for Hopf bifurcation are satisfied by the approximate linear system of equations (4.5) and (4.11) (Arrowsmith and Place 1982, pp. 212-16). However, without specifying the complete non-linear system, of which equations (4.5) and (4.11) are presumed to be only linear approximations, the remaining (and most difficult) condition that the origin ($B = 0$, $F = 0$) is a globally or asymptotically stable fixed point $n = n_c$ cannot be proved. (Note at $n = n_c$, the local linear system has $\Delta|_{n=n_c} > 0$ and $\tau = 0$, which has pure imaginary roots generating circles. But this local property is misleading for judging the global stability of the unspecified, complete non-linear system.)

Our formal discussion may be summarized roughly by considering a parametric variation of $n$ on the real line, where all the other parameters ($a$, $b$, $m$, $\theta$, $i$) are treated as constant coefficients in equations (4.5) and (4.11).

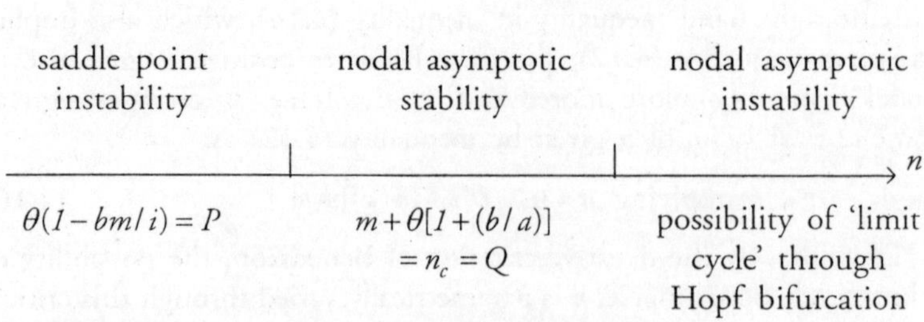


($n$ = lenders' sensitivity to change in reserves)

FIGURE 4.1

## ECONOMIC SIGNIFICANCE OF THE MODEL

To interpret the economic meaning of our preceding formal analysis, note first that a relatively large value of the parameter $n$ implies that the lenders react rather violently to any 'news' of a change in reserves. Thus, a relatively small decrease in external reserves leads to lenders' expectations of a large devaluation of the currency in the future. (Obversely also, a slight increase in reserve induces expectations of a large appreciation.) It is hardly surprising that the formal model suggests that such violent reactions to changes in reserves on the part of the lenders would lead to instability in capital flows and in the balance of payments position. The instability, however, might mean a deepening payments crisis; but it could also mean an 'embarrassment of riches'. An important aspect of the formal model is to suggest they are merely two sides of the same coin.

Thus, a small decrease in reserve may lead to the expectation of a large depreciation due to the assumed high value of the parameter $n$ [equation (4.8)]. This would mean that short-term capital inflow also falls sharply, induced by the fear of depreciation [equation (4.6)]. As a result, the current exchange rate depreciates [equation (4.4)] to improve the balance of payments [equation (4.3)]. However, if this improvement proves inadequate in relation to the decline in capital inflow [violation of inequality (4.12)], the reserve decreases further in an unstable spiral downwards. It is easy to work out the opposite scenario along the same line, when a small increase in reserves generates expectations of large appreciation in the exchange rate, and induces large capital inflows to build up even more reserve in an unstable upward spiral, indicating the 'embarrassment of riches'.

While the above discussion outlines how the model assigns a critical role to the lenders' reaction to the changes in reserves in stabilizing or destabilizing the balance of payments and exchange rate in a regime of massive short-term capital flow, it leaves open the important question: what factors influence or determine lenders' reactions to the changes in reserves? It is in answering this question that particular models and historical episodes seem to suggest diverse answers.

In order to focus on how a serious crisis in international payments position of a developing country is precipitated, it seems plausible to argue that the lenders' sensitivity to further depletion in the reserve held by the borrowing country assumes 'dangerously' high values [i.e. $n > n_c$ in equation (4.16)] when the level of reserve is perceived to be unsustainably low in relation to external debt obligations. This may happen because either reserves are seen as being depleted too fast (i.e. large current account deficit) or external debt accumulates rather dramatically. It has been theorized that such situations are brought about by the problems of 'moral hazard' on the part of either the borrowers or the lenders. The borrowers, e.g. domestic commercial banks and firms, may 'overborrow' on the presumption that they would be bailed out by their government in case of serious repayment difficulties, because both the domestic financial system and the international reputation of the country is at stake. 'Overborrowing' is often seen in this case as the result of investment in risky and dubious projects such as the real estate speculation of borrowing short to invest long. Similarly, the lenders may also 'push' loans. International banks and other financial institutions may overlend, again on the presumption that the International Monetary Fund (IMF) or the national government of their country of origin will come to their rescue in case of serious repayment difficulties.

The problem with this class of theories, relying on an asymmetry of information, which permits one side to overborrow or overlend, is that it may easily degenerate into fixing responsibility of the crisis almost entirely on one side. Thus, over-borrowing by the domestic banks was often depicted as 'crony capitalism' in the context of the East Asian crisis—a nexus of banks, corporations, and the government—which encouraged banks to presume that the government will rescue them. However, with equal justification one could turn the responsibility on the international lenders; their over-lending might have been sustained by their belief that either their national governments or the IMF would come to their rescue. It is not that the 'moral hazard' argument is irrelevant; but it loses much of its force if both sides are subject to it. After all it takes two to tango; and it certainly takes two sides to make financial deals that go wrong.

More conventional explanations of a crisis may centre around other parameters in our model [equation (4.15)]. Thus, a more cautious attitude to foreign borrowing (i.e. higher $m$), faster adjustment of the exchange rate in the face of persistent demand-supply disequilibrium in the foreign exchange market (i.e. higher $\theta$), and better trade performance through depreciation (i.e. higher $b$) may be factors that stabilize, but large doses of short-term capital flow driven by exchange rate expectations (higher $a$) destabilize the international payments position of a country [equation (4.15)]. Interestingly, the model suggests that raising the speed of adjustment ($\theta$) of demand to supply through decreased regulation on the exchange rate may help, when it is combined with greater regulation of movements in short-term capital (i.e. a lower value of parameter *a*), and perhaps complementary regulations enforcing a more cautious attitude towards growing debt (parameter *m*) by lenders as well as borrowers. These are also preventive measures against lenders becoming dangerously sensitive to small depletion in foreign reserves [i.e. $n > n_c$, see equations (4.14) to (4.16)] which, as identified by our stylized model, is the general triggering mechanism of payments crises. In short, the management of the balance of payments under capital flows should not be viewed simply as a debate between regulation and deregulation of the foreign exchange market. It is more a question of identifying which types of regulation (or deregulation), and formal modelling may be suggestive in this complex task of identification.

## REFERENCES

Arrowsmith, D.K. and C.M. Place (1982), *Ordinary Differential Equations*, Chapman & Hall, London, Ch. 5.

Batiz, F.L.R. and L.R. Batiz (1989), *International Finance and Open Economy Macroeconomics*, Macmillan, New York.

Diaz-Alejandro, C. (1985), 'Good-bye Financial Repression, Hello Financial Crash', *Journal of Development Economics*, vol. 19, nos. 1-2, pp. 1-24.

Dornbusch, R. (1976), 'Expectations and Exchange Rate Dynamics', *Journal of Political Economy*, vol. 84, no. 6, December, pp. 1161-76.

Eichengreen, B. (1991), 'Historical Research on International Lending and Debt', *Journal of Economic Perspectives*, vol. 5, no. 2, Spring, pp. 149-69.

Fishlow, A. (1985), 'Lessons from the Past: Capital Markets during the 19th Century and Interwar Period, *International Organization*, vol. 39, no. 3, Summer, pp. 383-439.

Flood, R.P. and P.M. Garber (1984), 'Collapsing Exchange Rate Regimes: Some Linear Examples' *Journal of International Economics*, vol. 17, nos. 1-2, August, pp. 1-13.

Frankel, J.A. and A.K. Rose (1995), 'Empirical Research on Nominal Exchange Rates' in G. Grossman and K. Rogoff (eds.), *Handbook of International Economics*, vol. 3, North Holland, Amsterdam, pp. 1689-1729.

Froot, K.A. and R. Thaler, (1990), 'Anomalies: Foreign Exchange', *Journal of Economic Perspectives*, vol. 4, no. 3, Fall, pp. 179-92.

Kindleberger, C.P. (1978), *Manias, Panics and Crashes*, Basic Books, New York.

Krugman, P.R. (1979), 'A Model of Balance of Payments Crisis', *Journal of Money, Credit and Banking*, vol. 11, August, pp. 311-25.

Neal, L. (1990) *The Rise of Financial Capitalism*, Cambridge University Press, Cambridge.

Strange, S. (1998), 'The New World of Debt', *New Left Review*, no. 230, July-August, pp. 91-113.

# 5 Increasing Returns, Trade, and Development

*Aditya Bhattacharjea*

In the last two decades, a number of advances have been made in economic theory that permit a more rigorous analysis of some of the issues that have concerned scholars writing on development for more than two centuries. One major innovation has been the modelling of scale economies and their role in economic progress. Krugman (1995) acknowledges that many of the essential insights can be credited to authors like Rosenstein-Rodan, Nurkse, and Hirschman who pioneered what he calls the 'High Development Theory' of the 1940s and 1950s, but attributes their limited impact on the profession to their inability to state their ideas in formal models as required by mainstream economics. Increasing returns to scale (hereafter, IRS) require a consideration of imperfectly-competitive market structures and the possibility of multiple equilibria, strategic complementarity in investment decisions, and coordination failures. The necessary theoretical techniques, Krugman argues, were developed only after the late 1970s, and are only recently being applied to development economics. In this chapter, I shall be making a highly selective and idiosyncratic survey of these contributions, concentrating on those that provide useful insights into developmental issues, and which can be manageably taught to students with diverse backgrounds and training in economic theory. Also, I confine myself to contributions that involve the role of trade and trade policy in an essential way. While there is much in the new literature that is stimulating, I argue that the dictates of a particular kind of formalization severely limit its relevance. In this context, I shall contrast the treatment of economies of scale in the new literature to earlier ideas in the history of economic thought, and also to more recent neo-Keynesian approaches.

Given the vastness and diversity of this literature, our first task is to attempt a taxonomy of different types of economies of scale, each of which requires a different approach. We can distinguish three types of scale economies that figure in this literature:

1. Economies of scale that are internal to each firm, arising from fixed costs that get spread over a larger volume of output, while marginal costs remain constant.
2. Economies that are external to each firm, but arise from the growth of the industry to which the firm belongs, either within the same region or country, or internationally. These are usually attributed to the 'Marshallian triad', comprising (*a*) knowledge spillovers between firms; (*b*) labour market pooling, which make it easier to match employers' requirements with the availability of workers when there are many firms and many workers; and (*c*) development of specialized input suppliers, which are viable only if the industry using their products is large enough.
3. A third approach combines elements of IRS of Types 1 and 2(*c*) above. It features Type 1 *internal* economies in the production of differentiated intermediate inputs ('components'). Although the downstream industry that uses them is modelled as facing constant returns to scale (hereafter CRS), its productivity is increased by the use of a wider variety of components. This enables the downstream industry to expand, which in turn supports a wider range of specialized firms to provide them. Consequently, the downstream industry benefits from *external* economies of scale of Type 2(c), arising from the increased division of labour in the production of components. The tradability of the components is crucial in determining whether the externality operates nationally or globally.

Students are likely to be puzzled to find that the type of IRS that they are most familiar with from introductory courses, i.e. internal economies arising from per-unit variable or prime costs varying inversely with output, is not a feature of this literature. This is because such economies necessarily imply imperfect competition, since any firm can reduce its costs below its rivals by expanding output. In oligopoly models, decreasing costs can result in problems for the existence and stability of equilibrium, unless they are more than offset by eventually diminishing returns due to some fixed input. Other manifestations of increasing returns that are also not dealt with in this literature are discussed below. I now review the major contributions in each category, beginning with their advent in trade theory and then their more recent incarnations as models of development.

## TYPE 1: INTERNAL ECONOMIES

Decreasing costs at the level of the firm are incompatible with perfect competition, and theorists (notably Helpman and Krugman 1985) have generally employed models of Chamberlinian monopolistic competition for internal economies of Type 1. An important role is played by Dixit-Stiglitz preferences (represented by a utility function in which utility increases with the number of varieties consumed, not just the quantity of each variety), which were used to generate consumers' 'love of variety' in new models of product differentiation in industrial organization in the 1970s. In such models, fixed costs associated with the production of each differentiated variety dictate that an autarkic economy—especially one with a small market—permits only a few varieties to be produced and consumed on a small scale, and therefore at high average cost. Trade then enables consumers to benefit from greater variety, the country saves on the fixed costs of those firms that shut down, and those that survive operate on a larger scale (thanks to greater competition and export possibilities) and lower average cost. In Chamberlinian models, free entry ensures that cost savings are passed through into reduced prices, again benefiting consumers. Scale and variety effects can outweigh adverse income distribution effects resulting from resource reallocation, so that (in contrast to the Stolper-Samuelson result in a constant-returns world) all factors of production may be better off.

However, the major claim to fame of the models of monopolistic competition is not in dealing with IRS *per se*, but in explaining the large volume of intra-industry trade in differentiated products that occurs between the similar economies of the OECD. This explains a feature of the real world that is incompatible with both the Ricardian and Heckscher-Ohlin theories of comparative advantage, according to which trade should involve the exchange of very different products between countries with very different technologies or resource endowments. The major results of the Helpman-Krugman model are obtained for the case when similarity in countries' technologies and relative resource endowments enables trade between them to 'reproduce the integrated economy' with international equalization of factor prices. Most authors in this tradition themselves doubt its applicability to developing countries,[1] for whom they believe trade is better explained by traditional constant-returns models.

## TYPE 2: EXTERNAL ECONOMIES

Alternatively, one can adopt scale economies of Type 2, in which individual competitive firms can be treated as facing constant returns to scale (CRS) with respect to their inputs, but with the cost level being reduced by the growth of the industry to which the firm belongs. Although the idea was conceived by Alfred Marshall, and is thus more than a century old, it took decades for it to be properly understood. The last ten pages of Chipman's survey (1965) give an entertaining account of how eminent theorists were unable to comprehend it between the 1920s and 1950s. In an influential paper, Sraffa (1926) did understand it, but held that economies of scale that were external to the firm but internal to the industry were the type least likely to be met with in practice. None the less, such Marshallian externalities have played a major role in recent work in international trade, in ways that Sraffa did not consider.

Most of the burgeoning literature in this area typically features a 'Manufacturing' sector subject to IRS and an 'Agricultural' sector with CRS. Unlike the product-differentiation models under my Type 1 rubric, this class of models is designed to be relevant to 'North-South' trade, where the distinction between the two regions lies in the larger size or initial head-start in industrialization in the North. This enables it to produce manufactures on a larger scale and lower cost, progressively displacing Southern production, enabling the North to produce on an even larger scale and undermine cumulatively the competitiveness of the shrinking Southern industry (see Krugman 1981 and Ethier 1982a for externality models yielding this outcome). Explicit in Ethier but implicit in Krugman are 'gains from trade', even if the South loses its IRS sector when exposed to foreign competition.[2] This is because in addition to a more efficient allocation of resources, its consumers benefit from the cheaper imports, which are further cheapened by the Northern industry being able to produce on an even larger scale. In this setting, the possibility of a welfare loss due to contraction of an IRS sector (emphasized by Frank Graham in a celebrated 1920s debate with Frank Knight) occurs when it is not *completely* shut down and therefore operates at reduced scale and high cost. In the theoretical literature, this is because the country where manufacturing tends to concentrate does not have a resource endowment large enough to produce enough of it for both countries. This is likely only when countries are fairly similar in size. Thus, like the Type 1 models, these Type 2 models reinforce the traditional view of the desirability of free trade for developing countries.

## TYPE 3: SYNTHESIS

Although the idea of greater division of labour in producing a wider range of intermediate inputs has been around for a long time, the proximate inspiration in modern trade theory is Ethier (1982b), who showed the way in using the production function analogue of the Dixit-Stiglitz utility function. This makes productivity a function of the number of specialized intermediate inputs ('components') that are used. Internal economies dictate that each type of component is produced by only one firm at one location, and fixed costs limit the number of components a closed economy can produce. If components can be imported, the externality is international in scope. Ethier is preoccupied with showing that this analysis makes very little difference to the standard theorems of trade theory, permitting inter-industry trade to be driven by factor endowments while intra-industry trade (IIT) occurs in components. The more dissimilar the trading countries' relative factor endowments, the less the volume of IIT.

Several recent papers have used this approach to demonstrate conditions under which trade may result in uneven development. This literature draws upon two other areas where modelling IRS has resulted in new ways of looking at old intuitions. One is the formalization by Murphy et al. (1989) of the 1940s and 1950s literature on the 'Big Push'. This literature, it may be recalled, pointed out that the indivisibility of investment interacts with small market sizes in developing countries to deter investment by individual entrepreneurs. But if a large enough number of them could somehow be induced to undertake their investments simultaneously, they would be justified *ex post* by the resulting widening of the market resulting from the additional incomes generated. The Murphy et al. paper was developed for a closed economy, and emphasized the idea—originally stated by Rosenstein-Rodan (1943)—of pecuniary externalities arising from the *horizontal* complementarity between investments in widening each other's market. This issue of the narrowness of the home market was shrugged off by later economic theorists not just because, as Krugman (1995) suggests, it was presented informally in the traditional literature, but because a later generation of economists believed that there could be no demand constraint on the inducement to invest, since a developing economy typically faced elastic world demand for any manufactured goods it was capable of producing. Opinions to the contrary were derided as either suffering from 'export pessimism', or a refusal to confront the anti-export bias built into protectionist import-substitution policies.

This is where the second new area comes in: the 'new economic geography', which was also initiated by Krugman (see Krugman 1991b for a relatively accessible introduction). This re-examines the role of space and transport costs in the location of economic activity. Increasing returns to scale acts as a centripetal force, cumulatively reinforcing cost advantages and thus tending to concentrate production in one firm, region, or country (geographical concentration is known as 'agglomeration'). On the other hand, transport costs act centrifugally, impelling producers to disperse in order to be near their suppliers or consumers.[3] This can restore a home-market effect even in an open economy. Helpman and Krugman (1985, Ch. 10) showed this in a Type 1 monopolistic competition model, with transport costs only for the differentiated products. However, Davis (1998) shows that such an assumption is empirically not well-founded, and the home market effect disappears if there are equal transport costs for the homogeneous product. But in a Type 3 model with transport costs for all commodities, we can get a pattern of cumulative causation within a country, in which a larger industry can support the production of more and cheaper inputs, which in turn raise productivity in the downstream industry, enabling it to expand, providing a positive feedback to the intermediate producers as well as generating incomes that broaden the market for other final goods producers.

This approach formalizes the *vertical* complementarities, or 'forward and backward linkages' emphasized by development writers of the 1950s such as Hirschman, along with the horizontal complementarities of Rosenstein-Rodan. Again, these make no sense for a small open economy in the absence of transport costs, since there is then no particular advantage to be gained from locating near existing suppliers or consumers. However, Ciccone and Matsuyama (1996), Rodriguez-

Clare (1996), and Rodrik (1996) make the specialized inputs non-traded (or involving services that are non-traded), and produced under Type 1 internal economies of scale. An individual input producer may then find that demand is insufficient to permit him to break even unless others simultaneously enter the market. A small market thus suffers from a 'shallow' division of labour, with a restricted range of inputs and consequently low productivity and income levels. However, if a coordinated 'Big Push' investment programme can be implemented, it can break out of this poverty trap and attain a superior equilibrium with a 'deep' division of labour that is self-justifying *ex post*. This multiplicity of equilibria is characteristic of models with IRS. Unlike Rosenstein-Rodan and Nurkse, few economists today are sanguine about the ability of central planning to overcome the coordination failure and bring about this desirable outcome. The three papers just cited suggest other possibilities: optimistic and self-fulfilling entrepreneurial expectations,[4] exogenous capital accumulation, or a minimum wage policy that acts as a deliberate disincentive to employment in the CRS sector (or, in another variant of the model, the less component- using sector) and forces it into the IRS (or more component-using) sector. Each of these seems to me as much of a *deus ex machina* as the discredited omniscient central planner.

The papers just cited in effect make transport costs for intermediate inputs prohibitive, so that they become non-tradable. Krugman and Venables (1995) consider variable levels of transport costs, and assume that the manufactured good is a Dixit-Stiglitz aggregation of intermediates, each produced under Type 1 IRS, and can be used for both intermediate production and final consumption. Assuming a single factor (labour) and identical technologies across countries rules out both Heckscher-Ohlin and Ricardian comparative advantage. For high levels of transport costs, there is only a symmetric equilibrium in which each country produces its own requirements of all goods. For intermediate levels (permitting trade but with a home market bias), size alone gives the country with an initially larger manufacturing sector (the North) a cost advantage, since it can support the production of a larger range of intermediate goods. The symmetric equilibrium becomes unstable, and the slightest perturbation induces industry to relocate to the North. Northern real wages increase, partly due to higher labour demand as its manufacturing sector expands, and partly from not having to pay the transport costs on imported manufactured goods consumed by workers. Southern wages initially fall, as they bear the burden of transport costs on the manufactured goods increasingly imported from the North. The world thus 'spontaneously' organizes itself into industrial and agricultural regions, or core and periphery.

However, further reduction of transport costs neutralizes the Northern industry's advantage of proximity to markets and component suppliers. Producers can access these benefits even if they relocate to take advantage of lower Southern wages, permitting the South to re-industrialize and its wages to catch up, with factor price equalization occurring in the limit as transport costs fall to zero. International labour immobility thus acts centrifugally, since rising Northern wages eventually reverse the agglomerating tendency of manufacturing activity if tranport costs are negligible. According to the authors, since falling transport costs is one way to capture the process of globalization, their model—immodestly subtitled 'The History of the World' in its original version—explains the initial divergence and subsequent convergence between countries. Protection in the North promotes industrialization there, enhancing the divergence and delaying the eventual convergence.

The idea is developed further by Puga and Venables (1999) in a more comprehensive paper with many countries and many products with different degrees of upstream and downstream linkage. Agriculture uses land as well as labour, and is perfectly competitive and subject to CRS; manufacturing again uses labour and differentiated intermediates, produced under IRS and monopolistic competition as before. Attention is focused on the role of IRS by assuming identical relative endowments and technology, thereby ruling out orthodox comparative advantage. Consumer preferences are modelled so that demand for manufactures increases disproportionately with income after a subsistence level of agricultural consumption is satisfied. Beginning with a situation in which the IRS manufacturing sector is confined to one country, Puga and Venables examine the consequences of neutral exogenous technological progress occurring simultaneously in all countries. Due to the interaction of IRS and the demand bias in favour of manufactures, this promotes further expansion of manufacturing in the leading country. Since the resulting backward and forward linkages are localized by international transport costs, productivity and wages rise in the leader. This is followed by successive waves of industrialization and convergence by other countries as manufacturing relocates in the face of rising wages in the leader(s): 'a story of breathtaking scope' as the authors describe it in a later version (Fujita et al. 1999, p. 277).[5] Allowing for many countries and many industries with different characteristics, a numerical simulation shows countries graduating from producing labour-intensive goods without significant linkages, to more sophisticated and densely-linked manufactures. This is illustrated by an empirical appeal to the stylized facts of international development experience.

Puga and Venables also examine trade policy by interpreting the transport cost parameter as the level of tariffs on manufactures. Industrialization of a follower country in their model can be induced by either high tariffs that encourage import-substitution, or by low tariffs that permit exploitation of the linkage effects from the foreign industry. A simulation shows that real income levels are higher in the latter case. There is also an intermediate zone of tariff levels where industrialization is not possible. This zone is enlarged, disproportionately downwards by protectionism in the advanced country (making export-promoting industrialization of the follower more difficult), and disproportionately upwards by the smaller initial size of a follower country (making import-substituting industrialization more difficult). The policy prescription that emerges from their approach is that developing countries can do no better than to lower their trade barriers and patiently await their turn for the spillover of manufacturing activity from developed countries.

## CRITICAL ASSESSMENT

Some obvious questions arise even from a casual acquaintance with the new development literature: Does the takeover of a small less developed country (LDC) market yield significant additional economies of scale for the foreign industry? Even if it does, do competitive pressures really force it to pass on the benefits in the form of lower prices? What proportion of consumers in low-income countries benefits from cheaper imports and a greater variety of consumer goods? Is there any direct evidence that productivity is enhanced by a wider range of intermediate goods that are imperfectly substitutable for each other? I raise these questions not merely to ask for empirical testing (on which see the penultimate section), nor to dismiss this literature out of hand (the concluding section attempts a balanced appraisal), but to draw attention to certain limitations that remain embedded in the 'new' theory because of its excessive fidelity to the 'old'.

The first such feature is the assumption of a representative consumer and/or homothetic preferences, so that more varied and/or cheaper imported consumer goods are necessarily a good thing. As a modern-day Marie Antoinette might say, the poor can have not just bread, but also several indigenous and imported varieties of cake! Puga and Venables do employ a non-homothetic linear expenditure system to generate a demand bias in favour of manufactures, but evade distributional issues by assuming that all consumers have the same income, above the subsistence level. In any case, mainstream trade theorists always sidestep questions of income distribution by invoking a mythical government armed with the ability to redistribute income through lump-sum taxes and transfers.

However, the neat parallelism established between consumers' putative 'love of variety' and the productivity-enhancing effect of differentiated components has also been carried too far. This means that a larger number of specialized inputs increases downstream productivity without any bound, and they have equal and constant elasticities of substitution for each other in the production of the final good. Correspondingly, market structure in the component-producing industry is also symmetric: all firms produce one component each, with identical fixed and marginal costs. For these and other reasons, industrial organization theorists (e.g. Tirole 1989) are extremely critical of the Dixit-Stiglitz approach to modelling competition between differentiated products. Krugman (1995) argues that theorists must be willing to be 'silly in the details' of their models in order to get results, but unless one has a Friedmanic disdain for approximate realism of assumptions, in this case their willingness seems to be going too far. These assumptions yield intermediate predictions (which even Friedman's shield should not protect from falsification) that are wildly at variance with casual observation. For example, the particular form assumed for the production function, combined with so-called 'iceberg' transport costs,[6] means that constant elasticities of demand face the component producers, resulting in prices that are constant and equal mark-ups over their identical marginal costs. They operate at a constant scale, with market expansion or contraction showing up only in changes in the number of varieties produced.

A second piece of traditional theoretical baggage carried by the new models is the need to provide a zero-profit closure, which limits them to perfect competition with external economies, or to monopolistic competition. This is why it does not matter if the home country loses its IRS sector, since the benefits of large-scale production abroad accrue at home: unless transport costs are significant, it does not matter where the IRS industry is located. However, studies in several different countries have shown that above-normal profits tend to persist, especially in differentiated product industries, even if there are many producers (Mueller 1990). Probably the most salient stylized fact about industrial organization in developing countries is the small size of markets relative to fixed costs of entry, so that oligopoly would seem to be the appropriate characterization. Then, trade liberalization has two contradictory effects: it benefits consumers by reducing industry mark-ups, but it reduces the scale of operation of domestic firms—the so-called 'business-stealing effect'. In Bhattacharjea (2002), I show that even if one uses the standard measure of social welfare (the sum of consumer and producer surplus), the adverse effect necessarily dominates over a certain range of foreign entry, regardless of the demand specification and mode of oligopolistic competition. The decline in welfare is sharper, the more concentrated the domestic industry, and the larger the gap between its social and private costs (on account of imperfect labour markets, for example)—both of which are likely to be characteristic of developing countries. I also show that in a Cournot model with linear demand, imports must capture at least 80 per cent of the domestic market for welfare to improve relative to autarky. I also summarize some empirical findings on the existence of a business-stealing effect in various countries. Of course, like most of the trade literature with oligopoly underpinnings, that paper deals with partial equilibrium, single-industry interaction rather than the broad economy-wide perspective adopted by the new development theory in its attempts to rival the grand narratives of the classical authors and the High Development Theory of the 1950s. In the neoclassical paradigm, this translates into a general equilibrium model, with externalities or monopolistic competition being used to reconcile competitive pricing with the non-convexity introduced by IRS.[7]

These general equilibrium models typically feature two sectors, with one characterized by IRS. This introduces two more limitations that the new literature carries over from the old. One is the assumption of clearing factor markets which results in full employment; I shall return to this when I come to the neo-Keynesian models below. The other is the modelling of the non-IRS sector ('Agriculture') as operating under CRS and perfect competition, enabling it to absorb the workers laid off from the contracting IRS sector at constant wages. Relaxing this assumption makes a major difference to models based on pure Marshallian externalities. In Panagariya (1981), where the second sector is subject to diminishing returns, contraction of the IRS sector has an ambiguous effect on welfare; in Panagariya (1986) where the two sectors each require a specific factor but employ intersectorally mobile labour, it adversely affects workers and also the rents on the specific capital of the IRS sector, even allowing for consumption of cheaper IRS goods. Panagariya's models allow for multiple equilibria, with the possibility that an equilibrium which retains some IRS production may be superior to one with complete specialization that abandons it.

Diminishing returns in agriculture have somewhat different implications in the spatial models. While Krugman and Venables (1995) do not examine this possibility, the extended version of the model in Fujita et al. (1999) does, while in Puga and Venables (1999) it results from the inclusion of land in the agricultural production function. In such a setting, diminishing returns in agriculture makes industrialization doubly beneficial, since it draws labour out of agriculture, raising productivity and wages there as well, damping and then reversing labour's incentive to move to the expanding manufacturing sector. However, the Fujita-Krugman-Venables parables are narrated only in terms of the advent of industrialization in follower countries where no industrial sector already exists. The story that remains untold, although equally possible in their models, is that reduction of transport costs or tariff levels from high to moderate (as in India in recent years?) can still bring about *de*industrialization, since the domestic industry loses its sheltered market while protection remains too high for it to benefit from international linkages. In this case diminishing returns in agriculture begins to bite, with wages falling over a certain range.

The Puga-Venables model suggests that trade liberalization should be pushed beyond this range. But this may have to be reconsidered if we examine the features that are central to a model by Eswaran and Kotwal (1993), where the characteristics of consumer demand and asset distribution are modelled in a manner that is more relevant to developing countries. Recall that Puga and Venables (1999) have a non-homothetic specification of consumer preferences, in the form of a linear expenditure system, and also a fixed endowment of land to generate diminishing returns in agriculture. However, they make all agents start out with incomes above the subsistence level, with land distributed equally amongst them. This dodges not just the normative aspects of income distribution, as mentioned above, but also the strictly 'positive' issue of how the composition of the demand influences the equilibrium outcome. In Eswaran and Kotwal (1993), on the other hand, when the low-productivity domestic industrial sector is exposed to trade, deindustrialization forces workers into an agricultural sector with diminishing returns, where they suffer declining wages. They miss out on the benefits of cheaper imported manufactures, since with non-homothetic 'hierarchical' preferences, their incomes are below the subsistence threshold at which manufactures are consumed. The combination of diminishing returns and heirarchical preferences also means that landlords benefit from rising rents and cheaper manufactured' imports. Eswaran and Kotwal do not model IRS on the production side, but doing so in conjunction with a more realistic characterization of consumer demand seems to be a promising avenue of enquiry.

Eswaran and Kotwal emphasize, especially in the more pedagogic exposition of their model in their 1994 book *Why Poverty Persists in India*, that the right lesson to draw from their model is to encourage greater openness and competition, so as to encourage faster productivity growth in the manufacturing sector, which will allow it to expand rather than contract when exposed to trade. What kind of openness has such benign rather than malign consequences is unexplained. The textbook prescription for promoting an externality-producing sector is a production subsidy rather than protection, but this is subject to well-known fiscal and informational limitations.

A fifth and final limitation the new literature carries over from its predecessors is in viewing change by comparing static equilibrium states, rather than as a process occurring in irreversible historical time. The two sources of IRS that are admitted into the analysis can work in both directions as scale expands or contracts; thus industrialization and deindustrialization are symmetric processes, cumulative causation can generate either a vicious or a virtuous circle, and configurations of the economy can in principle be made, unmade, and restored again with equal ease by varying the exogenous parameters of the model. The limitations of this approach were recognized by the authors who laid the foundations for the new theory: 'the comparison of equilibria involved in comparative statics exercises . . . should be understood as a comparison between two alternative histories, not as a change that takes place over time' (Helpman and Krugman 1985, p. 39).

The subsequent literature, including Krugman's own contributions, ignored this salutary warning. It used Marshallian externalities as a convenient way to reconcile IRS with competitive behaviour, forgetting that Marshall himself (particularly in Appendix H of his *Principles*) had emphasized the *irreversibility* of productivity increases. Other branches of modern economic theory do recognize the possibility of irreversibility, variously manifested as hysteresis, non-ergodicity, lock-in, and path-dependence in different contexts. These arise from sunk costs, network externalities and complementarities, research and development, or learning by doing, each of which involves IRS in different and crucial ways. These phenomena are excluded from the new trade-and-development literature, which does not allow for capital (human or physical, sunk or otherwise), much less its accumulation.

This last feature of the new literature is obviously not carried over from traditional trade theory; it arises, rather, from the need to focus narrowly on scale economies as the basis for trade. Countries are therefore treated as identical in respect of their endowments (usually labour alone), preferences, and technology, thereby purging the models of other sources of comparative advantage. One country is given a head start in industrialization for some unexplained reason, which remains conveniently open to different historical interpretations: the Protestant work ethic or colonial exploitation, for example. This 'purging', however, has the unfortunate consequence that there is nothing in the Puga-Venables multi-country model which explains the order in which follower countries industrialize. Also, the IRS manufacturing activity spreads from country to country through the relocation of ghostly 'firms' with no capital, and is immediately up and running at best-practice levels of productivity wherever it goes. Thus, despite its promising stylization in terms of Agriculture/ Manufacturing and North/South, and the several attractive features to which I return below, much of the new literature does not fit into a developmental perspective. It is, rather, concerned with examining how much difference increasing returns makes for traditional neoclassical trade theory regarding the pattern of trade, and its effects on the domestic allocation of (fully-employed) resources and the corresponding factor prices, within a context in which resource endowments, consumer preferences, and technological possibilities are either given or change exogenously. Endogenous resource accumulation and technological improvement lie beyond its horizon.

## GROWTH MODELS

Considerations of space as well as competence limit my ability to go into the rapidly expanding endogenous growth literature that investigates these phenomena. The driving force in most of these models is actually not IRS as such, but rather *non-diminishing* (constant) marginal returns in the production of some accumulable input such as knowledge or human capital. The models often rely on very similar devices to those of the literature surveyed above, such as fixed costs, externalities and monopolistic competition to ensure competitive pricing.[8] Some theorists (notably Grossman and Helpman 1991) think of IRS in terms of fixed costs of research and development resulting in the creation of new intermediate inputs or capital goods (in a manner very similar to the models discussed above), or a movement up the quality ladder with temporary monopoly power accruing to the innovator. In some models, R&D in the North is innovative while in the South it is imitative. The resulting new products are tradable, permitting international spillovers of the benefits. Productivity growth in a country is then linked to R&D taking place in its trading partners, transmitted through the import of new (horizontally or vertically differentiated) inputs, or simply through international communication of knowledge, which is hypothesized to be positively related to the volume of trade. In parallel with the static IRS models reviewed earlier, trade also eliminates wasteful duplication of R&D (although this is an equilibrium result pertaining to surviving innovations, and may be the outcome of 'patent races' in which the losers end up wasting resources on infructuous R&D). It also expands the customer base and hence the incentive for further research.

Other approaches are based on learning by doing, or on human capital formation resulting from individuals' rational decision to acquire skills outside the production process. In all these cases, trade theorists are led by their general-equilibrium training to examine the impact of trade on resource allocation as between R&D and production, or between sectors with more and less potential for learning, or with greater or less return to private investment in human capital. The consequences for the growth rate can then go either way, with at least some presumption that the static comparative advantage of developing countries will direct resources away from the human capital and knowledge intensive growth-promoting sectors into the labour and natural resource intensive sectors, with a consequent fall in the rate of growth and widening international disparities. This must be set off against the usual gains from specialization, including access to a wider range of intermediate goods.

## ALTERNATIVE APPROACHES

Capital accumulation remains the stepchild of these models, left to the savings decisions that result from the intertemporal optimization of consumption by households. Writers with a neo-Keynesian perspective believe instead that investment in a capitalist economy is governed by industrial profit rates, and model IRS as a Kaldorian 'technical progress function', with productivity an increasing function of the growth rate of manufacturing. This is a sort of reduced form that is meant to capture all types of IRS phenomena. A recent example is Skott and Larudee (1999), who modify Krugman (1981) in these two respects, as well as in allowing for labour force growth and exogenous productivity growth but diminishing returns to labour in agriculture. They assume (like Krugman and others) that wages are determined by productivity in the agricultural sector, which absorbs the labour force not taken up by industry, and (unlike them) a small price-taking economy. Profits and accumulation in an open economy are then governed by the gap between the exogenous world price and the unit labour costs in manufacturing. The dynamics of the model can result either in deindustrialization with rising incomes (if agricultural productivity grows more rapidly than the labour force), or self-reinforcing industrialization, or a deindustrialization trap with slow growth. The last possibility, interestingly, arises when labour costs are too high relative to the world price of manufactures, which can occur because agricultural productivity is growing too rapidly. Although I do not believe that optimizing microfoundations are absolutely essential for modelling, this approach sidesteps the question of market structure altogether, so that it is not clear why profits are not dissipated by entry. It could also benefit from the neoclassical models' emphasis on imported producer goods, which could have an impact along with labour costs on industrial profits.

Some of these issues are addressed by Ocampo and Taylor (1998), which allows for the other distinguishing characteristic of post-Keynesian models: unemployment and variable degrees of capacity utilization. Here, the investment associated with technical change increases capacity utilization, with a positive feedback to investment and growth. Protection of infant industries can thus stimulate technological investment, giving an impetus to growth from both supply and demand sides. Unlike most radical writers, Ocampo and Taylor (perhaps because of their 'structuralist' pedigree, which sensitizes them to the consequences of foreign exchange constraints, or 'external strangulation') recognize the possibility that the protected industries might produce more expensive or lower quality inputs and thereby undermine productivity growth. They argue strongly for Korea-style incentives contingent on export performance, and investment in human capital and 'development of public and private institutions to facilitate the transfer, adaptation, and diffusion of more productive technologies' (p. 1539), although this puts as much faith in the state as the neoclassical models do in the market.

## EMPIRICAL EVIDENCE

Like most attention-grabbing theoretical models, those surveyed here remained until recently far removed from empirical application, except for appeals to the pervasiveness of IRS and non-convergence between countries. In the last decade, a huge literature has emerged based on the results of cross-country regressions by various authors who seek to relate growth to a wide range of explanatory variables. However, apart from providing evidence of conditional convergence between countries (which is consistent with various IRS-based endogenous growth models) and the role of human capital, they do not illuminate the particular mechanisms surveyed above. Backus et al. (1992), who explicitly examine scale effects on labour productivity, find that they are confined to the manufacturing sector and not evident for GDP, and are detected only when output measures are used as the scale variable. A weak negative relationship is found when the working-age population, or manufacturing employment, are used instead. They also find that productivity growth at the aggregate level is also positively related to intra-industry trade in manufacturing. Antweiler and Trefler (2000), employing a theoretically-informed estimation procedure and a huge international database, find evidence of economies of scale in several individual industries, but are unable to disentangle Type 1 and 2 economies, or for that matter what they call 'scale-biased technical change', arising from the fact that new technologies are often embodied in large plants.

The latest papers I have surveyed in the two theoretical traditions, Puga and Venables (1999) and Skott and Larudee (1999), both offer simulations calibrated with crude estimates of the parameters of their models, for Korea and Mexico, respectively. The Puga-Venables paper is quite cavalier with its choice of stylized facts. They conclude that their model's prediction that tariff reduction promotes exports of only labour-intensive consumer goods is in accordance with the Korean experience since the 1980s. They do not seem to be aware that the more successful Korean exports in the liberalization period included automobiles and consumer electronics, which are not included in their exercise, and steel, whose production according to their simulation should not have been viable at low tariffs.

Coe and Helpman (1995) and Coe et al. (1997) seek to validate the Grossman-Helpman endogenous growth models, in which trade transmits the effects of R&D. They establish a statistical relationship between countries' total factor productivity growth (TFPG) and an import-weighted average of the R&D stocks of their trade partners, with the best results coming from a specification which interacts the latter with the ratio of machinery imports to GDP. This approach, however, received a knock from Keller (1998), who showed that the same relationship could be validated by using a set of *random* weights! Even in their own 1997 paper, Coe et al. found that the estimated coefficient on the foreign R&D stock was much too high to be credible when country-specific time trends were excluded, and negative when they were included, leading them to drop time trends in their preferred result All this is quite apart from conceptual problems in measuring TFPG, which involves assumptions of perfect competition and CRS inconsistent with the literature surveyed above.

Finally, the proliferating and contradictory evidence on the relationship between gross domestic product (GDP) or productivity growth rates and various contrived measures of 'outward-orientation' or 'openness' is interpreted selectively according to the predictions of the author's model or priors on the desirability of trade liberalization. Going into this would take me too far afield, but see Ocampo and Taylor (1998) for a fairly nuanced appraisal.

## FORGOTTEN ANCESTORS

Returning to where we began, with Krugman's faint praise for the 'High Development Theory' of the 1950s, our review of the new development theory brings to mind some forerunners who are not given the recognition due to them. Although it is conventional for writers on this subject to acknowledge Adam Smith as the first to recognize IRS, Bagchi (1993-4) has drawn our attention to Josiah Tucker's more comprehensive treatment a few years before the publication of *The Wealth of Nations*. In light of some of the modern theories that were surveyed above, it is especially significant that Tucker seems to have considered a wider range of scale phenomena, including what today would be called external economies, such as the development of better implements, infrastructure, non-appropriable know-how, and means of instruction, and applied these insights to predict a cumulative divergence between nations.

Two centuries later, there is the signal contribution of Nicholas Kaldor. It is strange that while the neoclassical authors reviewed above pay ritual obeisance to Allyn Young and the 1950s development theorists, none of them mentions Kaldor, who posed some of the issues raised by IRS far more sharply. Presumably, his disdain for 'microfoundations' and for equilibrium, and the informal style of his later work, puts him beyond the pale, despite a strong plea by a leading neoclassical theorist for taking his approach more seriously (Stern 1991). Kaldor drew his inspiration directly from Young (1928). This is a rather verbose paper, but its main conclusions were neatly summed up in its concluding paragraph, which is worth quoting at length:

> First, the mechanism of increasing returns is not to be discerned adequately by observing the effects of variations in the size of an individual firm or of a particular industry, for the progressive division and specialization of industries is an essential part of the process by which increasing returns are realized.... Second, the securing of increasing returns depends on the progressive division of labour, and the principle economies of the division of labour, in its modern forms, are the economies which are to be had by using labour in roundabout or indirect ways. Third, the division of labour depends on the extent of the market, but the extent of the market also depends upon the division of labour. In this circumstance lies the possibility of economic progress.... (Young, 1928, p. 539)

Although these arguments figure prominently in the new development literature, Kaldor saw in them an inherently *disequilibriating* process, in which each advance in the division of labour stimulates induced investment, which further expands the market and results in further division of labour. His writings from the mid-1960s onwards anticipate many of the models reviewed above, including their emphasis on regional polarization resulting from locally produced specialized inputs, and even the suggestion of an employment tax on the CRS sector to divert labour forcibly into the IRS sector. His early critique of Chamberlinian monopolistic competition anticipates that of the modern industrial organization theorists. However, it should be noted that he shared the new trade literature's scepticism of protectionism, and favoured what would today be called outward-oriented policies to take advantage of IRS.[9]

## CONCLUDING ASSESSMENTS

Even if we reconcile ourselves to using equilibrium models, much of the theoretical apparatus in the neoclassical literature seems contrived to provide 'microfoundations' for algebraically tractable behavioural specifications that are routinely assumed by structuralist or post-Keynesian theorists. Thus, Cobb-Douglas utility functions result in constant shares of consumer expenditure for each final good, while the constant elasticity functional forms and Chamberlinian market structure inspired by Dixit-Stiglitz, combined with convenient assumptions about transport costs, give mark-up pricing of their intermediate inputs. To neoclassical economists, starting from such relationships without deriving them from the first principles of individual maximizing behaviour is unacceptable ad hoc procedure; to those of other persuasions, it is simply starting from obvious 'stylized facts'. The Krugman-Venables 'History of the World', with IRS activities running into diminishing returns in each territory and then relocating in successive undeveloped regions, is an arresting metaphor for the impressive run enjoyed by the Dixit-Stiglitz specifications, beginning with industrial organization and then spilling over successively into trade, growth, geography, and now development models.

From yet another perspective, the excessive formalism of the 'new economic geography' also causes dismay amongst even technically-competent geographers, who decry its adherence to equilibrium rather than processes, logical rather than historical time, lack of empirical applicability at anything but the highest level of generality, blindness to local institutional specificities, and in general its 'neglect of real places' (Martin 1999). Krugman and his fellow authors would no doubt insist that these are inevitable and even desirable features of formal models, and that local particularities, whether of natural geography or social institutions, can be accommodated as needed. However, even Paul David (1998), no stranger to formal modelling of increasing returns in economics, is unhappy with the new 'spare and bare' formalism, with its search for deterministic, universally applicable principles. In particular, he points out that different types of inputs will typically have their transport costs—more broadly interpreted to include transactions costs—declining by different degrees, and some (such as services involving transmission of uncodified technical knowledge) may remain stubbornly localized. He also points out that investment in transport infrastructure is itself subject to indivisibilities, and therefore tends to favour existing concentrations of economic activity.

One might add that the revolution in information technology has substantially reduced search and transactions costs, and also made transport costs for certain kinds of products (including many of the 'producer services' which the Type 3 models explicitly or implicitly regard as the differentiated intermediate inputs) negligible and independent of distance. This, however, will asymmetrically benefit those countries with better telecommunications infrastructure. Therefore, instead of falling uniformly for all products and destinations as in the new geography/development models, transport costs are likely to evolve unevenly. In terms of the discipline's preferred metaphor (see n. 6), different icebergs melt at different rates, depending on their composition and location. Some, to adapt a classical phrase, may perish in the instant of their creation; others may be transported at high speed without melting at all.

The neoclassical models reviewed above capture some of the important stylized facts of development and of production subject to IRS that cannot be dealt with in traditional trade theory. They make it possible to highlight, in ways in which traditional theory did not, the self-reinforcing nature of competitive advantage, the tendency to concentration and agglomeration of industry, the role of trade in impelling structural shifts in resource re-allocation between CRS and IRS sectors and its implications for living standards, and the importance of the home market. In showing how small differences in scale between otherwise identical economies can lead to a cumulative divergence of their development trajectories, they provide an antidote to the view that under-development is the result of some innate deficiency in entrepreneurial ability, thrift, or work ethics. This new neoclassical literature can be credited for reconciling some very aggregative empirical features of development, and the insights of earlier generations of writers on the subject, with individual maximizing behaviour. While this certainly represents a major advance over traditional neoclassical trade theory, whether it has 'explained' those facts any better than the informal treatments of earlier authors, depends on one's idea of scientific progress.

At the same time, the alternative neo-Keynesian models could pay more attention to market structure and transportation and transactions costs, drawing upon various traditions including the neoclassical. And perhaps it is time that the venerable technical progess function acquired more structure, perhaps even rudimentary microfoundations? Acknowledging the relationship between income distribution and the composition of demand also needs to be on the agenda, for both schools. Also, while economies 'internal to the industry but external to the firm' have been modelled more inventively than Sraffa (1926) imagined, his central message regarding the need to face up squarely to the consequences of IRS for imperfect competition still rings true. Perhaps there are elements to be borrowed from each tradition for the next generation of models, and—bearing in mind the pedagogic mission of this volume—to be taught to the next generation of modellers.

## NOTES

1. In fact, Hummels and Levinsohn (1995) empirically discredit a standard model of this genre by showing that its predictions conform to the pattern of trade between low-income developing countries, which would not be expected to export differentiated products!
2. Ironically, this is despite Krugman's invoking Lenin, Baran, the doctrine of uneven development, and deindustrialization in nineteenth-century India! It is perhaps significant that he does not cite this paper in his later writings, including his work on development.
3. The original geography models were relevant to a single economy, in which labour was free to move to the growth centres, while immobile land or natural resources reinforced the centrifugal tendency, with dispersed farmer-consumers in the countryside and rising rents in the cities both counteracting the benefits from agglomeration. In the international trade models, countries become dimensionless points, between which goods can move at a cost but labour cannot move at all. This immobility of labour provides the counteracting effect in terms of rising wages, as we shall see below.
4. Related to this (although in a closed economy context) is Krugman's (1991a) rather difficult analysis of the relative roles of 'history versus expectations' in determining which of multiple equilibrium states comes about. He shows that high discount rates, weak IRS, or high adjustment costs all favour 'history' (i.e. the status quo) and prevent self-fulfilling expectations from propelling the economy to a superior equilibrium.
5. This monograph contains in chapters 14 and 15 a much clearer exposition of the Krugman-Venables (1995) and Puga-Venables (1999) models, integrated in a common

framework with the contributions of these and other authors to spatial economics. Chapter 7 allows for transport costs for agricultural goods, showing that it acts as an additional centrifugal force, counteracting the tendency to agglomeration. The book also deliberately and wisely refrains from drawing any policy implications.

6. This involves treating goods as if a part of them melts away in the process of shipping, so that for each unit exported, less than one unit arrives at the destination.
7. Helpman and Krugman (1985, Ch. 5) did embed Cournot competition in a general equilibrium model, and showed that trade in this setting can have a 'pro-competitive effect' on welfare, *provided* output per firm rises in decreasing-cost industries.
8. See the various essays in Coricelli et al. (1998) for a critical evaluation of the new growth literature's contribution to our understanding of development.
9. Kaldor's most important papers have been collected in Targetti and Thirlwall (1989). The most relevant are his 1935 *Econometrica* article criticizing Chamberlin, his 1972 Inaugural Lecture, and his 1985 *Economics Without Equilibrium.*

## REFERENCES


Antweiler, W. and D. Trefler (2000), 'Increasing Returns and All That: A View from Trade', NBER Working Paper, no. 7941, Cambridge, MA.

Backus, D.K., P.J. Kehoe and T.J. Kehoe (1992), 'In Search of Scale Effects in Trade and Growth', *Journal of Economic Theory*, vol. 58, no. 2, pp. 377-409.

Bagchi, A.K. (1993-94), 'Political Economy: A Discourse of Mastery or an Apparatus of Dissent?', *Indian Historical Review*, vol. 20, pp. 78-113.

Barro, R. and X. Sala-i-Martin (1995), *Economic Growth*, McGraw-Hill, New York.

Bhattacharjea, A. (2002), 'Foreign Entry and Domestic Welfare', *Journal of International Trade and Economic Development*, vol. 11, no. 2, pp. 143-62.

Chipman, J.S. (1965), 'A Survey of the Theory of International Trade, part 2: The Neo-Classical Theory', *Econometrica*, vol. 33, no. 4, pp. 685-760.

Ciccone, A. and K. Matsuyama (1996), 'Start-up Costs and Pecuniary Externalities as Barriers to Economic Development', *Journal of,Development Economics*, vol. 49, no. 1, pp. 33-59.

Coe, D.T. and E. Helpman (1995), 'International Research and Development Spillovers', *European Economic Review*, vol. 39, no. 5, pp. 859-87.

Coe, D.T., E. Helpman and A.W. Hoffmaister (1997), 'North-South R & D Spillovers', *Economic Journal*, vol. 107, no. 440, pp. 134-49.

Coricelli, F., M. di Matteo and F. Hahn (1998), *New Theories of Growth and Development*, Macmillan, London and Basingstoke.

David, P.A. (1998), 'Comment on "The Role of Geography in Development" by Paul Krugman', in B. Pleskovic and J.E. Stiglitz (eds.), *Annual World Bank Conference on Development Economics*, pp. 108-17, Washington, D.C.

Davis, D. (1998), 'The Home Market, Trade and Industrial Structure', *American Economic Review*, vol. 88, no. 5, pp. 1264-76.

Eswaran, M. and A. Kotwal (1993), 'A Theory of Real Wage Growth in LDCs', *Journal of Development Economics*, vol. 42, no. 2, pp. 243-69.

——— (1994), *Why Poverty Persists in India*, Oxford University Press, New Delhi.

Ethier, W.J. (1982a), 'Decreasing Costs in International Trade and Frank Graham's Argument for Protection', *Econometrica*, vol. 50, no. 5, pp. 1243-68.

——— (1982b), 'National and International Returns to Scale in the Modern Theory of International Trade', *American Economic Review*, vol. 72, no. 3, pp. 389-405.

Fujita, M., P. Krugman and A.J. Venables (1999), *The Spatial Economy: Cities, Regions and International Trade*, MIT Press, Cambridge and London.

Grossman, G.M. and E. Helpman (1991), *Innovation and Growth in the Global Economy*, MIT Press, Cambridge, MA.

Helpman, E. and P.R. Krugman (1985), *Market Structure and Foreign Trade*, MIT Press, Cambridge, MA.

Hummels, D. and J. Levinsohn (1995), 'Monopolistic Competition: Reconsidering the Evidence', *Quarterly Journal of Economics*, vol. 110, no. 3, pp. 799-836.

Keller, W. (1998), 'Are International R&D Spillovers Trade-Related?', *European Economic Review*, vol. 42, no. 8, pp. 1469-81.

Krugman, P. (1981), 'Trade, Accumulation and Uneven Development', *Journal of Development Economics*, vol. 8, no. 2, pp. 149-61.

——— (1991a), 'History versus Expectations', *Quarterly Journal of Economics*, vol. 105, no. 2, pp. 651-67.

——— (1991b), *Geography and Trade*, MIT Press, Cambridge, MA.

——— (1995), *Development, Geography, and Economic Theory*, MIT Press, Cambridge, MA.

——— (1998), 'The Role of Geography in Development', in B. Pleskovic and J.E. Stiglitz (eds.), *Annual World Bank Conference on Development Economics*, Washingon, D.C., pp. 89-107.

Krugman, P. and A.J. Venables (1995), 'Globalization and the Inequality of Nations', *Quarterly Journal of Economics*, vol. 110, no. 4, pp. 857-80.

Martin, R. (1999), 'The New "Geographical Turn" in Economics', *Cambridge Journal of Economics*, vol. 23, no. 1, pp. 65-91.

Mueller, D. (1990), *The Dynamics of Company Profits: An International Comparison*, Cambridge University Press, Cambridge.

Murphy, R., A. Schleifer and R. Vishny (1989), 'Industrialization and the Big Push', *Journal of Political Economy*, vol. 97, no. 5, pp. 1003-26.

Ocampo, J.A. and L. Taylor (1998), 'Trade Liberalisation in Developing Countries: Modest Benefits but Problems with Productivity Growth, Macro Prices and Income Distribution', *Economic Journal*, vol. 108, no. 450, pp. 1523-46.

Panagariya, A. (1981), 'Variable Returns to Scale in Production and Patterns of Specialization', *American Economic Review*, vol. 71, no. 1, pp. 221-30.

——— (1986), 'Increasing Returns and the Specific Factors Model', *Southern Economic Journal*, vol. 53, no. 1, pp. 1-17.

Puga, D. and A.J. Venables (1999), 'Agglomeration and Economic Development: Import Substitution vs. Trade Liberalisation', *Economic Journal*, vol. 109, no. 455, pp. 292-311.

Rodriguez-Clare, A. (1996), 'The Division of Labour and Economic Development', *Journal of Development Economics*, vol. 49, no. 1, pp. 3-32.

Rodrik, D. (1996), 'Coordination Failures and Government Policy: A Model with Applications to East Asia and Eastern Europe', *Journal of International Economics*, vol. 40, nos. 1-2, pp. 1-22.

Rosenstein-Rodan, P. (1943), 'Problems of Industrialization of Eastern and South-Eastern Europe', *Economic Journal*, vol. 53, no. 210, pp. 202-11.

Skott, P. and M. Larudee (1999), 'Uneven Development and the Liberalisation of Trade and Capital Flows: The Case of Mexico', *Cambridge Journal of Economics*, vol. 22, no. 3, pp. 277-95.

Solow, R. (1994), 'Perspectives on Growth Theory', *Journal of Economic Perspectives*, vol. 8, no. 1, pp. 45-54.

Sraffa, P. (1926), 'The Laws of Returns under Competitive Conditions', *Economic Journal*, vol. 36, no. 144, pp. 535-50.

Stern, N. (1991), 'The Determinants of Growth', *Economic Journal*, vol. 101, no. 404, pp. 122-33.

Targetti, F. and A.P. Thirlwall eds. (1989), *The Essential Kaldor*, Holmes and Meier, New York.

Tirole, J. (1989), *The Theory of Industrial Organization*, MIT Press, Cambrige, MA.

Young, A. (1928),'Increasing Returns and Economic Progress', *Economic Journal*, vol. 38, no. 152, pp. 527-42.

# 6 Wages, Labour Mobility, and International Trade

*Sugata Marjit and Saibal Kar*

## INTRODUCTION

Labour flows from the poor to the rich nations have been a crucial component of international economic relations at least to the extent that they affect political debate in the developed countries. While international wage differentials should be the major driving force behind such movements, mass migration has also been caused by political violence, oppression, and natural calamities. Although theoretical support for the relation between relative income and mass migration is easy to establish, empirical verification for such a connection has been difficult to find. Total international migration, as of present, is estimated at 100 million, i.e. less than 2 per cent of world population. About three-fourths of the world population lives in countries whose per capita income is less than one-tenth of the average in the capital rich countries. Yet, international migration in the aggregate has an extraordinarily low responsiveness (elasticity) to international income and wage differences. Changes in international wage differentials do not necessarily translate into changes in migration.

The attempt to find the answer to the above puzzle exclusively in the domain of economic incentives leads to failure. A recent study by O'Connor and Farsakh (1996) tries to do this precisely and reflects very little on the political issues that affect international migration. The fact that the capital-rich nations have never treated the issues of capital and labour mobility on the same footing seems to bypass a lot of the discussions on migration. Since a large part of our analysis will also evolve around economic issues, one should be aware of the limitations of such analyses.

This chapter aims to provide a broad overview of the literature on international migration, identify the major areas of research, and reflect on the contemporary policy perspective from the viewpoint of the developing world.

The next section deals with a survey of the conventional results. It mainly focuses on the aggregate welfare implications of factor flows in general and labour flows in particular. Empirical evidence, on trade reform, international mobility of labour, 'migration hump', and the long-run relationship between trade and migration, is briefly discussed.

Mobility of labour as a heterogeneous factor and the impact of such mobility on wage inequality, unemployment, and capital formation will be discussed in the third section. We shall attempt a simple and tractable way of understanding the problems associated with labour flows from developing countries.

The way emigration helps the process of development of a poor economy has to do with the expansion of capital stock—physical and human. This may entail a process of rising wages and savings. Such a mechanism may fail to operate due to various reasons. Also there is the issue of 'brain drain' which may be detrimental to the process of development. Large outflow of skilled people can promote or hurt local skill or capital formation. The penultimate section is devoted towards these issues. The last section concludes with some remarks.

## OVERVIEW

W.R. Bohning (1984) is precise in commenting that the effects of international migration depend crucially on the type of movement involved. Every type entails different effects on the receiving as well as the sending country. The typology that follows takes as its starting point the fact that it is the state as an institution rather than the migrant as an actor which determines contemporary patterns of migration, and it is based on the following definitions of regular migrants.

Regular migrants are non-nationals who possess the authorizations of the state in whose territory they are, that are required by law in respect of entry, stay, or work (if they are economically active) and who fulfil the conditions to which their entry, stay, or work are subjects.

Regular migration is shaped by economic, political, and social forces, primarily those of migrant-receiving countries, and looked at from their viewpoints, two broad categories, each having several sub-categories, can be distinguished. The first category relates to a policy that does not subject either the stay or the work of non-nationals to restrictions (except in respect of work that involves the exercise of official authority). Three sub-categories under this type can be identified:

(*a*) There are free migration policies under which countries abolish substantive entry, residence, and labour market controls for specified nationalities. This holds true in for instance, the European Economic Community (EEC), the Nordic Community Labour Market, the Trans-Tasman Agreement between Australia and New Zealand, and that for the Syrian Arab Republic in respect of Arab nationals;

(*b*) Foreigners may be admitted with a view to be granted permanent residence and in the hope that they would become future citizens. Australia and many English-speaking and Spanish-speaking countries of the Americas are perhaps best known for having pursued such a policy, although this was by no means the only type of policy they adopted at one time or another;

(*c*) Non-nationals may be permitted to stay indefinitely, in the cases where after a period of time the general restrictions on stay and work are lifted as in many West European countries or where the foreigners who do not qualify for naturalization or who do not wish to change their nationalities are enabled to stay, as in the US.

The other broad category, where regularly admitted migrants are subjected to limitations on stay or work can be divided into at least two sub-categories:

(*a*) Contract migration, which usually involves only wage and salary earners. It can once again take several forms: individual as opposed to collective contract migration; migration where the workers are employed on ordinary jobs or as project-tied migrants. Contract migration has been given such names as 'workers of distinguished merit and ability', or such labels as 'guest worker'.

(*b*) Official and business migration is the other sub-category. It

> covers all economically active persons and comprises, for example, diplomatic or assimilated personnel, transport or media representatives, entertainers or sportsmen, investors or traders, and the great variety of employees moving under the auspices of multinational corporations (MNCs).

This brief excursion into the typology indicates how diverse contemporary migration is. Visibly, this is a shift from the classical theory of labour migration, in which economists tended to make the simplifying assumptions that labour could be regarded as homogenous and in the long run perfectly mobile within one country. Apart from that, there was a tendency of making the generalization that more attention to capital than labour as a factor of production was bestowed upon by the classical approach, and most models of economic change based on this approach presuppose very similar behaviour of capital and labour insofar as geographical movement is concerned. They also regarded labour in the same way as they regarded capital—as a supply ready to meet a demand initiated exogenously and that such supply could vary independently. If the concept of maximization of returns holds good in this connection, it would be observed that a migration model based on the shifting advantages over different geographical locations is well developed. In this classical theory, the advantage was probably thought of as fertile land, later mineral resources and, still later advantages derived from the size of the market. These would primarily attract employers, who would then generate a certain demand for labour and cause the initiation of a migratory process.

Nevertheless, even a rigorous classical model would admit that in the short run, labour is to be paid higher wages in order to be attracted to a certain country, while such induced or maybe even autonomous movements in the long run would cause wages to equalize across nations. This stands out as an equilibrium system in the sense that, except for exogenous shocks, regional wage differentials will tend to be lowered, and the optimum system where each worker receives exactly his marginal product will be continually approached. Models of the kind presuppose that exogenous shocks can be taken care of without forcing the system too far out of equilibrium, and that all migratory patterns might be self-correcting, such that following any shock (for example, a change in the export market for a particular industry or a natural resources discovery as North Sea gas), the wages in the migrant-sending countries will eventually increase and cause to reverse the direction of migration. However, a situation like this might emerge only with a static population or with a fixed growth in population, at a rate which does not adversely affect the causes and consequences of migration.

Evidently this might sound too simplistic and a variant of the structure is brought forth in another set of models which are essentially Keynesian, showing that capital was likely to move in the same direction as labour and in effect would intensify and perpetuate the disequilibrium between the gaining and the losing areas. In Great Britain, the depressed areas of the 1920s, which then had much higher unemployment and much higher emigration rates than the remainder of the country were still mainly the depressed areas of the 1930s in spite of a very large net loss of migration over the 20 years. A solution to this problem was sought in Barlow's *Report*[1] demanding government intervention in the form of assisting or persuading firms to move into declining regions so that the continuing process of decline would be halted and then reversed.

The above two models take it for granted that the level of employment (possibly through its effect on the wage rate) is the determinant of migration. So, the question as to whether migration is self-correcting or cumulative translates itself into a question of migration's effect on future employment and wages. It may be trivially true that few people wishing to remain in employment move to new areas beyond the commuting distance of their existing jobs without having good reasons to believe that they will find employment there. But the models would apply only if employment or wage levels determined net migration flows, and most country experiences suggest strongly that there is no such simple relationship.

Once it is accepted that the causes of migration patterns are more complex than and not necessarily related to employment, it becomes easier to understand why the economic models of the above types appear to help so little in evaluating questions about either economic causes or effects of migration and why newer sophisticated analyses are necessitated. In other words, to move towards a more realistic explanation of migration, one has to take into account a number of other economic variables, viz., congestion of the state of an area's infrastructure; geographical factors, viz., the distance from the nearest major population centre; psychological factors, viz., the image of an area and political factors, like new towns or development area policy (Lind 1969). Naturally, this multiplicity of factors produce a far more complex picture and allows for new approaches to the central question about migration trends—whether they are self-correcting and economically efficient or cumulative and undesirable—to interpret on the whole, the features in terms of present and future policies.

Gerking and Mutti (1983) are of the opinion that the 'guest worker' programmes initiated by Western European nations and the more recent surge of illegal immigration into the US from Latin America are but two examples of movements of predominantly unskilled workers from less developed countries (LDCs) to developed countries (DCs). Understandably, such labour movements suggest that the wages paid to unskilled workers in the receiving countries should fall whereas that paid to their counterparts in the country of emigration should rise. This appears to explain in a straightforward manner, why the proposed liberalization of immigration restrictions in developed countries is often met with strenuous objections from labour groups, while at the same time, government officials in LDCs tend to view emigration as a vent for surplus unskilled labour. Gerking and Mutti (1989) established that, in the context of a static general equilibrium model, when there is a movement of unskilled workers from LDCs to DCs:

(i) wages paid to this type of labour are likely to fall in both countries, while the returns to all capital owners rise; and
(ii) the developed country accumulates capital at the expense of the LDCs.

Gerking and Mutti (1983) also predicted that if production technologies differ sufficiently across countries, then the absolute disparity between the wage rates paid to unskilled labour in the two countries may actually increase. This combined with other results is indicative of the fact that the then dilemma regarding illegal immigration into the US could be persistent—and in reality it has been because 'even leaving aside the compounding factor of divergent population growth rates, incentives for entry brought about by international wage rate differences may not tend to disappear when emigration to the U.S. occurs'.

Sapir (1993) also states that during the 1960s and 1970s employment of foreign labour became an important aspect of Western European economies. The fact suggests that immigration policies might have been used by Western European capitalists in structurally weak sectors as a means of remaining competitive. Clearly, one way for industries in the industrialized countries to resist the competition from the less developed labour-abundant countries is to try to reduce their labour costs, and therefore between trade competition and immigration from labour-abundant countries there has to be a crucial relationship in a capital-abundant economy. In this regard, Sapir proposed that

> within the Ricardo-Viner (sector-specific) model, a host country protecting its importable sector might experience a welfare gain or loss from an inflow of foreign labour which receives its full (tax-free) marginal product. If workers are paid only in terms of the importable good there will be a gain; if they are paid only in terms of the exportable good, there might be either a loss or a gain. Moreover, these results hold regardless of whether the host country is labour-or-capital-abundant.

While Sapir's conclusion remains conditional and therefore open-ended, Wong (1983) rank-orders a set of policies or 'regimes' from the viewpoint of overall welfare impact and considers two possibilities:

1. Given a well-behaved social utility function and diversification in production, the more the national factor-price ratio deviates from and on the same side of the autarkic factor-price ratio, the higher will be the welfare level that the country will have.
2. Given a well-behaved social utility function and diversification in production, the more the combined (national and foreign) factor endowment ratio deviates from and on the same side of the national factor endowment ratio, the higher will be the welfare level that the country will have.

Schiff (1996) offers three scenarios under which trade and migration are complements rather than substitutes, i.e. when trade liberalization will temporarily lead to more migration, not less, creating the 'migration hump'. Intuitively, trade liberalization, by creating new employment in migrant-sending countries, provides families with a means to finance international migration which they could not afford in the past. Secondly, following trade reforms, with sectors showing specificity in factor usage, there would be some economic costs involved in switching resources from one sector to another. This would lead to some transitional unemployment and therefore increased migration pressure. Finally, if (and in reality, it is) the most protected import-competing sector is labour-intensive, then trade liberalization renders labour unemployed.

It follows from the concept of 'migration hump', that in the aftermath of a trade reform at time zero, the assumed short run complementarity between trade and migration will cause an increase in migration above the status quo trajectory line, which is rising at a decreasing rate. On the other hand, the assumed long-run substitutability between trade and migration will cause a downslide of the hump much below the trajectory line. So, the migration hump in the short-run suggests a net long-run 'savings' in unwanted migration as a result of trade reforms.

It is also assumed in this regard that the duration and amplitude of the hump are relatively small. Thus, when viewed over a long enough period of time, there is less migration with trade than without it.

If, however, trade and migration are substitutes both in the short-run and in the long-run, the migration hump becomes a migration trough. This view is supported by standard trade theory, whereby specific endowment labour (L) and capital (K) rich countries end up specializing in the commodities they have comparative advantage in. On the other hand, if the standard neoclassical assumptions are relaxed, then even the traditional 2 × 2 × 2 framework might evoke complementarity between trade and migration and henceforth a migration plateau. These are, however, based on the underlying assumptions that markets are perfect, adjustments are instantaneous, trade is not due to scale economics, and there is no disparity in factor productivity. These features are illustrated in Fig. 6.1.

The market imperfection induced migration underlies the 'New Economics of Labour Migration' pioneered by Oded Stark, where migrants are viewed as financial intermediaries who provide their families with liquidity and income insurance. Stark (1991) argues that the desire to overcome the risk and capital constraints is a primary motivation for migration. Previously, Katz and Stark (1986) examined the effect of migratory opportunities for children on fertility, when the decision by the child whether or how much to remit is endogenous to the analysis. International migration under asymmetric information has also been extensively dealt with in Katz and Stark (1987), where they introduce a migration model in the absence of costly 'signalling' and in the presence of time-consuming revelation of true productivity of the migrant workers. Koo and Stark shows that asymmetric information will tend to reduce the skill level of migrants, by changing qualitatively as well as quantitatively the distribution of migrant groups in the population. The restoration of informational symmetry reinforces the possibility of migration only by the high-skill and the low-skill groups, with the middle group not migrating. With the same structure,

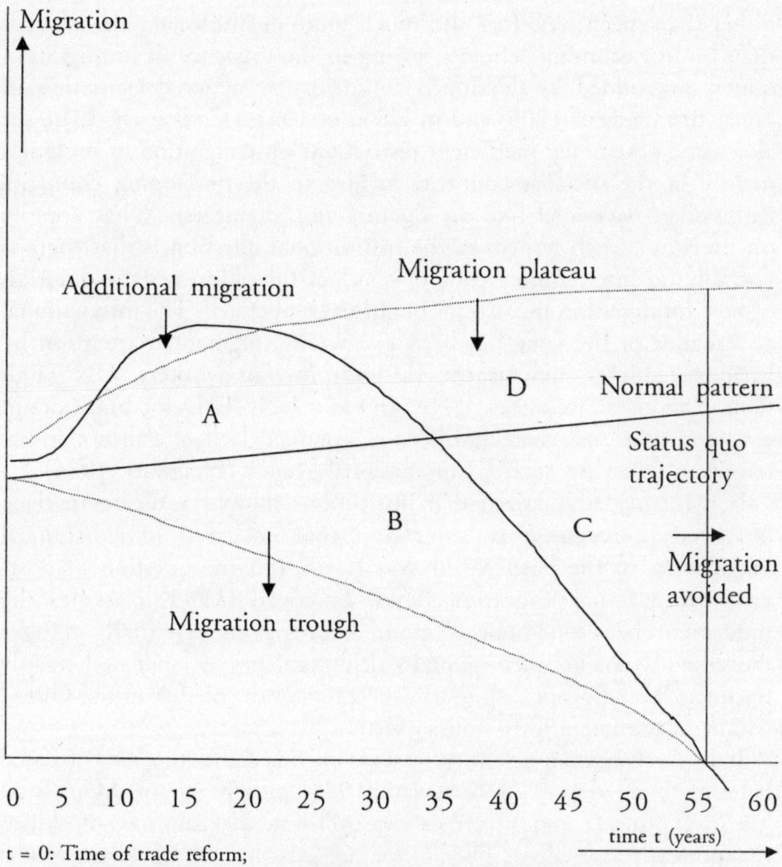


t = 0: Time of trade reform;
A = Migration hump, short-run complementarity between trade and migration;
B = Migration avoided, long-run substitutability between trade and migration;
Area (A + D) = Migration plateau; Area (B + C) = Migration trough.

FIG. 6.1: MIGRATION HUMP, PLATEAU AND TROUGH

Katz and Stark (1989) also show that when migration is desirable at the lowest skill level, introduction of asymmetric information results in a reduction of the quality and quantity of international migration or has no effect at all. Contrarily, when at the lowest skill level migration is not desirable, introduction of asymmetric information will result in migration by all or by none.

By another strand of analysis, however, the phenomenon of international migration is the one that is characterized by disincentives rather than incentives. It is also much more institutionally determined than by free economic choices, owing to the existence of immigration quotas sanctioned by developed countries (by national legislation in Great Britain as of 1905, and in US as of 1921). Conversely, there are also some potentially inefficient restrictions on emigration of nationals mainly in the socialist countries as also in the developing countries (for skilled personnel like the doctors and engineers). What appears on the whole with respect to the institutional question is that there is virtually no international code of conduct that addresses the question of how immigration restrictions ought to be operated. The international governance of the issue has been given only fragmented attention by various agencies such as the ILO for foreign workers, UN High Commission for Refugees, UNESCO and UNCTAD for brain drain, etc., and above all there has been a sustained lack of concern in attempting to set up such a supranational agency (Bhagwati, 1984).

It is further emphasized that institutions showed a 'deliberate' lack of speed in response to migration that occurred in substantial magnitudes in the post World War II era. On the question of post-war international migration flows, Bhagwati (1988) classifies the movement between 'poor to poor' countries as essentially refugee movement, that between 'poor to rich' countries as emanated mainly from the West European 'gastarbeiter' programme or that in the OPEC region in the late 1970s, and so forth.

It is also very important to discuss in this light, the long-debated issue of 'brain drain'. As Bhagwati (1988) puts it, 'brain drain' is an 'emotive phrase', and preserves the overtone that outflow of skilled manpower is a problem. The author suggests that a brain drain model and a spillover model can be identically treated and according to the empirical judgement it appears that substantial outflows often create difficulties for small source countries with limited educational opportunities. He further points out that, for large countries, with wide educational network, emigration of doctors or engineers may not really be a problem, although emigration of 'talented' individuals might stall the domestic institution building process. However, such emigration can pave the path for improving the productivity of distinguished nationals as part of prestigious foreign institutions and enhance opportunities for other nationals to train abroad.

The issue of 'return migration' also requires some attention in this context. Piore (1979) notes that contributions by migrants in terms of the regional economics development or as a source of significant industrial skills have been generally elusive for the source countries. For the developing countries on the path of industrialization, it is expected that the technical requirements of the job structure would follow the technical evolution of the labour force. The process is such that increasing levels of education and training are required of the labour force as development proceeds in order to bridge the gap between the skills of the labour force and the requirement of the technology that the countries are introducing. Return migrants in general have not contributed sufficiently towards overcoming this gap.

To see empirically the issue in question, an explicit link between trade reforms and migration is found in Faini and de Melo (1996), who ran a macro simulation for Morocco, revealing that the removal of import restrictions in Morocco shifted the composition of demand in favour of foreign goods. The total impact on employment in the short-run depends critically on the labour-intensity of exports to import-competing goods and in the Moroccan case labour-intensive exports expanded (because of real exchange rate depreciation) quickly. There was a reduction of total output on account of the now dearer imported inputs and despite all this no distinct effect on employment is visible. The reason for this is that textiles, being the major item of trade, provided local employment as an alternative to short-run migration.

Lee and Roland-Holst (1996) attempt a 10-country computable general equilibrium model (CGE) to estimate the impacts of various trade reform measures on employment in the Pacific basin. Though the model does not link countries on the labour side through migration, trade induced changes in employment and wage disparities across countries suggest the direction, if not the magnitude, of changes in migration pressure resulting from trade reform. The remarkable finding of this study is the surprisingly small impact of trade liberalization on total employment in the region, the reason being the fact that for all these countries imports were more labour-intensive than exports.

Other empirical support for the analysis with respect to the labour market effects of migration and trade comes from Borjas et al. (1992) in the North American context. They base their analysis on the 1980s finding that the wage and employment-population rate of less-skilled Americans, particularly young men, fell relative to the more-skilled workers. The real earnings of 25–34 year old male high school graduates and drop-outs declined, beginning from 1973 and reversing the historic trend. They empirically support the two suggested causes: (*a*) inflow of less-skilled immigrants, including illegal migrants and (*b*) the trade deficit. In a later article, Borjas and Freeman (1997) concluded that 44 per cent of the said decline in wages (1980-95) resulted from immigration. Their study contradicts the findings of Altonji and Card (1991), who computed the correlation between the fractions of immigrants in a city and the employment and wage outcomes of natives for 120 major SMSAs (Standard Metropolitan Statistical Areas) over the 1970 and 1980 censuses. Here, the basic finding is that a 1 per cent increase in the fraction of immigrants in a SMSA reduces less-skilled native wages by roughly 1.2 per cent. The least squares estimates imply wage reductions of 3 per cent. These were not significant.

According to Rivera-Batiz (1998), the US economy has absorbed millions of workers during this century and yet earnings and living standards have generally gone up. The explanation is that increased labour supply tends to generate other mechanisms in the economy that increase the demand for labour and therefore employment. Any influx that significantly reduces wage in a particular labour market also tends to attract industries in that market, given the cheaper labour. Over time then, the downward pressure on wages exerted by labour is reversed as demand rises.

Lastly, Kuhn and Wooton (1991) estimate the effect of immigration on the US workers. Based on 430 4-digit manufacturing industries for the years 1960, 1970, 1980 and 1984, their estimate indicated that at least since 1970, factor intensities in US manufacturing show consistent pattern; unskilled and skilled labour are used intensively in import-competing and export industries respectively. They conclude that increased immigration of either skilled or unskilled workers to the US will, in the long run, hurt US workers of both types and benefit owners of capital.

## HETEROGENEOUS SKILL AND WELFARE IMPACT OF MIGRATION

An easy way to capture the issue of emigration in the context of a developing country is to construct an example where different types of labour are used for producing different types of goods. Skilled labour and capital produce a skilled good ($X$) while unskilled labour and capital produce an unskilled good ($Y$).

Following equations denote competitive conditions before the citizens decide to emigrate. The 'benchmark' model assumes a simple neoclassical world into competitive markets, full employment, and free trade. None of these assumptions is really necessary to derive the basic conclusions.

$$w_S a_{SX} + r a_{KX} = P_X \tag{6.1}$$

$$w a_{LY} + r a_{KY} = P_Y = 1 \tag{6.2}$$

where ($w_S$, $w$) are (skilled, unskilled) wages, $r$ is the return to capital, $P_X$, $P_Y$ are prices, and $a_{ij}$s are input–output ratios dependent on factor prices. The structure here is drawn from Jones (1971) exhibiting a specific-factor model. This is a 'small' economy which faces exogenously given $P_X$ in the rest of the world.

Consider a case where the rest of the world unskilled wage $w^*$ is greater than $w_0$, the initial one prevailing within the economy. This calls for labour outflow. Since $w^*$ cannot be affected by such a movement as the country concerned is small, $w_0$ has to rise up to $w^*$.

As unskilled labour emigrates, local supply of labour falls and $w$ rises. Under the standard 'Inada' type conditions,

$\underset{L \to 0}{Lt} \dfrac{\partial Y}{\partial L} = \infty$, $w$ will rise up to $w^*$ for a finite level of outflow.

If $L_m$ is the extent of labour outflow, then $(w^* - w_0)\, L_m$ will be the addition to 'real income' of this nation and hence the gain in welfare. $L_m$ is basically export of labour and $(w^* - w_0)$ is the additional income per unit of such exports.

A crucial presumption in such analysis is that the economy under consideration has command over this extra income. Suppose a fraction of $(w^* - w_0)\, L_m$ is remitted, that will mean greater real income. Typically, the consumption standards of migrants may improve once they locate themselves abroad. This will tend to reduce the amount of remittance.

Such emigration will reduce $r$ since the local unskilled worker becomes more expensive to hire. As $r$ goes down, $w_S$ moves up, given $P_X$. In fact, if the technology in the rest of the world is the same as in the local economy, $w_S$ should go up to $w_S^*$ and $r$ should fall to $r^*$. Thus the movement of just one type of labour leads to factor price equalization. Skilled labour does not need to move further since cheaper rental on capital leads to greater skilled wages for the local economy.

An interesting implication of such an outflow can be traced to the relative income between the skilled and the unskilled. It can be easily checked from equations (6.1) and (6.2) that $\dfrac{w_{s0}}{w_0}$ adjusts towards

$\frac{w_s^*}{w^*}$ where $\frac{w_s^*}{w^*} > \frac{w_{s0}}{w_0}$. In other words the distribution of income between the skilled and the unskilled can very well worsen by exporting unskilled labour. Since $\frac{W_s^*}{W^*}$ is given in the rest of the world and the technology is identical across the globe, the condition $\frac{w_s^*}{w^*} > \frac{w_{s0}}{w_0}$ boils down to the comparison of the share of capital in production costs of each sector, $\theta_{KX}$ relative to $\theta_{KY}$. If $\theta_{KX} > \theta_{KY}$, $w_S$ will rise more, thus widening the gap between $w_S$ and $w$.[2]

Movement of unskilled labour eliminates the incentive for skilled labour to move. If the technological differences across the globe are not so prominent, relative factor abundance becomes crucial in dictating the wage differential and the consequent movement of labour. If the technological gap is considerable, reflecting the productivity gap of similar type of labour, factor prices will not be equalized between the source country and the rest of the world. But there will be a tendency for the wages to come together. A lot more labour has to flow out in that case to bring the wages into line. But once $w_S$ are the same, '$r$' in the source country should still be lower than $r^*$ due to the 'productivity' gap. If the skill sector of the source country exhibits similar productivity with the rest of the world, $w_S$ will go up even more relative to the case with no productivity-gap. In fact, $w_S$ is likely to be greater than $w_S^*$, worsening the pattern of wage distribution. However, increase in $w$ always improves aggregate real income of the small trading nation and therefore should be encouraged. But emigration of unskilled labour may not lead to the evaporation of class-based conflict in the society.

The appealing property of this class of general equilibrium model is that they allow for imperfect factor flows within an economy, unlike the standard 'long-run' type models. This also in a way captures the case of developing nations where smooth sectoral adjustments are difficult to conceive. Our small economy exploits further gains from trade allowing emigration. Note that once $w_0$ is allowed to adjust up to $w^*$ through a continuous process of labour outflow, skilled production continues to expand and the local unskilled sector contracts. If this country has been exporting $Y$, factor movement substitutes for commodity trade—a well-known result due to Mundell (1957).

One interesting and much discussed result in trade theory has to do with the effect of changes in factor endowments in tariff-distorted economies. Papers by Johnson (1967), Brecher and Diaz-Alejandro (1977), Findlay (1985), Jones (1997), Neary and Ruane (1988), Beladi and Marjit (1992), Marjit et al. (1997), etc., discuss different facets of the problem of growth and welfare in 'protected' economies.

As unskilled labour emigrates and as a result the skilled sector expands, the small economy may face an adverse welfare effect if the sector producing the 'skilled' good is protected to start with. Taxing imports causes distortion in consumption and a further reduction in the volume of imports will accentuate the welfare loss. This has to be offset against the remittance income received from the non-residents. It is obvious that allowing skilled labour to go is doubly beneficial in the presence of protection, although protection may curtail the incentive for emigration. However, the standard welfare reducing effect of growth in the protected sector may not hold with imported intermediates. This has been recently expressed in Marjit and Beladi (1996, 1999). Since the standard textbook principle for a small economy is not to restrict trade of any kind, the 'adverse' welfare effect of restricting commodity trade can be mitigated by opening up of trade in factors.

The results discussed so far change with unemployment. Consider a little twist to our existing framework. Suppose the unskilled wage is fixed at $\overline{w}$ to reflect union-pressure in the presence of unemployment. So given $\overline{w}$, $r$ is determined from equation (6.2), and that in turn determines $w_S$. The amount of skilled labour determines output in the skilled sector and the capital to be employed there. The rest of the capital employs unskilled labour and in the presence of $\overline{w}$ cannot absorb the entire unskilled labour force. It is obvious that if the unemployed unskilled labour starts moving out, nothing happens to the factor returns and the gains are enormous because for some of them the opportunity cost may be close to zero.

It is instructive to provide the list of the possible welfare impact of outward migration.

1. Migration directly increases national welfare by expanding the set of consumption possibilities available to the locals through increased remittances.
2. With unemployment it is likely that the gain will be more since the opportunity cost of emigration should be very low.
3. Typically movement of one type of labour should improve wages of other types by inducing a fall in the cost of capital.

4. Apart from the static welfare effect, remittances may constitute an important contribution towards capital information.

It is also instructive to look at the representative empirical evidences on some of the issues discussed so far. In a fairly detailed discussion on migration, remittances, and capital flows in the context of the Indian economy, Nayyar (1994) reports certain interesting facts, as elaborated in table 16 therein.

In 1980s remittances were equivalent to about 2 per cent of aggregate private consumption expenditure, 67 per cent of the gross domestic savings and capital formation. However, the division of remittances into consumption and investment are not available from the macro-economic data. Gulati and Mody (1985) provide an analysis which suggests that for the state of Kerala, remittances were about 25 per cent of the state domestic product. This proportion was estimated to be as high as 40-50 per cent in some districts of the state that experienced higher volumes of out-migration.

## MIGRATION AND CAPITAL FORMATION

Static welfare effects do not provide a complete picture of the welfare implications of emigration. To the extent that capital formation assumes a crucial role in the process of growth and development, one must elaborate the avenues through which remittances stimulate the pace of investment. Remittances are likely to increase both consumption and savings of the local population. Empirically it is very difficult to isolate the impact of remittances on saving and investment at an aggregate level. As elaborated in Nayyar (1994), at least in the context of the Indian economy, this has been a compelling task. Close scrutiny of the regions that supply substantial number of migrants to the outside world over a specific time period can be a better strategy to evaluate the investment impact of remittances. It will be interesting to reflect on the structural features of the relationship between migration and capital formation. This can be done by focusing on both the supply side and demand side of the problem. We consider the supply side first.

As argued earlier the inflow of amount $(w^* - w_0)\ L_m$ adds to the real national income of the trading nation. A part of $(w^* - w_0)L_m$ can go to augment the capital stock. In that case growth takes place through an increase in investment. But $(w^* - w_0)L_m$ can be quite small relative to the size of the capital stock and nothing should change much. Also the fraction of $(w^* - w_0)L_m$ set apart for raising $K$ can be very low depending on the time preference of the people deciding on the intertemporal consumption pattern of remittances. One interesting exercise will be to check whether priorities to invest vary across income groups. It is possible that a dollar which lands in the hands of poor people representing the local community of unskilled migrants will be utilized differently from the one which goes to the richer income group. The presumption related to the break up of the remittance into consumption and savings for each of the group can go either way and, therefore, the net impact on investment is anybody's guess.

Following the recent work of Galor and Zeira (1993) or Banerjee and Newman (1998), one can forcefully argue that remittances to the poor segment of the population can achieve a lot in terms of human capital formation. It is now well known that 'inequality' of income can hamper 'growth' in a world with imperfect capital markets. Remittances can be an effective means of bypassing the 'entry-barrier' caused by financial constraints. In a model with multiple equilibria, unskilled migration can get the economy out of a 'low level equilibrium'.

Typically, the extra income received from the migrant workers settled or temporarily working abroad can contribute towards local capital formation if and only if the investment is constrained from the supply side. It is quite possible that there might not be sufficient demand for investable funds since investment depends on a set of medium and long term factors. Thus the prevailing macroeconomic investment should dictate whether investment is resource constrained. But clearly, remittances can improve local infrastructural conditions, which in turn may lead to more investments. Again a way of evaluating such an impact is to look for case studies since the aggregate data may not be suited for such an exercise. Whether remittances have helped the growth of small business in places like Kerala is still an open question. Even if one admits that the process of human development in Kerala must have been influenced by the remittances from the Middle East, yet Kerala has not shown remarkable progress in terms of industrial investment and employment. These issues require substantial applied work at the micro level.[3]

One important contribution of net factor income from abroad is to allow the government to make adjustments to periodic balance of payment problems. The oil boom in the mid-1970s led to a massive temporary emigration of workers, skilled and unskilled, to the Middle

East. Export of labour was a major source of foreign exchange earnings for India, and it helped to curb the negative impact of trade deficits. Nayyar (1994) observes that the per capita remittance from the unskilled workers has been greater than the same received from the skilled workers.

It is well known that in the developing world, the state heavily subsidizes higher education and therefore promotes the growth of human capital. This is justified by the 'social return' on human capital which private financiers are not likely to internalize. The large exodus of skilled engineers, managers, scientists, and technical personnel away from the developing world does not allow the local economy to recover the social costs of training. In a way, the developing world indirectly subsidizes the higher education system in the richer nations with high quality undergraduate training. It is needless to say that a large chunk of such emigration eventually leads to permanent settlements. Apart from the fact that such 'brains' do not produce the required externality effects on the local economy, valuable tax payers' money is hardly recovered. The pricing of higher education is a politically sensitive issue. Often sound economic judgement has to take a back seat because of the shameless hypocrisy of the so-called egalitarian student movement. Higher education invariably accommodates students coming from more privileged segments of the society and they always protest vehemently if the subsidy is reduced even by a bit. It will be interesting to study the impact of subsidized education on the 'net resource inflow' to the local economy and the role of emigration in dictating the magnitude of such an impact.

## NOTES

1. Barlow Report, Royal Commission on 'Distribution of the Industrial Population', Cmd. 6153, HMSO (London 1940).
2. For effects of immigration on wages in one-commodity simple model and n-commodity generalization thereof, see Jones and Engerman (1997).
3. For related work on remittances of Asian workers from Gulf countries, see Gardezi (1997).

## REFERENCES

Altonji, J.G. and David Card (1991), 'The Effects of Immigration on the Labour Market Outcomes of Less-Skilled Natives', in J.M. Abowd and R.B. Freeman (eds.), *Immigration, Trade and the Labor Market*, University of Chicago Press, Chicago, London, pp. 201-34.

Banerjee, Abhijit, V. and Andrew F. Newman (1998), 'Information, the Dual Economy and Development', *Review of Economic Studies*, vol. 65, no. 4, October, pp. 631-53.

Beladi, Hamid and Sugata Marjit (1992), 'Foreign Capital and Protectionism', *Canadian Journal of Economics*, vol. 25, no. 1, pp. 233-8.

Bhagwati, J.N. (1984), 'Incentives and Disincentives: International Migration', *Weltwirtschaftliches Archiv,* vol. 120, no. 4, pp. 678-700.

——— (1988), 'Global Interdependence and International Migration', in J. Cassing and S. Husted (eds.), *Capital, Technology and Labour in the New Global Economy*, Washington, AEI, pp. 149-83.

——— (1997), *Writings on International Economics*, ed. V. Balasubramanyam, Oxford University Press, Oxford.

Bhagwati, J.N. and T.N. Srinivasan (1983), 'On the Choice Between Capital and Labour Mobility', *Journal of International Economics,* vol. 14, nos. 3-4, pp. 209-21.

Bohning, W.R. (1984), 'International Migration: Implications for Development Policies in Population Distribution, Migration and Development', Department of International Economic and Social Affairs, United Nations.

Borjas, G.J. and R.B. Freeman (1997), 'Findings We Never Found', *The New York Times,* 10 December.

Borjas, G.J., R.B. Freeman and L.F. Katz (1992), 'On the Labor Market Effects of Immigration and Trade', in J.M. Abowd and R.B. Freeman (eds.) *Immigration, Trade and the Labor Market*, University of Chicago Press, Chicago, London, pp. 213-44.

Brecher, Richard and C. Diaz-Alejandro (1977), 'Tariffs, Foreign Capital and Immiserizing Growth', *Journal of International Economics*, vol. 7, no. 4, pp. 317-22.

Caves, R and R.W. Jones (1985), *World Trade and Payments: An Introduction*, Little Brown and Company, Boston.

Faini, R. and J. de Melo (1996), 'Trade Liberalization, Employment and Migration: Some Simulations for Morocco', Discussion paper 1198, Centre for Economic Policy Research, London.

Findlay, Ronald (1985), 'Growth and Development in Trade Models', in R.W. Jones and P.B. Kennen (eds.), *Handbook of International Economics*, vol. 1, pp. 185-236, North Holland, Amsterdam.

Galor, Oded and Joseph Zeira (1993), 'Income Distribution and Macro-economics', *Review of Economic Studies*, vol. 60, no. 1, pp. 35-52.

Gardezi, Hassan N. (1997), 'Asian Workers in the Gulf States of the Middle East', in B.S. Bolaria and R.V.E. Bolaria (eds.), *International Labour Migrations,* Oxford University Press, Oxford, pp. 99-120.

Gerking, Shelby D. and John H. Mutti (1983), 'Factor Rewards and the International Migration of Unskilled Labor: A Model with Capital Mobility', *Journal of International Economics*, vol. 14, nos. 3-4, pp. 367-80.

Gulati, Iqbal and Ashoka Mody (1985), 'Remittances of Indian Migrants to the Middle East: An Assessment with Special Reference to Migrants from Kerala State', ESCAP, DP/RILM/4, July, Bangkok.

Johnson, Harry G. (1967), 'The Possibility of Income Losses from Increased Efficiency or Factor Accumulation in the Presence of Tariffs', *The Economic Journal,* vol. 77, no. 306, pp. 151-4.

Jones, Ronald W. (1965), 'The Structure of Simple General Equilibrium Models', *Journal of Political Economy*, vol. 73, no. 6, December, pp. 557-72.

——— (1971), 'A Three-Factor Model in Theory, Trade and History', in J.N. Bhagwati, et al. (eds.), *Trade, Balance of Payment and Growth*, North Holland, Amsterdam, pp. 39-57.

——— (1997), 'Trade, Technology and Income Distribution', *Indian Economic Review,* vol. 32, no. 2, pp. 129-40.

Jones, R.W. and Stanley L. Engerman (1997), 'International Labor Flows and National Wages', *American Economic Review,* vol. 87, no. 2, May, pp. 200-4.

Katz, Eliakim and Oded Stark (1986), 'On Fertility, Migration and Remittances in LDCs', *World* Development, vol. 14, no. 1, pp. 133-5.

——— (1987), 'International Migration under Asymmetric Information', *The Economic Journal,* vol. 97, no. 387, September, pp. 718-26.

——— (1989), 'International Labour Migration under Alternative Informational Regimes: A Diagrammatic Analysis', *European Economic Review*, vol. 33, no. 1, pp. 127-42.

Kuhn, Peter and I. Wooton (1991), 'Immigration, International Trade and Wages of National Workers', in J.M. Abowd and R.B. Freeman (eds.), *Immigration, Trade and the Labor Market*, University of Chicago Press, Chicago, London, pp. 285-304.

Lee, H. and David Roland-Holst (1996), 'CGE Modelling of Trade and Employment in Pacific Rim Countries', in J.E. Taylor (ed.), *Development Strategy, Employment and Migration*, OECD Development Centre, Paris, pp. 107-48.

Lind, Harold (1969), 'International Migration in Britain'. in J.A. Jackson (ed.), *Migration: Sociological Studies* 2, Cambridge University Press.

Marjit, Sugata, U. Broll and S. Mitra (1997), 'Targeting Sectors for Foreign Capital Inflow in Small Open Economy', *Review of International Economics,* vol. 5, no. 1, February, pp. 101-6.

Marjit, Sugata and H. Beladi (1996), 'An Analysis of Rural-Urban Migration and Protection', *Canadian Journal of Economics*, vol. 29, no. 4, November, pp. 930-40.

——— (1999), 'Complementarity between Import Competition and Import Promotion', *Journal of Economic Theory*, vol. 86, no. 2, pp. 280-5.

Martin, L. Philip and J.E. Taylor (1996), 'The Anatomy of a Migration Hump', in J.E. Taylor (ed.), *Development Strategy, Employment and Migration*, OECD Development Centre, Paris, pp. 43-62.

Mundell, Robert A (1957), 'International Trade and Factor Mobility', *The American Economic Review*, vol. 67, no. 3, June, pp. 321-5.

Nayyar, Deepak (1994), *Migration, Remittances and Capital Flows: The Indian Experience,* Oxford University Press, New Delhi, Oxford, New York.

Neary, Peter and F.P. Ruane (1988), 'International Capital Mobility, Shadow Prices and the Cost of Protection', *International Economic Review*, vol. 29, no. 4, pp. 571-85.

O'Connor, David and L. Farsakh (1996), 'Development and Migration—An Overview', in O'Connor and Farsakh (eds.) *Development Strategy, Employment and Migration—Country Experiences*, OECD Development Centre, Paris, pp. 9-34.

Piore, Michael J. (1979), *Birds of Passage: Migrant Labour and Industrial Societies*, Cambridge University Press, London.

Rivera-Batiz, Francisco L. (1998), 'Migration and the Labor Market: Sectoral and Regional Effects in the United States', in *Migration, Free Trade and Regional Integration in North America*, OECD Proceedings, OECD, Paris.

Sapir, Andre (1983), 'Foreign Competition, Immigration and Structural Adjustment', *Journal of International Economics*, vol. 14, nos. 3-4, pp. 381-94.

Schiff, Maurice (1996), 'Trade Policy and International Migration: Substitutes or Complements?', in J.E.Taylor (ed.), *Development Strategy, Employment and Migration*, OECD Development Centre, Paris, pp. 23-42.

Stark, Oded (1991), *The Migration of Labour*, Basil Blackwell, Oxford.

Stark, Oded and J.E. Taylor (1991), 'Migration Incentives, Migration Types: The Role of Relative Deprivation', *The Economic Journal*, vol. 101, no. 408, September, pp. 1163-78.

Taylor, J. Edward (1996), 'International Migration and Economic Development: A Micro Economy–Wide Analysis', in J.E. Taylor (ed.), *Development Strategy, Employment and Migration*, OECD Development Centre, Paris, pp. 11-28.

Wong, Kar-Yiu (1983), 'On Choosing Among Trade in Goods and International Capital and Labor Mobility—A Theoretical Analysis', *Journal of International Economics*, vol. 14, nos. 3-4, pp. 223-50.

APPENDIX 6.1

The basic welfare function algebra involves the 'change in welfare' function (Caves and Jones, 1985):

$$d\Omega = P_X dD_X + dD_Y$$

$$= dw_0(\overline{L} - L_e) - w_0 dL_e + w^* dL_e + dr\overline{K} + dw_s\overline{S} \ ,$$

where $w_0$ is the initial pre-emigration unskilled wage and $D_X$, $D_Y$ are demands. Note that

$$dw_0(\overline{L} - L_e) + dr\overline{K} + dw_s\overline{S} = P_X dD_X + d_Y$$

since $L_e$ stands for export of labour. One needs to add $(w^* - w_0)dL_e$ as the change in income due to emigration. If we use the competitive equilibrium and full employment conditions, we get $d\Omega = (w^* - w_0)dL_e$, as $P_X dD_X + d_Y$ vanishes due to the familiar 'envelope' conditions. Since $w > w_0$ it pays to send unskilled people abroad.

7

# Export Diversification, Market Shares, and Issues of North–South Terms of Trade

*Prabirjit Sarkar*

## INTRODUCTION

During the period of the Industrial Revolution in the North, the colonization of the South led to to the colonial pattern of North–South trade—raw materials and food moved from the colonies and semicolonies in the South to the industrial centre in the North. In many parts of the South, artisan activities declined due to competition from the machine-made goods of the North. This was also a part of the design of the colonial rulers. Some economic historians have described this phenomenon as de-industrialization (Bagchi 1976; see also Sarkar 1992). Artisan activities declined also in the North. But decline in these activities in the North was more than counter-balanced by increased industrial activities. Hence the North experienced industrialization while the South faced de-industrialization.

Mainstream economists hail this phenomenon as international division of labour according to comparative advantages. It was expected that the fruits of technical progress taking place in the industrial centre of the North would be transmitted to the peripheral agrarian countries (constituting the South) in the form of favourable terms of trade. The expectation of a favourable terms of trade of the South is based on the so-called classical law of improvements in the terms of trade of primary products *vis-à-vis* manufactures under the conditions of diminishing returns in agriculture and increasing returns in manufactures.

In the early post-Second World War period, Prebisch (1950) and Singer (1950) launched an opposite hypothesis—the hypothesis of secular decline in the (commodity) terms of trade of primary products and primary producing South *vis-à-vis* manufactures and the industrial North (respectively). Their hypothesis implies a secular decline in the factoral terms of trade of the South because of their presumption that technical progress had been taking place at a higher rate in the industrial North than in the agrarian South.

On the basis of the hypothesis of secular decline in the (commodity and factoral) terms of trade of the South, it was argued that the classical mechanism of transmitting the fruits of technical progress from the industrial North to the agrarian South did not operate. So the Southern countries were advised to suspend free play of international market forces through import restrictions and tariffs and to follow a path of import-substituting industrialization (Prebisch 1959, 1964).

Under the influence of UN Economic Commission for Latin America (ECLA) led by Raul Prebisch, many Latin American countries followed the path of import substituting industrial development. Many other countries such as India also followed this path guided by economic nationalism (independent of the policy implication of the Prebisch-Singer hypothesis).

However, import-substituting industrialization in basically agricultural countries required imports of machines and technology. So in the process of industrialization these countries started to face acute balance of payments problem. For financing the balance of payments deficit, these countries became dependent on the countries of the North and the international financial institutions such as the Interntional Monetary Fund (IMF) and the World Bank dominated by the rich countries of the North.

This scenario generated the dependency school of thought in Latin America which highlights the problem of development in the South under various forms of dependence on the North. The writings of Paul Baran, Gunder Frank, and many others on uneven development and neocolonization highlight more or less the same problem of development of the Southern countries.

The failure of the import-substituting strategy led many Southern countries to follow the path of export-oriented industrialization. Dependence on a few primary product exports was reduced and primary product exports increasingly began to be substituted by manufactured goods. The question that then arises: does this diversification of the export structure of the Southern countries change the declining course of the terms of trade of the South *vis-à-vis* the North? The present study is concerned with this question. It shows that the manufacture exports to pay for manufacture imports did not help the countries of the South to suspend the operation of the Prebisch-Singer law of terms-of-trade deterioration (thereby supporting the conclusion of Sarkar and Singer, 1991).

## IMPORTANCE OF MANUFACTURED GOODS IN EXPORTS FROM THE SOUTH TO THE NORTH, 1950-96

Available data (see Sarkar 1986a, Table 3) show the rising importance of manufactured goods in total exports of the South ('Developing Market Economy Region') to the North ('Developed Market Economy Region')[1] over the period, 1950-79. During 1950-4, the annual average value of total exports of the South to the North was $15.2 billion, and exports of manufactured goods (SITC sections 5 to 8) constituted 10.5 per cent of this total. In the process of steady growth the annual average value of this flow of goods reached $30.3 billion during 1965-9 and the share of manufacture exports rose to 19 per cent. During the period of the unprecedented oil price hike in the 1970s, the value of exports from the South to the North showed a manifold increase while the share of manufactures stagnated. During 1975-9, the average share of manufactured exports was 18.2 per cent of the total $203.7 billion.

Excluding the exports of 'fuels' (SITC section 3 that includes mineral oil), it was observed that the annual average value of total exports of the South to the North rose rapidly, particularly in the 1970s, along with the share of manufactures. The average value of this trade flow was $12.8 billion during 1950-4 and $20.1 during 1965-9; it rose to $38.1 billion during 1970-4 and jumped to a new high, $82.9 billion, during 1975-9. At the same time, the average share of manufacture exports also showed a rapid growth: from a figure of 12.5 per cent during 1950-4 it reached 28.7 per cent during 1965-9 and jumped to 38.6 per cent during 1970-4 and further to 45.9 per cent during 1975-9.

The last two decades experienced a further rise in the share of manufactures in the total exports of the South. Between the two periods 1983-6 and 1993-6, the average share of manufactures in the total exports of the South rose from 36 per cent to 67 per cent. The corresponding figures in the case of fuel-excluded total exports of the South were 62 per cent and 81 per cent as (calculated from the data available in United Nations 1986, p. 704; 1997, pp. S104-5).

## DIVERSIFICATION OF EXPORT STRUCTURES OF THE SOUTH, 1980-94: SELECTED COUNTRIES

The increasing importance of manufactured exports from the South to the North is associated with export diversification: the Southern countries relied less and less on a small number of export goods for their foreign exchange earnings. This is shown in our study below.

To measure diversification or commodity concentration of exports, a number of indices are available for a number of countries for the two selected years, 1980 and 1994 (see UNCTAD, 1997). One is simply the number of products exported at the 3 digit SITC (Rev. 2) level (call it $Nx$). The figures include only those products, the exports of which are greater than \$50,000 in 1980 or \$1,00,000 in 1994 or more than 0.3 per cent of the country's total exports. The idea is: the higher the number of products exported by a country, the more diversified is its export structure.

The second index is called the Diversification Index, D, which measures the absolute deviation of the country's export structure from the world structure. It assumes the value 0 for the minimum concentration and 1 for the most extreme concentration. The formula for the $j$th country, $D_j$, is the following:

$$D_j = \Sigma\ (|\ h_{ij} - h_i\ |)/2 \qquad (7.1)$$

where $h_{ij}$ = share of commodity $i$ in total exports of country $j$, $h_i$ = share of commodity $i$ in total world exports, and $|\ h_{ij} - h_i\ |$ is the absolute deviation between the two.

The third index is the Hirschman Concentration Index, $C$, normalized to take values ranging from 0 (minimum concentration) to 1 (maximum concentration). The formula for the $j$th country, $C_j$ is the following:

$$C_j = [\{\Sigma\ (X_i/X)^2\}^{1/2} - \{1/N\}^{1/2}]/[1 - \{1/N\}^{1/2}] \qquad (7.2)$$

where $X_i$ = the value of exports of the $i$th commodity, $X = \Sigma X_i$ (Total Exports), and $N$ = the number of products exported at the 3 digit SITC (Rev. 2) level = 239.

In Table 7.1, the three measures of export diversification are reported for 24 countries of the South (excluding major oil exporters) for the two years 1980 and 1994. These show that Thailand experienced dramatic changes between the two dates. Its diversification index fell from 0.77 to 0.49 (implying an increased diversification of its export structure); the concentration index fell from 0.2 to 0.09 (implying less commodity concentration of exports); and the number of products exported rose from 176 to 214 (supporting the conclusion of the two other measures) between the two dates. For some countries such as

TABLE 7.1: COMMODITY CONCENTRATION OF EXPORTS OF SELECTED SOUTHERN COUNTRIES IN 1980 AND 1994

| Country | Diversification Index, D | | Concentration Index, C | | No. of Goods Exported, Nx | |
|---|---|---|---|---|---|---|
| | 1980 | 1994 | 1980 | 1994 | 1980 | 1994 |
| Argentina | 0.71 | 0.58 | 0.15 | 0.14 | 198 | 217 |
| Burkina Faso | 0.89 | 0.93 | 0.48 | 0.60 | 43 | 28 |
| Brazil | 0.56 | 0.51 | 0.15 | 0.09 | 225 | 217 |
| Bolivia | 0.88 | 0.84 | 0.39 | 0.22 | 47 | 102 |
| Chile | 0.82 | 0.76 | 0.41 | 0.28 | 181 | 204 |
| Colombia | 0.78 | 0.64 | 0.58 | 0.24 | 162 | 201 |
| Costa Rica | 0.76 | 0.71 | 0.32 | 0.29 | 144 | 138 |
| Dominican Republic | 0.85 | 0.75 | 0.32 | 0.17 | 94 | 108 |
| Honduras | 0.85 | 0.84 | 0.37 | 0.38 | 99 | 91 |
| India | 0.69 | 0.60 | 0.11 | 0.14 | 211 | 219 |
| Kenya | 0.81 | 0.83 | 0.38 | 0.31 | 143 | 148 |
| Korea | 0.66 | 0.44 | 0.09 | 0.12 | 207 | 217 |
| Malaysia | 0.64 | 0.52 | 0.30 | 0.16 | 214 | 225 |
| Mauritius | 0.91 | 0.86 | 0.69 | 0.32 | 55 | 111 |
| Morocco | 0.81 | 0.76 | 0.31 | 0.17 | 113 | 166 |
| Pakistan | 0.78 | 0.85 | 0.24 | 0.24 | 157 | 132 |
| Panama | 0.73 | 0.81 | 0.26 | 0.40 | 136 | 73 |
| Papua New Guinea | 0.91 | 0.90 | 0.48 | 0.41 | 60 | 71 |
| Paraguay | 0.88 | 0.88 | 0.28 | 0.32 | 63 | 78 |
| Peru | 0.61 | 0.83 | 0.26 | 0.25 | 176 | 165 |
| Philippines | 0.78 | 0.65 | 0.22 | 0.32 | 175 | 189 |
| Sri Lanka | 0.86 | 0.77 | 0.39 | 0.22 | 97 | 152 |
| Thailand | 0.77 | 0.49 | 0.20 | 0.09 | 176 | 214 |
| Tunisia | 0.66 | 0.67 | 0.48 | 0.22 | 142 | 184 |

SOURCE: UNCTAD (1997), *Handbook of International Trade and Development Statistics, 1995.*

Burkina Faso and Panama, all the indices indicate increasing commodity concentration of exports.

For many countries, the different measures do not tally. For Korea, for example, the diversification index fell significantly from 0.66 to 0.44 along with a rise in the number of commodities exported from 207 to 217; but the concentration index rose slightly from a very low position of 0.09 to 0.12. Many other such instances can be brought out from Table 7.1.

In terms of the diversification index, 18 countries can be said to have experienced increased diversification in their export structures (implying movements closer to the world export structure). In terms of the concentration index, 16 countries can be said to have experienced reductions in the commodity concentration of their exports. Altogether 17 countries experienced increases in the number of products exported. Hence, in spite of the confusion created by different measures, it can be said that most of the countries covered in the study experienced more diversified export structures between the two dates.

## TRENDS IN THE TERMS OF TRADE OF THE SOUTH *VIS-À-VIS* THE NORTH SINCE 1950

The important question that crops up is: what has been the terms-of-trade experience of the South during the post-Second World War period? Are these declining in spite of its diversified and manufacture-dominated exports? These are the questions addressed here.

From UN sources (UNCTAD 1972; United Nations 1981, 1982) two series on the terms of trade between the South and the North are available over the period 1950-80. One series includes and the other series excludes fuels (SITC section 3) from the exports of the South: here the series are called South/North and South (-3)/North (respectively). These series were used in an earlier study to support the Prebisch-Singer hypothesis (Sarkar 1986b). An attempt is made here to update that study.

In the construction of the series mentioned above, the terms of trade (commodity terms of trade, CTT) are defined as unit values of exports of the South to the North as percentages of the unit values of exports of the North to the South. The series are not available for the period beyond 1980. So for the period, 1981-95, the unit values of exports of the South (including or excluding Major Petroleum Exporters) and the unit values of exports of the North (all the series are available in UNCTAD 1997) are used as proxies respectively of the numerator and denominator of the two series.

Fitting a log-linear trend equation on these series over different periods, it is observed that the rise and fall of OPEC in the 1970s and the 1980s, respectively, obscured the picture of a deteriorating trend in the terms of trade of the South *vis-à-vis* the North. The South/North series, showed no trend of statistical significance during 1950-80 and 1950-95 (Table 7.2, rows 1 and 3).

Adding intercept and slope dummies for the period of oil price hike, 1973-80, and fitting a multiple regression over the period 1950-80 showed that the terms of trade of the South deteriorated during 1950-72 and changed its course later due to the impact of the monopoly power of the OPEC and the consequent increase in oil prices. The situation changed in the 1980s as the OPEC lost much of its monopoly power and oil prices started falling. Use of an additional intercept and slope dummies for the period 1981-95 showed that the deteriorating trend of the period 1950-72 accentuated during 1981-95 (Table 7.2 rows 2 and 4). This is confirmed by fitting the simple regression (the log-linear trend) over the period 1981-95 (Table 7.2, row 5).

The South (-3)/North series exhibited trends of deterioration over the whole period, 1950-95, and also over the sub-period 1950-80: the rate of deterioration is more or less 1 per cent per annum. There is no evidence of acceleration or deceleration during 1973-80, the period of oil price hike under the influence of OPEC (none of the coefficients of intercept and slope dummies for 1973-80 are found to be statistically significant). There is, however, some evidence of accentuation of the deteriorating trend during 1981-95: the coefficient of slope dummy for 1981-95 is negative and statistically significant (Table 7.2, rows 6-10). Therefore the annual rate of terms-of-trade deterioration during 1981-95 is found to be 2 per cent (Table 7.2, row 11).

Terms-of-trade experience of individual Southern countries (24 countries mentioned in Table 7.1) since 1970 have also been examined. Due to lack of data on the terms of trade of individual Southern countries *vis-à-vis* the North, the following proxy is used: the export unit value of each Southern country is taken as percentage of the export unit value of the North. This procedure has the added advantage over the use of the terms-of-trade data of individual Southern countries (defined as the export unit values of these countries as percentages of

TABLE 7.2: TRENDS IN THE TERMS OF TRADE OF THE SOUTH *VIS-À-VIS* THE NORTH, 1950-95

| | Regression Coefficients[1, 2] | | | | | | Adj. $R^2$ | DW | F |
|---|---|---|---|---|---|---|---|---|---|
| | a | b | c | d | e | f | | | |
| I. Terms of Trade of the South *vis-à-vis* the North, South/North | | | | | | | | | |
| | | | | **1950-80** | | | | | |
| 1. | 3.83 | 0.02 | | | | | 0.70 | 1.87 | 36.19 |
| | (20.04) | (1.68) | | | | | | | |
| 2. | 4.03 | -0.01 | -123.21 | 0.06 | | | 0.84 | 2.13 | 55.16 |
| | (108.37) | (-3.75) | (-4.59) | (4.61) | | | | | |
| | | | | **1950-95** | | | | | |
| 3. | 3.95 | 0.007 | | | | | 0.81 | 1.88 | 94.24 |
| | (22.22) | (1.14) | | | | | | | |
| 4. | 4.03 | -0.01 | -123.22 | 0.06 | 1.97 | -0.03 | 0.84 | 1.52 | 56.70 |
| | (95.12) | (-3.29) | (-4.03) | (4.04) | (8.42) | (-4.94) | | | |
| | | | | **1981-95** | | | | | |
| 5. | 5.98 | -0.04 | | | | | 0.79 | 1.78 | 26.97 |
| | (13.93) | (-3.84) | | | | | | | |
| II. Terms of Trade of the South (less fuels) *vis-à-vis* the North, South (-3)/North | | | | | | | | | |
| | | | | **1950-80** | | | | | |
| 6. | 4.77 | -0.007 | | | | | 0.56 | 1.94 | 20.36 |
| | (121.31) | (-3.39) | | | | | | | |
| 7. | 4.81 | -0.01 | - 22.13 | 0.02 | | | 0.60 | 1.98 | 12.25 |
| | (133.72) | (-4.55) | (-0.94) | (0.95) | | | | | |
| | | | | **1950-95** | | | | | |
| 8. | 4.81 | -0.01 | | | | | 0.86 | 1.99 | 137.55 |
| | (107.56) | (-6.47) | | | | | | | |
| 9. | 4.77 | -0.01 | | | -0.48 | -0.02 | 0.87 | 1.87 | 73.32 |
| | (122.58) | (-3.48) | | | (-2.17) | (-2.37) | | | |
| 10. | 4.81 | -0.01 | -20.08 | 0.01 | 0.51 | -0.01 | 0.87 | 1.90 | 52.52 |
| | (127.42) | (-4.37) | (-0.86) | (0.87) | (2.59) | (-2.10) | | | |
| | | | | **1981-95** | | | | | |
| 11. | 5.37 | -0.02 | | | | | 0.88 | 1.61 | 36.96 |
| | (32.88) | (-6.01) | | | | | | | |

NOTES:

1. Figures in parentheses are t-ratios.
2. A log-linear trend equation is fitted: $\log y = a + b.t$

where $y$ = terms of trade, $a$ = intercept, $b$ = time coefficient and $t$ = time.
In order to examine shifts in the parameters ($a$ and $b$) during 1973-80 and/or during 1981-95, intercept and slope dummies are added. The coefficients of the intercept and slope dummies are $c$ and $d$ for the period 1973-80, and $e$ and $f$ for the period 1981-95 (respectively).

An appropriate error process is chosen in each case through the Lagrange Multiplier (LM) and the log-likelihood ratio tests. An AR (1) error process is found to be appropriate in each case excepting cases 2 and 11. In case 2, the Ordinary Least Square (OLS) method is applied. In case 11, the error process is found to be AR (2). The Maximum Likelihood (ML) technique is used to fit the regression in all the cases excepting in case 2. The computer programme used here is Microfit 3.0 (see Pesaran and Pesaran, 1991).

their import unit values): minimization of the impact of the dramatic rise and fall in oil prices in the 1970s and the 1980s respectively.

As before, a log-linear trend equation is fitted to the terms-of-trade data of each country. The estimates are reported in Table 7.3. It is observed that out of 24 countries, 5 countries (Bolivia, Malaysia, Mauritius, Sri Lanka and Tunisia) experienced no significant trend in their terms of trade. All other countries experienced significant deteriorating trends. Countries with highly diversified export structures (the concentration index ranging from 0.09 to 0.20 in 1980) such as Argentina, Brazil, Korea, and Thailand experienced highly significant deteriorating trends in their terms of trade. For Korea, the annual average rate of deterioration was 1 per cent during 1970-97; for Brazil and Thailand it was 2 per cent during the period 1970 to 1995-6; and for Argentina, it is as high as 4 per cent during 1973-92. Some other countries facing very high annual rates of deterioration in their terms of trade are the Philippines (4 per cent), Panama (5 per cent), and Paraguay (7 per cent).

## EXPORT DIVERSIFICATION AND TERMS OF TRADE

In the perspective of the general experience of terms-of-trade deterioration, the question that arises is whether the countries with less commodity concentration of exports faced lower rates of terms-of-trade deterioration and *vice versa*. To answer this question, a cross-country study is undertaken: a linear regression equation is fitted between the cross-country variation in the annual rates of change in the terms of trade during 1980-9 (obtained by fitting a log-linear relationship to each country's terms of trade series) and the cross-country variation in the diversification index for 1980.

The study found no statistically significant relationship between the rate of changes in the terms of trade and export diversification. Replacing the diversification index by either the concentration index for 1980 or the number of commodities exported in 1980 does not alter the result (Table 7.4, rows 1-3).[2] It then seems that export diversification provides no relief to terms-of-trade deterioration.

Does export diversification reduce terms-of-trade fluctuations? To answer this question, a log-linear trend equation is fitted to the terms-of-trade series of each of the 24 countries studied here for the period 1980-9. The standard error (SE) of the regression in each case (call it SE8089) is taken as a measure of the terms-of-trade fluctuations around

TABLE 7.3: TRENDS IN TERMS OF TRADE OF SELECTED SOUTHERN COUNTRIES *VIS-À-VIS* THE NORTH SINCE 1970

| Country | Period | Estimates[1] | | | |
|---|---|---|---|---|---|
| | | a | b | Adj. $R^2$ | DW Statistic |
| Argentina[2] | 1973-92 | 6.19 | -0.04 | 0.92 | 1.46 |
| | | (40.96) | (-8.35) | | |
| Burkina Faso | 1970-96 | -5.83 | -0.04 | 0.85 | 2.21 |
| | | (17.26) | (-3.70) | | |
| Brazil | 1970-96 | 5.65 | -0.02 | 0.85 | 1.66 |
| | | (29.94) | (-3.82) | | |
| Bolivia | 1970-96 | 5.09 | -0.01 | 0.82 | 1.36 |
| | | (5.32) | (-0.51) | | |
| Chile | 1973-92 | 5.91 | -0.04 | 0.78 | 1.74 |
| | | (17.51) | (-3.52) | | |
| Colombia | 1970-97 | 5.84 | -0.02 | 0.80 | 1.64 |
| | | (13.36) | (-2.02) | | |
| Costa Rica | 1971-93 | 5.86 | -0.03 | 0.83 | 1.59 |
| | | (26.86) | (-4.09) | | |
| Dominican Republic[3] | 1970-97 | 5.44 | -0.02 | 0.42 | 1.33 |
| | | (33.51) | (-4.51) | | |
| Honduras[3] | 1975-97 | 5.89 | -0.03 | 0.51 | 1.11 |
| | | (26.44) | (-4.87) | | |
| India[3] | 1970-95 | 5.17 | -0.01 | 0.72 | 1.26 |
| | | (87.46) | (-8.03) | | |
| Kenya | 1970-96 | 5.72 | -0.02 | 0.81 | 1.81 |
| | | (17.60) | (-2.28) | | |
| Korea[3] | 1970-97 | 5.09 | -0.01 | 0.71 | 1.55 |
| | | (104.03) | (-7.95) | | |
| Malaysia | 1970-91 | 5.92 | -0.02 | 0.61 | 1.78 |
| | | (10.32) | (-1.04) | | |
| Mauritius | 1970-96 | 4.31 | 0.009 | 0.40 | 1.60 |
| | | (14.11) | (1.00) | | |
| Morocco[2] | 1970-96 | 5.61 | -0.02 | 0.74 | 1.93 |
| | | (34.73) | (-4.99) | | |
| Panama | 1970-91 | 6.61 | -0.05 | 0.94 | 1.68 |
| | | (42.46) | (-9.96) | | |
| Pakistan | 1970-97 | 5.17 | -0.01 | 0.71 | 1.84 |
| | | (28.26) | (-2.1) | | |
| Papua New Guinea[3] | 1973-97 | 5.47 | -0.02 | 0.43 | 1.41 |
| | | (39.84) | (-4.38) | | |
| Paraguay[2] | 1970-89 | 7.48 | -0.07 | 0.77 | 1.83 |
| | | (21.23) | (-5.89) | | |
| Peru | 1970-97 | 5.53 | -0.02 | 0.60 | 1.73 |
| | | (27.99) | (-3.76) | | |
| Philippines[2] | 1970-91 | 6.24 | -0.04 | 0.87 | 2.03 |
| | | (63.03) | (-12.27) | | |

(contd.)

Table 7.3 (contd.)

| | | | | | |
|---|---|---|---|---|---|
| Sri Lanka[2] | 1970-97 | 4.99<br>(31.86) | -0.01<br>(-1.34) | 0.32 | 1.82 |
| Thailand[2] | 1970-95 | 5.29<br>(48.22) | -0.02<br>(-4.56) | 0.70 | 1.87 |
| Tunisia[2] | 1970-94 | 4.33<br>(9.94) | 0.01<br>(0.61) | 0.73 | 1.82 |

NOTES: 1. Estimates are obtained by fitting a log-linear trend equation

$$\log y = a + b.t$$

The LM (12) and log-likelihood ratio tests are used to choose the appropriate error process. Unless otherwise stated, an AR (1) error process is chosen and the Maximum Likelihood (ML) procedure is used to fit the equation. Figures in parentheses are t-ratios of the parameters. The computer programme used here is Microfit 3.0 as in Table 7.2.

2. An AR (2) error process is chosen and the equation is fitted through the ML procedure.

3. Ordinary Least Square (OLS) technique is used to fit the trend equation.

SOURCES: Calculated from data available in IMF, *International Financial Statistics Yearbook* (IMF, Washington), various issues and World Bank, *World Tables 1995* (Washington).

the trend. The cross-country variation in the SE is regressed on the three alternative measures of export diversification for 1980 (D80, C80, and N80).

In no case do we get a statistically significant relationship between the two (Table 7.4, rows 4-6). Using the diversification index (D80), a weak evidence of direct relationship (implying higher terms-of-trade fluctuations for more export concentration) is found; but the regression coefficient is not significant even at the 10 per cent level of significance. The same type of relationship can be found if the two other measures of diversification are used but the degree of confidence that can be attached to these results are very low. Hence the conclusion is: there may be some glimpse of truth in the contention that a diverse export structure reduces the risk of terms-of-trade fluctuations but the present sample cannot establish that with sufficient statistical rigour.

## EXPORT DIVERSIFICATION AND MARKET PENETRATION

Export diversification, however, helps market penetration as is evident from our following cross-country regression study. As before, export diversification is measured by the three alternative indices for 1980—the diversification index (D80), the concentration index (C80), and

TABLE 7.4: EXPORT DIVERSIFICATION, MARKET SHARE AND TERMS OF TRADE: A CROSS-COUNTRY STUDY

| | Estimates[1] Independent Variables | | | | | |
|---|---|---|---|---|---|---|
| | A | D80 | C80 | N80 | Adj. $R^2$ | F Stat. |
| *Dependent Variables:* | | | | | | |
| I. Rate of Changes in Terms of Trade, 1980-9 | | | | | | |
| 1. | -0.07 | 0.04 | | | -0.02 | 0.56 |
| | (-1.8 ) | (0.75) | | | | |
| 2. | -0.04 | | -0.005 | | -0.04 | 0.02 |
| | (-3.26) | | (-0.15) | | | |
| 3. | -0.04 | | | -0.00 | -0.04 | 0.00 |
| | (-3.21) | | | (0.04) | | |
| II. Fluctuations in Terms of Trade around Trends, 1980-9 | | | | | | |
| 4. | -0.03 | 0.17 | | | 0.06 | 2.51 |
| | (-0.32) | (1.58) | | | | |
| 5. | 0.09 | | 0.05 | | -0.02 | 0.56 |
| | (3.24) | | (0.68) | | | |
| 6. | 0.15 | | | -0.0003 | 0.09 | 3.13 |
| | [3.93] | | | [-1.42] | | |
| III. Country Share in Total World Exports, 1980-9 | | | | | | |
| 7. | 2.4 | -2.73 | | | 0.4 | 16.63 |
| | [3.29] | [-3.16] | | | | |
| 8. | 0.82 | | -1.65 | | 0.31 | 11.51 |
| | [3.12] | | [-2.5 ] | | | |
| 9. | -0.4 | | | 0.005 | 0.43 | 18.68 |
| | [-2.81] | | | [3.71] | | |

NOTE: [1] The fitted equation is

$$Y = A + BX$$

where $Y$ is the rate of changes in the terms of trade (during 1980-9) or the SE of the linear trend regressions fitted to the terms of trade series (SE8089) or the country share in total world exports (average of 1980-9), X is 1980-diversification index (D80) or concentration index (C80) or the number of commodities exported in 1980 (N80).

The OLS technique is used to fit the regression. Figures in parentheses are t-values of the parameters. Figures in the square brackets are t-values based on adjusted White's heteroscedasticity-consistent standard errors (SEs). As before, the Microfit 3.0 package is used for computation.

the number of commodities exported (N80).[3] The market penetration of a country is measured by its share in total world exports during 1980-9; it is the annual average value of total exports of a country as a percentage of the average world total exports over the period 1980-9 (call it Xshare80s).

Fitting a simple linear regression (between cross-country variations in D80 or C80 or N80 and those in Xshare80s), an interesting conclusion can be derived: the higher the diversification or concentration index of a country (the more the commodity concentration of exports), the lower is its share in total world exports and vice versa (Table 7.4, rows 7 and 8). Similarly, the higher the number of commodities exported by a country (a crude measure of increased diversification), the higher is its market share (Table 7.4, row 9).

This finding does not alter if the size factor is taken into consideration. The population figure of a country as a ratio to total world population in 1980 (call it Popshare) is taken as a measure of the size factor. It is expected to have little interaction with the measures of diversification and concentration. A multiple regression equation is fitted with Popshare and the measure of export concentration (D80 or C80 or N80) as explanatory variables and Xshare80s as the dependent variable. In each case, the coefficient of Popshare is statistically insignificant while that of the export concentration is highly significant (as observed in Table 7.4). To save space, only one result is reported below:

$$\text{Xshare80s} = \underset{[2.82]}{2.34} - \underset{[-2.74]}{2.67}\ \text{D80} + \underset{[0.49]}{0.0069}\ \text{Popshare} \qquad (7.3)$$

where Adjusted $R^2 = 0.38$, $F = 8.01$ (the t-ratios based on White's heteroscedasticity-consistent standard errors are reported in brackets).

Thus, at the cross-country level, one result is robust: the more a country diversifies its export structure, the more it will penetrate the world market and acquire a larger market share. The intuitive logic is that a country with more diversified export structure can cater more to the needs of different countries with diverse tastes and preferences.

## CAUSES OF DETERIORATING TRENDS IN THE TERMS OF TRADE OF THE SOUTH

It has been observed in an earlier study (see Spraos 1983; Sarkar 1986b) that the terms of trade of the South deteriorated in the past when primary products dominated their exports to the North. In the earlier part of the present study (also in Sarkar 1986a & b), it is further observed that even in the present day the terms of trade of the South have been deteriorating although manufactured goods have been increasingly dominating the exports of the South to the North.

In our sample of 24 countries, only five countries faced no trend of statistical significance in their terms-of-trade series; all others experienced deteriorating trends. Analysing the data available in Sarkar and Singer (1991, Table 7.3) it can be observed that many countries facing deteriorating trends in their terms of trade experienced rapid fall in the share of primary products in their export structures: between 1971-3 and 1983-5, the average share of primary products fell from 79 per cent to 55 per cent for Brazil, from 16 to 8 per cent for Korea, and from 88 to 52 per cent for the Philippines. For countries such as Argentina and India, no major change was noticed during this period.

Out of five countries facing no significant trend in their terms of trade, the data for Bolivia show a large increase in the share of primary products from 46 per cent during 1971-3 to 73 per cent during 1983-5, while for Tunisia, the share fell from 77 per cent to 52 per cent and for Malaysia the share remained constant around 70 per cent between the same two periods.

Data available in Tables 7.1 and 7.3 showed that all types of countries—those with highly diversified export structures and those with highly concentrated export structures—faced deteriorating trends in their terms of trade. The five cases of exceptions cannot be explained in terms of export diversification or concentration. At the cross-country level (see Table 7.4), it cannot be said that the higher (or lower) the export diversification, the higher (or lower) is the rate of change (+ or -) in the terms of trade.

Thus, in the foregoing analysis, the fundamental question remains unresolved: what explains the deteriorating trends in the terms of trade of the South? One explanation that can be offered is in terms of product cycles (see Vernon 1966 and Krugman 1979) in the context of North–South trade. A new product is often introduced in the North. Initially there is a craze for this product and its income elasticity is very high. Due to a lack of knowledge of its production technique, the South cannot start its production. The South produces comparatively older goods with a lower income elasticity. By the time the South acquires the knowledge, the North has introduced another new product.

In such a product cycle scenario, the income elasticity of Southern demand for Northern goods is likely to be higher than that of the

Northern demand for Southern goods. Under these circumstances, if both the North and the South grow at the same rate (or the South tries to catch up by pressing for a higher rate of growth), the global macro balance requires a steady deterioration in the terms of trade of the South *vis-à-vis* the North. This is shown in Sarkar (1997) through a North-South macroeconomic framework.

For a stable terms of trade in the process of growth and trade, the South should grow at a sufficiently lower rate. Given that the standard of living (as measured by per capita real income) of the Northern population is higher than that of the Southern population, a stable terms of trade (which requires a lower rate of growth of Southern output) implies a further widening gap between the standards of living of the two sets of population. This is particularly true in view of the higher rate of population growth in the South.

The available evidence points out a growing divergence in the standards of living (as measured by per capita real income) of the North and the South (Sarkar 1999). The present study observed deteriorating trends in the terms of trade of the South. Combining the two findings it could be argued that a stable terms of trade would imply a further divergence, or a catching up would imply a further terms-of-trade deterioration than what has been observed.

This dilemma of policy prescription would not exist if the whole product cycle scenario could be reversed. In that case, the South could catch up without any loss in the terms of trade. The reversal in the product cycle scenario is an Herculean task, particularly in the present global politico-economic scenario. It is not expected to take place in the foreseeable future. The Prebisch-Singer hypothesis seems to be now an inexorable law.

## WELFARE IMPLICATION OF A DETERIORATION IN TERMS OF TRADE

Lastly, why should the South bother about a deterioration in their (commodity) terms of trade (CTT)? Critics often point out that a loss in the terms of trade of a country or region may lead to a gain in the purchasing power of its exports through a rise in the volume of exports (or what is known as gain in its income terms of trade, ITT = CTT multiplied by its export volume). But it is not often clear as to how much of the gain in ITT is due to a loss in CTT because export volume often increases more due to a growth in global income. Hence, a loss in the CTT is often taken as a loss in the ITT compared to what could have been the case had there been no loss in the CTT.

On the basis of the same logic, Prebisch (1964) as the first Secretary General of UNCTAD calculated the loss incurred by the South due to a deterioration in their CTT during 1950-61. According to his estimate, the fall in the purchasing power of total exports from the South during 1950-61 due to a deterioration in the CTT was about $13.1 billion, which wiped out half of the net inflows of all types of resource inflow from the North (loans, investment, and grants-in-aid net of remittances of interest and profits). He further estimated that had there been no deterioration in the terms of trade the import capacity generated by exports together with the inflow of Northern resources—again minus the cost of servicing—would have increased by 4.5 per cent a year. Because of the deterioration, this did not happen; the Southern capacity to import expanded by only 3.5 per cent a year.

Moreover, the issue of terms of trade raised by Prebisch and Singer was basically concerned with relative gains from trade, not the absolute gains from trade. Gains in income terms of trade (ITT) are absolute gains from trade. The ITT of both the North and the South can rise simultaneously as shown in Sarkar (1986a); this implies that both regions experienced absolute gains from trade. Studying the behaviour of the ratio of ITTs of the two regions, it was observed that the North gained more during the post-Second World War period before the rise of OPEC (Sarkar 1986a). Sarkar and Singer (1991), however, observed that the South gained more in terms of ITT in the case of its exports of manufactures to pay for imports of manufactures during 1970-87.

Studying the economic history of Britain it has been observed that its CTT had been declining during the first half of the nineteenth century due to technological progress mainly in its cotton textile sector but its trading partners, the colonies, while experiencing terms-of-trade gains, faced the misery of deindustrialization (Sarkar 1986c).

The concept of double factoral terms of trade (DFTT) takes into account the impact of technological progress on CTT. It is defined as CTT multiplied by the ratio of labour productivity indices of the two regions. If the whole of the loss in CTT of a country or region can be accounted for by technological progress and labour productivity improvements in its export sector, it is not a loser; in that case its DFTT will not show any decline.

It is difficult to get data for the DFTT of the South *vis-à-vis* the North. The available data (see Sarkar and Singer 1991, Table 7.2) indicate that there exists a considerable and widening gap in the growth of labour productivity in manufacturing sectors of the North and the South. During 1960-70, the annual average rate of growth of labour productivity in the manufacturing sector of the North was 4.1 per cent while for the South, it was 2.3 per cent. This gap widened further in the next decade, 1970-80: while labour productivity grew more slowly, at an annual average rate of 2.8 per cent in the North, it declined even more sharply to a mere 0.4 per cent in the South.

Given the fact that the South has experienced a lower rate of growth in labour productivity, an observed decilne in the CTT of the South implies a more acute decline in their DFTT. Hence it was argued in Sarkar and Singer (1991) that the DFTT in the case of North-South trade in manufactures 'deteriorated even more' as the CTT was observed to decline during 1970-87.

The DFTT is intended to measure the relative gains from trade. Following Spraos (1983), the DFTT can be shown to be equal to the real income ratio. Let the prices of goods produced in the North and the South be $P_n$ and $P_s$ and the levels of output be $Y_n$ and $Y_s$, respectively. The levels of their money incomes are $P_nY_n$ and $P_sY_s$, respectively. Let $m$ and $m^*$ be the shares of import goods in the consumption baskets of the Southern and Northern populations, respectively. Using geometric average, the price indices ($P$ and $P^*$) faced by the Southern and Northern consumers can be given by the following: $P = P_s^{(1-m)} P_n^{m}$ and $P^* = P_n^{(1-m^*)} P_s^{m^*}$, respectively. The South–North real income ratio, $y$, is $P_sY_s/P \,/\, P_nY_n/P^* = (Y_s/Y_n)\ (P_s/P_n)^{(m+m^*)}$. If $l_s$ and $l_n$ are the labour productivities and $L_s$ and $L_n$ are the levels of total employment in the South and the North, respectively, $Y_s = l_sL_s$ and $Y_n = l_nL_n$ . The real income ratio $y$, becomes $kP^{(m+m^*)}l_s/\,l_n$ where $P = P_s/P_n$ (the South-North CTT) and $k = L_s/L_n$. Assuming that the employment levels are constant, $k$ will drop out when the real income ratio is taken as an index number. The real income ratio $y = P^{(m+m^*)}l_s/l_n$ and this is equivalent to the DFTT if $m + m^* = 1$. This condition is satisfied when the two countries have identical consumption patterns, meaning that the two goods enter their consumption baskets in the same proportion.

If the two regions do not have identical consumption patterns, the changes in the CTT component of the DFTT should be weighted by the factor $(m + m^*)$ to get changes in the DFTT to reflect changes in relative real incomes. The above analysis is based on the assumption of constant employment levels; this holds specially under full employment condition in both the regions. If one region faces a pool of chronically unemployed labour, Spraos (1983) suggested some correction for a gain in employment and introduced the concept of employment-corrected weighted DFTT (ECWDFTT). The index of real income ratio, $y$, or ECWDFTT equals $P^{(m + m^{*})} l_s \ L_s / \ l_n$ on the assumption that the South is a labour surplus economy (and the North is not). A similar correction is needed if the North is also a labour surplus economy, so that the index will be $(Y_s/Y_n) \ (P_s/P_n)^{(m + m^{*})}$.

Under the usual assumption of perfect competition and the neoclassical marginal productivity theory of distribution, the DFTT is nothing but the wage ratio. This is also true in the classical political economy framework of the world economy which Emmanuel (1969) had in mind. Emmanuel assumed perfect capital mobility which ensures an uniform rate of profit and imperfect labour mobility which implies unequal wages.

Let $P_s$ and $P_n$ be the prices of the goods produced in the South and the North, respectively, so that the CTT of the South is $P_s/P_n$. Let $l_s$ and $l_n$ be the respective labour productivities so that the DFTT = $P_s l_s \ / \ P_n l_n$. If $W_s$ and $W_n$ are the wage rates and $r_s$ and $r_n$ are the rates of profit prevailing in the two regions, respectively, the CTT is given by the following:

$$P_s/P_n = W_s \ (1 + r_s)/ \ l_s \ / \ W_n \ (1 + r_n)/ \ l_n = l_n W_s / l_s W_n \qquad (7.4)$$

since $r_s = r_n$ due to perfect capital mobility between the North and the South.

From equation (7.4), the DFTT = $P_s \ l_s \ / \ P_n \ l_n = W_s/W_n$, the wage ratio. In Emmanuel's concept of equal exchange, the CTT should be equal to the ratio of labour embodied in the commodities: $P_s/ \ P_n = 1/l_s \ / \ 1/l_n = l_n \ / \ l_s$. That is to say, under equal exchange, the DFTT should be equal to one. In Emmanuel's framework, equal exchange implies equalization of North–South wage rates. At any point of time, a positive North–South wage gap implies unequal exchange against the South (its DFTT is less than one).

If over time, the existing North–South wage gap rises, the DFTT of the South will fall over time (increasingly less than one). Following Emmanuel (1979), this situation of declining DFTT can be called dynamic unequal exchange. The idea of dynamic unequal exchange converges with the essence of the Prebisch-Singer thesis: a secular decline in the DFTT of the South.

## CONCLUSION

This chapter has observed that the commodity terms of trade (CTT) of the South continued to deteriorate in the post-Second World War period in spite of the increasing importance of manufactures in their exports to the North. Individual country cases confirm this result irrespective of whether their export structures are diversified and/or dominated by manufactures. Export diversification has, however, helped market penetration. The more diversified is a country's export structure, the more is its share in world exports but not less is its rate of deterioration in the CTT. The phenomenon of CTT-deterioration reduces the purchasing power of exports of the South and their relative gains from trade as measured by their double factoral terms of trade.

Before concluding it should be noted that in the present days of neocolonization, intra-firm trade of transnational corporations has dominated much of the trade flows. It is difficult to ascertain how much of changes in the terms of trade is due to their transfer pricing and other designs to bypass the national rules and regulations. The issue of North–South terms of trade once raised by Prebisch and Singer was not meant for this scenario.

## NOTES

1. The category, 'Developed Market Economy' constitutes West Europe, North America (USA and Canada), New Zealand, Australia, Japan, Israil and South Africa. This is our North. All other countries excepting former socialist countries including China constitute the 'Developing Market Economy', the South.
2. The findings do not alter if the 1994 indices are used instead of 1980 indices.

## REFERENCES

Bagchi, Amiya Kumar (1976), 'De-industrialisation in India in the Nineteenth Century: Some Theoretical Implications', *Journal of Development Studies*, vol. 12, no. 2, pp. 135-64.

Emmanuel, A. (1969), *Unequal Exchange*, Monthly Review Press, New York (English Translation, 1972).

——— (1979), 'The Dynamics of Unequal Exchange/Unequal Development', paper presented to a conference on Dependence at the London School of Economics.

Krugman, Paul (1979), 'A Model of Innovation, Technology Transfer and the World Distribution of Income', *Journal of Political Economy*, vol. 87, no. 2, pp. 253-66.

Pesaran, M. Hashem and Bahram Pesaran (1991), *Microfit 3.0*, Oxford University Press, London.

Prebisch, Raul (1950), *The Economic Development of Latin America and Its Principal Problems*, United Nations, New York.

——— (1959), 'Commercial Policy in the Underdeveloped Countries', *American Economic Review,* vol. 49, no. 2, pp. 251-73.

——— (1964), *Towards a New Trade Policy for Development,* United Nations for UNCTAD, New York.

Sarkar, Prabirjit (1999), 'Convergence of Real Income, 1950-1992', *Economic and Political Weekly,* vol. 34, no. 3, pp. 500-4, 20-27 February.

——— (1997), 'Growth and Terms of Trade: A North-South Macro-economic Framework', *Journal of Macroeconomics,* vol. 19, no. 1, pp. 117-33.

——— (1992), 'De-industrialisation through Colonial Trade', *Journal of Contemporary Asia,* vol. 22, no. 3, pp. 297-302.

——— (1986a), 'Patterns of Trade and Movements of Interregional Terms of Trade between the Developing and the Developed Market Economies, 1950-1980', *Economic Bulletin for Asia and the Pacific,* vol. 37, no. 2, pp. 1-13.

——— (1986b), 'The Singer-Prebisch Hypothesis: A Statistical Evaluation', *Cambridge Journal of Economics,* vol. 10, pp. 355-71.

——— (1986c), 'Terms of Trade Experience of Britain since the Nineteenth Century', *Journal of Development Studies,* vol. 23, pp. 20-39.

Sarkar, Prabirjit and Hans Singer, (1991), 'Manufactured Exports of Developing Countries and their Terms of Trade since 1965', *World Development,* vol. 19, pp. 333-40.

Singer, Hans (1950), 'The Distribution of Gains between Investing and Borrowing Countries', *American Economic Review,* vol. 40, no. 2, pp. 473-85.

Spraos, John (1983), *Inequalising Trade?*, Clarendon Press, London.

United Nations (1997), *International Trade Statistics Yearbook, 1996,* United Nations, New York.

——— (1986), *Statistical Yearbook, 1985-86,* United Nations, New York.

——— (1981, 1982), *Yearbook of International Trade Statistics, 1980, 1981,* United Nations, New York.

UNCTAD (1997), *Handbook of International Trade and Development Statistics, 1995,* United Nations, New York.

——— (1972), *Handbook of International Trade and Development Statistics, 1972,* United Nations, New York.

Vernon, Richard (1966), 'International Investment and International Trade in the Product Cycle', *Quarterly Journal of Economics,* vol. 80, no. 2, pp. 190-207.

# 8

# Changing Food Preferences, Nutritional Intake, and Nutritional Status: Emerging Perspectives and Issues

*R. Radhakrishna, S. Inderkant and C. Ravi*

## INTRODUCTION

It is generally believed that the solution to the widespread malnutrition in India lies in the overall growth of the economy or even in raising the incomes of the poor through public intervention. Studies on consumer demand reveal a large income elasticity of demand for food. These provide support for income augmentation programmes for improving the nutritional status of the poor. The large negative price elasticity of demand for food calls for the intervention of the state in the form of subsidized food. However, a cursory glance at the trends in food consumption and prices, and real incomes of the poor, indicates that cereal and calorie consumption have not risen despite an improvement in the real incomes of the poor and favourable movements in food prices. The question that arises is: are the poor in India moving along the necessary path to improve their nutritional status in the long run?

The per capita expenditure during 1970-89 in rural areas at 1990-1 prices increased at the rate of 1.54 per cent per annum, poverty declined at 2.50 per cent and real prices of cereals declined at 0.67 per cent per annum. Yet, contrary to expectations, the per capita cereal consumption and calorie intake decreased by 0.5 per cent and 0.18 per cent per annum, respectively. In urban areas, during 1970-90, per capita real expenditure increased at the rate of 1.45 per cent per annum, and both poverty and the real price of cereals declined at 1.96 per cent and at 0.82 per cent per annum, respectively. But per capita cereal consumption declined at the rate of 0.18 per cent per annum, while the per capita calorie intake increased at a low rate of 0.21 per cent per annum. These trends are not consistent with the estimated income and price elasticities of demand. With the growth in per capita total expenditure and favourable cereal price trends, one expects substantial improvement in food energy intake. This questions the widely held belief that the nutritional intake and therefore the nutritional status will improve automatically with increases in income.

In the post-liberalization period, the annual per capita real expenditure in rural areas increased at a lower rate of 1.18 per cent per annum, real cereal prices increased at 1.20 per cent, and the per capita cereal consumption declined sharply at 2.14 per cent as also the calorie intake at 1.53 per cent per annum. There is a need to assess whether the nutritional status of the rural poor has deteriorated. In urban areas, the annual growth rate of per capita expenditure accelerated to 2.77 per cent, real cereal price rose at 1.17 per cent per annum, and per capita cereal consumption and calorie intake declined, respectively, by 0.28 per cent and 0.44 per cent per annum. An intriguing question that arises is: why is the substantial increase in per capita expenditure not reflected in the nutritional intake?

Nutritionists prefer to assess the nutritional status in terms of outcome rather than food intake. They argue that food energy intake is a poor measure of nutritional status because it depends not only on nutrition intake but also on non-nutrient food attributes as well as the health status (Mortorell and Ho 1984). The outcome measures include anthropometric measures, clinical signs of malnutrition, and biochemical indicators. These are closely related to health and functional capacity. Among these, anthropometric measures are considered to have an advantage over other indicators since body measurements are sensitive to even minor levels of malnutrition whereas biochemical and clinical indicators, on the other hand, are useful only when the level of malnutrition is extreme. This chapter reviews the trends in food and nutrition deprivation using a wide range of input and output measures.

## FOOD AND NUTRIENT INTAKE

### CEREAL CONSUMPTION

Consumption data of the National Sample Survey (NSS) reveal that the per capita consumption of cereals has been declining since the early 1970s (Radhakrishna and Ravi 1992; Rao and Radhakrishna 1997; Rao 2000). Between 1970-1 and 1997-8, the per capita cereal consumption declined by 0.72 per cent per annum in the rural areas and by 0.74 per cent per annum in the urban areas. The cereal consumption in rural areas fell from 15.35 kg per capita per month in 1970-1 to 12.5 kg in 1997-8 while the same in urban areas fell from 11.36 kgs to 10.4 kg during the same period. The declining trend is visible across all the states with the exception of Kerala, West Bengal, and Orissa. The decline is very prominent in Punjab and Haryana where the decline is as much as about 6 kg per capita per month in rural areas. What is most striking is the low per capita intake of cereals in the most prosperous Punjab state (9.8 kg in the rural areas and 9.7 kg in the urban areas in 1997-8) and the converse in the backward state of Orissa (16 kg in the rural areas and 13.25 kg in the urban areas). This is partly due to the diversification of the food basket in Punjab and Haryana in favour of superior non-cereal food, particularly milk and milk products, vegetables and fruits, etc. Can these changes be viewed in a positive light? The striking decline in cereal consumption is attributed to changes in consumer tastes and preferences from food to non-food items, within the food group from cereals to non-cereal food, and from 'coarse' to 'fine' cereals (Radhakrishna and Ravi 1992). More recently, Rao (2000) has shown that the decline in cereal consumption has been sharper in the rural areas where improvements in rural infrastructure have made other food and non-food items available to the rural households and hard manual work has been greatly reduced in agriculture due to farm mechanization. Rao further observes that a reduction in the intake of food grain on this account should not be taken as a deterioration in human welfare.

### FOOD CONSUMPTION AND CALORIE INTAKE

Data from NSS surveys show that per capita consumer expenditure at constant (1990-1) prices has increased since 1970 both in rural and urban areas (Table 8.1). Though it increased at around 1.5 per cent per annum in both the areas during 1970-89, it increased at a lower rate during the 1990s in rural areas but at a substantially higher rate in urban areas. It appears that the 1990s liberalization process benefited more the urban households than the rural ones. However, even in urban areas, the increase in expenditure did not get reflected in food expenditure. Per capita food expenditure at constant prices increased at around 0.9 per cent per annum during 1970-89. During the 1990s it declined at 0.9 per cent per annum in rural areas and remained stagnant in urban areas.

Per capita cereal expenditure at constant prices declined both in

TABLE 8.1: GROWTH RATES OF TOTAL EXPENDITURE, FOOD EXPENDITURE AND THE CEREAL EXPENDITURE AT 1990-1 PRICES AND PER CAPITA CALORIE INTAKE

*(per cent per annum)*

| | Bottom 30% | Middle 40% | Top 30% | All classess |
|---|---|---|---|---|
| *Rural* | | | | |
| Per capita cereal expenditure | | | | |
| 1970-89 | 0.09 | -0.58 | -1.28 | -0.69 |
| 1990-8 | -1.38 | -2.34 | -2.43 | -2.14 |
| Per capita food expenditure | | | | |
| 1970-89 | 1.34 | 0.87 | 0.74 | 0.89 |
| 1990-8 | -0.48 | -0.78 | -1.12 | -0.88 |
| Per capita calorie intake | | | | |
| 1970-89 | 0.16 | 0.15 | 0.40 | 0.23 |
| 1990-8 | -0.96 | -1.63 | -1.76 | -1.53 |
| Per capita total expenditure | | | | |
| 1970-89 | 1.71 | 1.40 | 1.45 | 1.54 |
| 1990-8 | 1.19 | 1.11 | 1.23 | 1.18 |
| *Urban* | | | | |
| Per capita cereal expenditure | | | | |
| 1970-89 | 0.07 | -0.33 | -0.18 | -0.18 |
| 1990-8 | -0.67 | -0.55 | 0.30 | -0.28 |
| Per capita food expenditure | | | | |
| 1970-89 | 1.29 | 1.19 | 0.69 | 0.97 |
| 1990-8 | 0.08 | 0.03 | -0.23 | -0.08 |
| Per capita calorie intake | | | | |
| 1970-89 | 0.31 | 0.05 | 0.32 | 0.21 |
| 1990-8 | -0.58 | -0.74 | -0.05 | -0.44 |
| Per capita total expenditure | | | | |
| 1970-89 | 1.44 | 1.50 | 1.40 | 1.45 |
| 1990-8 | 1.70 | 2.27 | 3.31 | 2.77 |

SOURCE: Ravi (2000).

rural and urban areas throughout this period for all the expenditure classes, except the bottom 30 per cent during the first two decades and the urban top 30 per cent during the last decade. During the 1990s, the decline is more in rural areas than in urban areas. The fall in cereal consumption is more than compensated by increased consumption of non-cereal foods during the first two decades and as a result, per capital calorie intake increased by 0.2 per cent per annum during this period both in rural and urban areas. However, this did not continue during the 1990s when the per capita calorie intake fell by about 1.5 per cent per annum in rural areas and by 0.4 per cent per annum in urban areas. It implies that the consumption of non-cereal food items could not compensate the loss of food energy intake due to fall in cereal consumption during this period. There is substantial variation in energy intake among different expenditure segments of the population. While the top 30 per cent of the population is well-fed, both in rural and urban areas, the middle 40 per cent is barely close to the nutritional requirement both in rural and urban areas (Table 8.2). Strangely, the energy intake of this section, like that of the well-fed top 30 per cent, is slowly declining even though they are close to the norms. The most alarming aspect is that the energy intake of the bottom 30 per cent is very deficient both in rural and urban areas. The energy intake of this section increased marginally during 1970-89, but it started declining in the post-reform period.

For the bottom 30 per cent of the population, the per capita cereal expenditure at constant prices was stagnant during 1970-89 but

TABLE 8.2: AVERAGE PER CAPITA CALORIE INTAKE AND ITS GROWTH RATES IN INDIA

*(kcal per capita per day)*

| | Rural | | | | Urban | | | |
|---|---|---|---|---|---|---|---|---|
| Expenditure classes | 1972-73 | 1977-78 | 1993-94 | 1972-94 AGR* | 1972-73 | 1977-78 | 1993-94 | 1972-94 AGR* |
| Lower 30 per cent | 1504 | 1630 | 1678 | 0.5 | 1579 | 1701 | 1682 | 0.3 |
| Middle 40 per cent | 2170 | 2296 | 2119 | -0.1 | 2154 | 2438 | 2111 | -0.1 |
| Top 30 per cent | 3161 | 3190 | 2672 | -0.8 | 2572 | 2979 | 2405 | -0.3 |
| All classes | 2268 | 2364 | 2152 | -0.2 | 2107 | 2379 | 2071 | -0.1 |

NOTE: * Annualized Growth Rate (percentage).
SOURCE: Computed from NSS Report No. 405.

declined during 1990-8 (Table 8.1). It seems that the improvement in economic access to food made possible by income growth did not result in a higher consumption of cereals. The declining cereal consumption would not be a major cause of concern if the food energy intake levels of the poor were nutritionally adequate. The per capita calorie intake in 1993-4 was 1678 kcal per day in rural areas and 1682 kcal per day in urban areas (Table 8.2). This section of the population was deprived of an adequate diet that would provide the required food energy of about 2200 kcal per person per day. Their low nutrient intake would have an adverse effect on the health and nutritional status of both adults and children.

There has also been a substantial diversification of the consumption basket of the poor in favour of non-cereal items, particularly non-food items. The changes in the composition of diet have increased the cost of calories (Radhakrishna and Ravi 1992). The per capita non-food expenditure at constant prices has been expanding among all income groups of rural and urban areas throughout but its rate of expansion was higher in the 1990s, even among the poor (Ravi 2000). A question of topical interest is: are the poor households not buying food items from a nutritional perspective? Studies suggest that the poor generally suffer from micro-nutrient (iron, vitamin A, riboflavin, and niacin) deficiencies due to lack of variety in their diet [National Nutrition Monitoring Bureau (NNMB) reports]. It is therefore important to analyse the implications of the changes in dietary preferences on the nutritional and health status of the poor. So long as the diversification of the consumption basket improves nutritional status, even though it may not add calories, it should not be a cause of concern. Another important issue that evokes interest is: what would be the impact of economic reforms and liberalization on food habits? There is hardly any study which throws light on these issues.

## DETERMINANTS OF NUTRITIONAL INTAKE

Cereal food is the cheapest source of calories for both poor and non-poor households (Table 8.3). The calories derived from a rupee of expenditure tend to be higher for the poor. For instance, in rural areas, very poor households obtained 556 kcal per rupee spent on cereals in 1998 and the non-poor higher group obtained 500 Kcal. The higher income households generally substitute fine cereals for coarse cereals and prefer quality food. Due to significant increases in

TABLE 8.3: CALORIE CONTAINED IN ONE RUPEE EXPENDITURE ON FOOD ITEMS

*(in kcals per rupee at 1998 prices)*

| Commodity Group | Rural | | | | | Urban | | | | |
|---|---|---|---|---|---|---|---|---|---|---|
| | VP | MP | NPL | NPH | All | VP | MP | NPL | NPH | All |
| *Calorie from rupee expenditure* | | | | | | | | | | |
| Cereals & Subst. | 556 | 508 | 489 | 482 | 500 | 494 | 452 | 425 | 371 | 406 |
| Milk & Milk Products | 90 | 90 | 89 | 90 | 89 | 63 | 61 | 60 | 56 | 57 |
| Meat, Fish & Eggs | 228 | 227 | 228 | 230 | 229 | 236 | 225 | 217 | 197 | 207 |
| Edible Oils | 25 | 26 | 26 | 26 | 26 | 21 | 21 | 20 | 19 | 19 |
| Sugar & Gur | 217 | 215 | 215 | 216 | 236 | 236 | 230 | 225 | 207 | 216 |
| Other Food | 116 | 111 | 103 | 91 | 100 | 99 | 95 | 93 | 85 | 88 |

NOTES: VP = Very poor, i.e. households whose PCE is below 75 per cent of the poverty line.

MP = Moderately poor, i.e. households whose PCE is below the poverty line but above 75 per cent of it.

NPL = Non-poor lower, i.e. households whose PCE is above the poverty line but below 150 per cent of it.

NPH = Non-poor higher, i.e. households whose PCE is above 150 per cent of poverty line.

SOURCE: Ravi (2000).

the price of cereals, the real cost of calories has increased during the 1990s (Ravi 2000).

Cereals, the cheapest source of calories, accounted for 75-80 per cent of the calorie intake of very poor households both in rural and urban areas (Table 8.4). Improved income and urbanization result in significant diversification in the sources of food energy. For instance, non-cereal food accounted for nearly half of the calorie intake of the urban higher income households and one-third of that of their rural counterparts.

The expenditure elasticities for cereals is markedly lower for non-poor households in both rural and urban areas (Tables 8.5 and 8.6). The elasticity for food exceeds the elasticity for energy (calories) for non-poor households. This may be due to the fact that households at higher income levels prefer variety and better quality of food.

The expenditure elasticity for cereals is substantial for the very poor households (0.7–0.8) in both rural and urban areas but low for moderately poor households in urban areas, at around 0.18. As in the

TABLE 8.4: CALORIE INTAKE BY SOURCE IN 1998, MARGINAL AND AVERAGE PROPENSITY TO CONSUME CALORIES

*(at current prices)*

| Commodity Group | Rural | | | | | Urban | | | | |
|---|---|---|---|---|---|---|---|---|---|---|
| | VP | MP | NPL | NPH | All | VP | MP | NPL | NPH | All |
| Cereals & Substitutes | 1289 | 1403 | 1484 | 1628 | 1472 | 1092 | 1137 | 1228 | 1296 | 1229 |
| Milk & Milk Products | 22 | 53 | 102 | 218 | 109 | 30 | 59 | 96 | 186 | 124 |
| Meat, Fish & Eggs | 73 | 99 | 129 | 177 | 126 | 110 | 134 | 157 | 219 | 176 |
| Edible Oils | 4 | 6 | 11 | 20 | 11 | 5 | 9 | 12 | 20 | 14 |
| Sugar & Gur | 34 | 50 | 70 | 120 | 73 | 55 | 71 | 84 | 111 | 91 |
| Other Food | 131 | 182 | 230 | 325 | 228 | 154 | 214 | 280 | 518 | 363 |
| Total (All Foods) | 1551 | 1795 | 2026 | 2488 | 2019 | 1445 | 1624 | 1855 | 2350 | 1997 |

NOTE: Abbreviations same as in Table 8.3.
SOURCE: Ravi (2000).

TABLE 8.5: PRICE AND EXPENDITURE ELASTICITIES OF CALORIE INTAKE AND BROAD COMMODITY GROUPS IN RURAL AREAS

| Commodity/ Expenditure group | Elasticity with respect to prices | | | | |
|---|---|---|---|---|---|
| | Cereals | Non-cereal Food | All Food | Non-food | Expenditure Elasticities |
| *Cereal* | | | | | |
| Very Poor | -0.88 | 0.01 | -0.87 | -0.01 | 0.87 |
| Moderately Poor | -0.43 | -0.01 | -0.44 | 0.01 | 0.44 |
| Non-poor lower | -0.21 | -0.02 | -0.22 | 0.00 | 0.22 |
| Non-poor high | -0.19 | 0.00 | -0.19 | 0.07 | 0.11 |
| All groups | -0.34 | -0.00 | -0.34 | 0.03 | 0.32 |
| *Non-cereal Food* | | | | | |
| Very Poor | -0.08 | -1.03 | -1.11 | -0.01 | 1.12 |
| Moderately Poor | -0.29 | -0.97 | -1.26 | 0.02 | 1.24 |
| Non-poor lower | -0.27 | -0.89 | -1.16 | 0.02 | 1.14 |
| Non-poor high | -0.09 | -1.07 | -1.17 | 0.47 | 0.70 |
| All groups | -0.17 | -0.98 | -1.16 | 0.22 | 0.94 |
| *All Food* | | | | | |
| Very Poor | -0.51 | -0.47 | -0.98 | -0.01 | 0.99 |
| Moderately Poor | -0.36 | -0.52 | -0.87 | 0.01 | 0.86 |
| Non-poor lower | -0.24 | -0.54 | -0.78 | 0.01 | 0.77 |
| Non-poor high | -0.12 | -0.74 | -0.86 | 0.35 | 0.51 |
| All groups | -0.24 | -0.56 | -0.81 | 0.14 | 0.67 |

(contd.)

| | | | | | |
|---|---|---|---|---|---|
| *Non-food* | | | | | |
| Very Poor | -0.08 | 0.02 | -0.06 | -0.98 | 1.04 |
| Moderately Poor | -0.31 | -0.03 | -0.34 | -1.03 | 1.37 |
| Non-poor lower | -0.35 | -0.13 | -0.48 | -1.02 | 1.50 |
| Non-poor high | -0.21 | 0.06 | -0.15 | -1.39 | 1.54 |
| All groups | -0.24 | -0.00 | -0.24 | -1.20 | 1.45 |
| *Calories* | | | | | |
| Very Poor | -0.74 | -0.16 | -0.90 | -0.01 | 0.91 |
| Moderately Poor | -0.40 | -0.20 | -0.60 | 0.01 | 0.59 |
| Non-poor lower | -0.22 | -0.24 | -0.45 | 0.01 | 0.45 |
| Non-poor high | -0.16 | -0.36 | -0.51 | 0.21 | 0.31 |
| All groups | -0.29 | -0.26 | -0.55 | 0.08 | 0.48 |

SOURCE: Ravi (2000).

TABLE 8.6: PRICES AND EXPENDITURE ELASTICITIES OF CALORIE INTAKE AND BROAD COMMODITY GROUPS IN URBAN AREAS

| Commodity/ Expenditure group | Elasticity with respect to prices | | | | |
|---|---|---|---|---|---|
| | Cereals | Non-cereal Food | All Food | Non-food | Expenditure Elasticities |
| *Cereal* | | | | | |
| Very Poor | -0.72 | 0.02 | -0.71 | 0.01 | 0.70 |
| Moderately Poor | -0.22 | -0.00 | -0.22 | 0.04 | 0.18 |
| Non-poor lower | -0.11 | -0.01 | -0.11 | 0.02 | 0.09 |
| Non-poor high | -0.15 | -0.02 | -0.16 | 0.03 | 0.13 |
| All groups | -0.20 | -0.01 | -0.21 | 0.03 | 0.18 |
| *Non-cereal Food* | | | | | |
| Very Poor | -0.12 | -1.03 | -1.15 | 0.01 | 1.13 |
| Moderately Poor | -0.19 | -0.99 | -1.18 | 0.22 | 0.96 |
| Non-poor lower | -0.14 | -0.88 | -1.02 | 0.19 | 0.83 |
| Non-poor high | -0.05 | -0.73 | -0.78 | 0.16 | 0.62 |
| All groups | -0.09 | -0.79 | -0.88 | 0.16 | 0.72 |
| *All Food* | | | | | |
| Very Poor | -0.37 | -0.59 | -0.96 | 0.01 | 0.95 |
| Moderately Poor | -0.20 | -0.57 | -0.76 | 0.14 | 0.62 |
| Non-poor lower | -0.13 | -0.62 | -0.75 | 0.14 | 0.61 |
| Non-poor high | -0.07 | -0.58 | -0.65 | 0.13 | 0.52 |
| All groups | -0.12 | -0.56 | -0.68 | 0.12 | 0.56 |
| *Non-food* | | | | | |
| Very Poor | -0.11 | 0.03 | -0.09 | -1.03 | 1.12 |
| Moderately Poor | -0.32 | -0.01 | -0.32 | -1.27 | 1.58 |
| Non-poor lower | -0.28 | -0.14 | -0.42 | -1.23 | 1.65 |
| Non-poor high | -0.11 | -0.18 | -0.29 | -1.11 | 1.40 |
| All groups | -0.15 | -0.15 | -0.30 | -1.12 | 1.42 |

(contd.)

| | | | | | |
|---|---|---|---|---|---|
| *Calories* | | | | | |
| Very Poor | -0.57 | -0.22 | -0.79 | 0.01 | 0.78 |
| Moderately Poor | -0.20 | -0.27 | -0.47 | 0.09 | 0.38 |
| Non-poor lower | -0.11 | -0.27 | -0.38 | 0.07 | 0.31 |
| Non-poor high | -0.10 | -0.31 | -0.41 | 0.08 | 0.33 |
| All groups | -0.16 | -0.29 | -0.44 | 0.08 | 0.37 |

SOURCE: Ravi (2000).

case of higher income households, the expenditure elasticity for food exceeds the expenditure elasticity for calorie intake.

A rise in cereal prices adversely affects the calorie intake of the very poor households since the absolute value of the cereal price elasticity is close to one. What is more, a cereal price increase hurts the poor households the most. In the case of the higher income groups, whose sources of calorie intake are more diversified, an increase in cereal prices will have a marginal effect.

## CHANGING CONSUMER PREFERENCES

The above evidence reveals that expenditure and price elasticities are large for the poor households. With the significant growth in the income of the bottom segment of the population during 1970-89 and favourable cereal price movements (Table 8.7, Fig. 8.1 and 8.2), one expects an improvement in the cereal consumption of the poor. But no such improvement had taken place. For explanation, one may have to consider exogenous factors which affect food consumption. These include the introduction of new products, marketing, advertisements, etc.

In the absence of changes in consumer preferences, the per capita cereal consumption of the bottom 30 per cent of the rural population would have increased during 1970-89 at an annual rate of 1.12 per cent due to growth in per capita real expenditure and at 0.44 per cent per annum due to the decline in real price of cereals (assuming for the bottom 30 per cent, the average of the elasticities of the very poor and moderately poor groups). Income growth and favourable price movement together would have increased the real expenditure on cereal by 1.56 per cent per annum (in the absence of changes in tastes); the changes in the tastes reduced the growth rate to 0.09 per cent per annum. In the urban areas, in the absence of changes in tastes, per capita real expenditure on cereals of the bottom 30 per cent of the population would have risen by 1.23 per cent per annum.

TABLE 8.7: REAL PRICES OF COMMODITY GROUPS

| Index Year | Rural: Relative Price: Cereals | Non-cereal food | Food | Non-food | Consumer price index | Urban: Relative Price: Cereals | Non-cereal food | Food | Non-food | Consumer price index |
|---|---|---|---|---|---|---|---|---|---|---|
| 1969-70 | 1.13 | 0.77 | 0.96 | 1.08 | 0.24 | 1.17 | 0.79 | 0.92 | 1.12 | 0.23 |
| 1970-1 | 1.08 | 0.81 | 0.95 | 1.09 | 0.25 | 1.11 | 0.83 | 0.92 | 1.12 | 0.24 |
| 1971-2 | 1.08 | 0.79 | 0.94 | 1.11 | 0.25 | 1.10 | 0.80 | 0.91 | 1.14 | 0.25 |
| 1972-3 | 1.11 | 0.81 | 0.97 | 1.06 | 0.28 | 1.14 | 0.83 | 0.93 | 1.10 | 0.27 |
| 1973-4 | 1.13 | 0.86 | 1.00 | 1.00 | 0.32 | 1.14 | 0.88 | 0.97 | 1.05 | 0.30 |
| 1974-5 | 1.25 | 0.79 | 1.03 | 0.95 | 0.41 | 1.31 | 0.84 | 1.00 | 1.00 | 0.38 |
| 1975-6 | 1.16 | 0.79 | 0.98 | 1.03 | 0.40 | 1.20 | 0.82 | 0.95 | 1.07 | 0.38 |
| 1976-7 | 1.06 | 0.81 | 0.94 | 1.11 | 0.39 | 1.09 | 0.84 | 0.92 | 1.11 | 0.38 |
| 1977-8 | 1.04 | 0.88 | 0.96 | 1.06 | 0.42 | 1.06 | 0.90 | 0.95 | 1.07 | 0.41 |
| 1978-9 | 1.02 | 0.86 | 0.94 | 1.10 | 0.41 | 1.05 | 0.86 | 0.93 | 1.11 | 0.41 |
| 1979-80 | 1.03 | 0.84 | 0.94 | 1.11 | 0.45 | 1.06 | 0.85 | 0.92 | 1.12 | 0.44 |
| 1980-1 | 1.06 | 0.85 | 0.96 | 1.07 | 0.50 | 1.08 | 0.85 | 0.93 | 1.10 | 0.48 |
| 1981-2 | 1.07 | 0.84 | 0.96 | 1.07 | 0.55 | 1.08 | 0.85 | 0.93 | 1.10 | 0.53 |
| 1982-3 | 1.10 | 0.84 | 0.97 | 1.05 | 0.59 | 1.12 | 0.86 | 0.95 | 1.08 | 0.57 |
| 1983-4 | 1.10 | 0.89 | 1.00 | 1.00 | 0.64 | 1.11 | 0.91 | 0.98 | 1.03 | 0.63 |
| 1984-5 | 1.03 | 0.93 | 0.98 | 1.04 | 0.65 | 1.02 | 0.93 | 0.96 | 1.06 | 0.65 |
| 1985-6 | 1.05 | 0.90 | 0.98 | 1.04 | 0.68 | 1.04 | 0.91 | 0.96 | 1.07 | 0.67 |
| 1986-7 | 1.03 | 0.95 | 0.99 | 1.02 | 0.73 | 1.02 | 0.95 | 0.98 | 1.04 | 0.73 |
| 1987-8 | 1.03 | 0.98 | 1.01 | 0.99 | 0.79 | 1.02 | 0.97 | 0.99 | 1.01 | 0.78 |
| 1988-9 | 1.06 | 0.95 | 1.01 | 0.98 | 0.86 | 1.07 | 0.94 | 0.98 | 1.02 | 0.84 |
| 1989-90 | 1.03 | 0.96 | 1.00 | 1.00 | 0.91 | 1.02 | 0.97 | 0.99 | 1.02 | 0.91 |
| 1990-1 | 1.00 | 1.00 | 1.00 | 1.00 | 1.00 | 1.00 | 1.00 | 1.00 | 1.00 | 1.00 |
| 1991-2 | 1.06 | 1.00 | 1.03 | 0.94 | 1.17 | 1.07 | 1.00 | 1.02 | 0.97 | 1.14 |
| 1992-3 | 1.10 | 0.97 | 1.04 | 0.93 | 1.29 | 1.10 | 0.98 | 1.02 | 0.97 | 1.25 |
| 1993-4 | 1.09 | 0.97 | 1.03 | 0.94 | 1.36 | 1.10 | 0.97 | 1.02 | 0.98 | 1.34 |
| 1994-5 | 1.10 | 0.96 | 1.03 | 0.94 | 1.51 | 1.11 | 0.96 | 1.01 | 0.99 | 1.48 |
| 1995-6 | 1.08 | 0.99 | 1.03 | 0.94 | 1.65 | 1.07 | 0.98 | 1.01 | 0.98 | 1.61 |
| 1996-7 | 1.11 | 0.97 | 1.05 | 0.92 | 1.79 | 1.13 | 0.97 | 1.02 | 0.97 | 1.73 |
| 1997-8 | 1.12 | 0.98 | 1.06 | 0.90 | 1.84 | 1.12 | 0.98 | 1.03 | 0.96 | 1.81 |
| 1971-80 | -0.83 | 0.69 | -0.19 | 0.32 | 6.86 | -0.82 | 0.59 | 0.01 | -0.01 | 7.03 |
| 1981-90 | -0.52 | 1.57 | 0.48 | -0.87 | 4.34 | -0.86 | 1.43 | 0.63 | -0.95 | 4.46 |
| 1991-8 | 1.20 | -0.27 | 0.52 | -1.03 | 8.61 | 1.17 | -0.38 | 0.19 | -0.29 | 8.46 |

SOURCE: Ravi (2000).

During the 1990s, the bottom 30 per cent of the rural population experienced both a slowdown in the growth rate of per capita real expenditure and a sharp rise in the real price of cereals (Tables 8.1

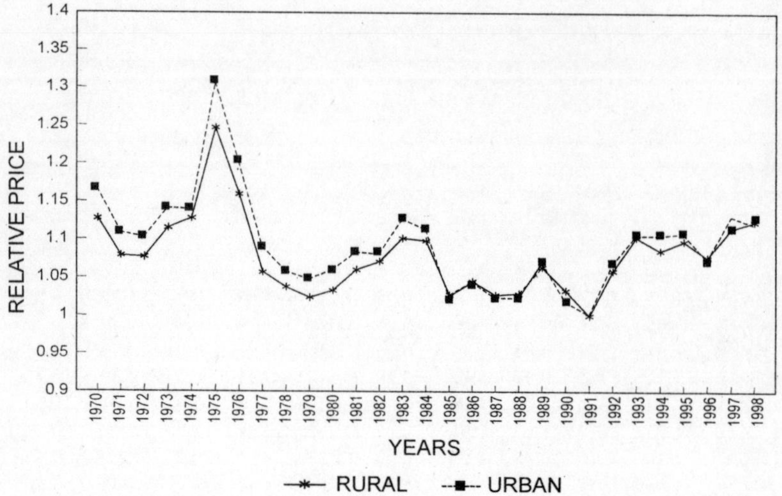


SOURCE: Derived from Table 8.7.

FIG. 8.1: RELATIVE PRICE OF CEREALS: RURAL AND URBAN

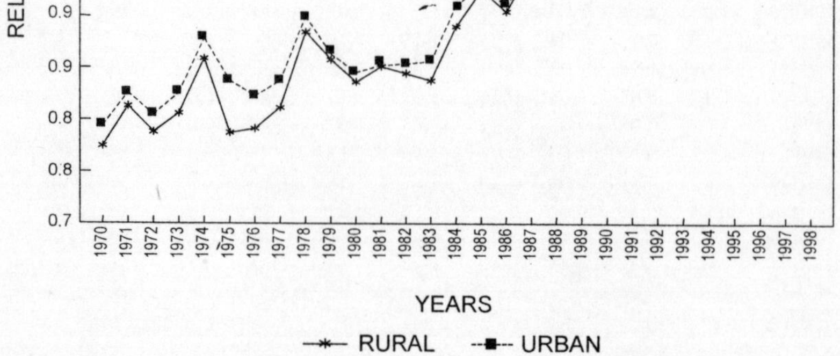


SOURCE: Derived from Table 8.7.

FIG. 8.2: RELATIVE PRICE OF NON-CEREAL FOOD: RURAL AND URBAN

and 8.2). In the absence of changes in tastes, the per capita expenditure on cereals of the bottom 30 per cent of the rural population would have stagnated, but due to changes in tastes, it declined by -1.38 per cent per annum. This had an adverse effect on their calorie intake.

## NUTRITIONAL STATUS OF RURAL HOUSEHOLDS

The National Nutrition Monitoring Bureau provides the nutritional status of rural households in seven sample states for the periods 1975-80, 1990-1 and 2000-1. The NNMB classified rural children aged 1-5 years into different nutritional grades based on weight for age (Gomez classification). The results show that the percentage of children suffering from severe malnutrition declined from 15 in 1975-9 to 11.1 in 1990-1 and further to 6.4 in 2000-01 (Table 8.8). If those classified in moderate and severe malnutrition ranges are considered together, the percentage of children afflicted by malnutrition declined from 62.5 in 1975-9 to 56.2 in 1990-1 and further to 47.7 in 2000-1. It is thus evident that in spite of some improvement in nutritional status, nearly half of the rural children suffer from malnutrition. State-wise, the decline in the percentage of severely malnourished children is very visible across all NNMB sample states except Madhya Pradesh and Orissa, and the improvement is very striking in Kerala.

There are substantial inter-state variations in the malnutrition levels of children aged below five years. In 2000-1, the percentage of moderately/severely malnourished children varied between 29 in Kerala and 64 in Madhya Pradesh. In terms of the nutritional status of children, middle income states such as Kerala, Tamil Nadu, and Andhra Pradesh performed better than higher income states like Gujarat and Maharashtra. Not surprisingly, poorer states such as Madhya Pradesh and Orissa showed the worst performance. It is noteworthy that despite the low food energy intake of children in Kerala and Tamil Nadu, these states could perform better. The National Family Health Survey (NFHS) data also reveal more or less similar patterns (Table 8.9).

The NNMB data indicate that 49 per cent of the rural adult population in the seven sample states suffered from chronic energy deficiency (CED) in 1994 (Table 8.10), and that the extent of malnutrition among the adults was closer to that of children. The regional patterns are similar to those of malnutrition among the children (NNMB, 1996). Chronic energy deficiency (CED) was found to be lower in Kerala (33 per cent) and Tamil Nadu (37 per cent) and higher in Orissa (57 per cent).

TABLE 8.8: PER CENT DISTRIBUTION OF CHILDREN (AGED 1-5 YEARS) BY NUTRITIONAL STATUS IN RURAL AREAS OF SELECTED STATES

| State | Period | Normal | Mild | Moderate | Severe |
|---|---|---|---|---|---|
| Kerala | 1975-9 | 7.5 | 35.7 | 46.5 | 10.3 |
| | 1991-2 | 17.6 | 46.7 | 29.6 | 6.0 |
| | 2000-1 | 20.8 | 50.4 | 26.9 | 1.9 |
| Tamil Nadu | 1975-9 | 6.2 | 34.2 | 47.0 | 12.6 |
| | 1991-2 | 8.0 | 39.7 | 41.7 | 5.7 |
| | 2000-1 | 10.5 | 50.6 | 35.3 | 3.7 |
| Karnataka | 1975-9 | 4.6 | 31.1 | 50.0 | 14.3 |
| | 1991-2 | 3.6 | 33.6 | 54.5 | 8.3 |
| | 2000-1 | 7.2 | 45.2 | 45.2 | 2.4 |
| Andhra Pradesh | 1975-9 | 6.1 | 32.4 | 46.1 | 15.4 |
| | 1991-2 | 9.9 | 39.2 | 41.9 | 8.9 |
| | 2000-1 | 11.5 | 48.6 | 35.8 | 4.1 |
| Maharashtra | 1975-9 | 3.2 | 25.4 | 49.5 | 21.9 |
| | 1991-2 | 4.5 | 33.3 | 44.9 | 17.3 |
| | 2000-1 | 8.2 | 39.6 | 48.0 | 7.2 |
| Gujarat | 1975-9 | 3.8 | 28.1 | 54.3 | 13.8 |
| | 1991-2 | 2.4 | 34.9 | 50.8 | 11.8 |
| | 2000-1 | 7.4 | 43.7 | 40.0 | 8.9 |
| Madhya Pradesh | 1975-9 | 8.4 | 30.3 | 45.1 | 16.2 |
| | 2000-1 | 5.8 | 30.4 | 49.2 | 14.7 |
| Orissa | 1975-9 | 7.5 | 35.9 | 41.7 | 14.9 |
| | 1991-2 | 6.0 | 38.2 | 42.5 | 13.3 |
| | 2000-1 | 6.7 | 38.9 | 47.2 | 7.2 |
| West Bengal | 1991-2 | 9.3 | 30.1 | 42.7 | 17.9 |
| | 2000-1 | 7.4 | 43.0 | 42.9 | 6.7 |
| All states* | 1975-9 | 5.9 | 31.6 | 47.5 | 15.0 |
| | 1991-2 | 7.2 | 36.3 | 45.1 | 11.1 |
| | 2000-1 | 9.0 | 43.3 | 41.3 | 6.4 |

NOTES: Based on National Centre for Health Statistics (NCHS) standards.
*Pooled estimates for Kerala, Tamil Nadu, Karnataka, Andhra Pradesh, Maharashtra, Gujarat, Madhya Pradesh and Orissa.

SOURCE: National Nutritional Monitoring Bureau, Technical Reports 18 and 21, National Institute of Nutrition, Hyderabad.

Inter-state comparisons reveal a weak correlation between nutritional status and per capita state domestic product (SDP) as well as between nutritional status and per capita calorie consumption. The state level mismatch between the food intake and nutritional status could be attributed to the differences in education, health, availability of safe drinking water, and environmental sanitation, which intervene between

TABLE 8.9: NFHS ESTIMATES OF MALNUTRITION AMONG CHILDREN

*(weight-for-age)*

| State | 1993 (Children under age 4 years) | | | 1998-9 (Children under age 3 years) |
|---|---|---|---|---|
| | Rural | Urban | All | All (Rural+Urban) |
| Andhra Pradesh | 52.1 | 40.2 | 49.1 | 37.7 |
| Assam | 51.8 | 37.3 | 50.4 | 36.0 |
| Bihar | 64.1 | 53.8 | 62.6 | 54.4 |
| Gujarat | 45.8 | 40.5 | 44.1 | 45.1 |
| Haryana | 39.4 | 33.0 | 37.9 | 34.6 |
| Himachal Pradesh | 48.3 | 30.2 | 47.0 | 43.6 |
| Jammu & Kashmir | NA | NA | 44.5 | 34.5 |
| Karnataka | NA | NA | NA | 43.9 |
| Kerala | 30.6 | 22.9 | 28.5 | 26.9 |
| Madhya Pradesh | 59.4 | 50.1 | 57.4 | 55.1 |
| Maharashtra | 57.5 | 45.5 | 52.6 | 49.6 |
| Orissa | NA | NA | 55.3 | 54.4 |
| Punjab | 47.4 | 40.0 | 45.9 | 28.7 |
| Rajasthan | 41.1 | 43.9 | 41.6 | 50.6 |
| Tamil Nadu | 52.1 | 32.3 | 46.6 | 36.7 |
| Uttar Pradesh | NA | NA | 49.8 | 51.7 |
| West Bengal | NA | NA | 56.8 | 48.7 |
| Arunachal Pradesh | 40.3 | 36.2 | 39.7 | 24.3 |
| Manipur | 31.6 | 25.9 | 30.1 | 27.5 |
| Nagaland | 30.5 | 19.7 | 28.7 | 24.1 |
| Tripura | 53.0 | 31.6 | 48.8 | NA |
| Meghalaya | 47.2 | 37.5 | 45.5 | 37.9 |
| Mizoram | 34.5 | 22.0 | 28.1 | 27.7 |
| All India | 59.9 | 45.2 | 53.4 | 47.0 |

NOTES: Children below 2 S.D. from the international reference population median are treated as suffering from malnutrition. NA: not available.

SOURCE: National Family Health Survey (NFHS), 1993 and 1998-9.

food and nutritional status (Seckler 1982; Pelletier et al. 1995). A better environment would reduce food wastage caused by infections and diseases. The improved nutritional status at a comparatively lower level of consumption of food energy as observed in Kerala and Tamil Nadu could be due to better health care and nutritional intervention.

*Does all this imply that the calorie intake matters little*? While empirical evidence tends to suggest a positive association between the calorie intake and nutritional status, the responsiveness is likely to be affected

TABLE 8.10: ESTIMATES OF DISTRIBUTION OF PERCENTAGE OF ADULTS BY BMI GRADE IN RURAL AREAS OF SELECTED STATES

| State | BMI Grade | | |
|---|---|---|---|
| | CED | Normal | Obesity |
| Kerala | 33.2 | 56.5 | 10.3 |
| Tamil Nadu | 37.3 | 53.1 | 9.6 |
| Karnataka | 53.8 | 41.9 | 4.3 |
| Andhra Pradesh | 49.4 | 46.4 | 4.2 |
| Maharashtra | 51.0 | 44.6 | 4.4 |
| Gujarat | 53.1 | 42.1 | 4.8 |
| Madhya Pradesh | 53.3 | 46.0 | 0.7 |
| Orissa | 57.3 | 41.1 | 1.6 |
| Pooled | 48.5 | 46.5 | 5.0 |

NOTES: BMI – Body Mass Index.
CED – Chronically Energy Deficient.
SOURCE: NNMB Report, 1996.

by the factors relating to health and environment. What is a desirable diet from a nutritional perspective thus remains unsettled in view of the controversies. It is also unclear as to how much of the malnutrition is due to an inadequate diet and how much due to the environment.

## CONCLUDING OBSERVATIONS

While India could achieve some success in reducing the income poverty during the last three decades, it has failed to make much dent in reducing the widespread malnutrition. As many as half of the pre-school children suffer from malnutrition and close to half of the adult population suffer from chronic energy deficiency in the rural areas.

The per capita calorie intake of the population as a whole declined marginally during the last three decades despite significant increase in per capita expenditure in real terms. There have been substantial changes in the consumer preferences from food to non-food, within food from cereal to non-cereal food, and from 'coarse' to fine cereals. The bottom 30 per cent of the rural population had a per capita intake of only about 1670 kcal per day, compared to the nutritional requirement of 2200 kcal per day.

Despite the disquieting trend in food energy intake, the nutritional status has improved though at a slow rate. What is more important, middle income states such as Kerala, Tamil Nadu and Andhra Pradesh have performed better than higher income states such as Maharashtra, West Bengal and Gujarat. Not surprisingly, lower income states such as Madhya Pradesh and Orissa had the worst performance.

Improvement in food consumption is a necessary but not a sufficient condition for overcoming the problem of malnutrition in India. Apart from inadequate consumption, the other important causes of malnutrition are high incidence of gastrointestinal and respiratory infections and behavioural factors such as faulty breast-feeding and weaning practices, all of which contribute to the low absorption of nutrients from the food consumed. Economic growth, left to itself, may not have a dramatic impact on the nutritional situation in the near future, although it provides greater opportunities for public intervention. Effective and efficient food and environmental interventions are needed until the poor are freed from food and nutritional deprivation.

## REFERENCES

Mortorell, R. and T.J. Ho (1984), 'Malnutrition, Morbidity and Mortality', *Population and Development Review*, Supplement to vol. 10, pp. 49-68.

Pelletier, D.L., E.A. Frongillo, Jr., D.G. Schroeder and J.P. Habicht (1995), 'The Effects of Malnutrition on Child Mortality in Developing Countries', *Bulletin of the World Health Organisation*, vol. 73, no. 4, pp. 443-8.

Radhakrishna and C. Ravi (1992), 'Effects of Growth, Relative Price and Preferences on Food and Nutrition', *Indian Economic Review*, vol. 27, Special Number, pp. 303-23.

Rao, C.H.H. and R. Radhakrishna (1997), 'National Food Security: A Policy Perspective for India', Plenary paper, 27th International Conference of Agricultural Economists, 10-16 August, Sacramento, California and published in G.H. Peter and J.V. Braun (ed.) *Food Security, Diversification and Resource Management: Re-focussing the Role of Agriculture,* Ashgate, London.

Rao, C.H.H. (2000), 'Declining Demand for Foodgrains in Rural India: Causes and Implications', *Economic and Political Weekly*, vol. 35, no. 4, 22 January, pp. 201-6.

Ravi, C. (2000), *Complete Demand Systems, Welfare and Nutrition: An Analysis of Index Consumption Data,* Centre for Economic and Social Studies, Hyderabad.

Seckler, D. (1982), 'Small but Healthy', in P.V. Sukhatme (ed.), *Newer Concepts in Nutrition and their Implications for Policy,* Maharashtra Association for the Cultivation of Science, Pune.

# 9

# Socio-economic Analysis of Reproduction and the Family

*Nirmala Banerjee*

## INTRODUCTION

The concepts of reproduction and family still sit somewhat uneasily on the periphery of the discipline of economics. It is not that the entire area has been ignored; since classical times, reproduction in some sense has been a widely discussed issue in economics. It continues to dominant, but in a different context, the neoclassical theories of Home Economics. However, the treatment of these concepts so far by economists has not been found satisfactory for dealing with issues both in development economics and in feminist studies. Opponents criticize the classists for homogenizing the reproductive behaviour of all families according to their class. On the other hand, the treatment by the neoclassical home economists of intra-family relations as market dealings between free individuals is also unacceptable to them. The Marxist-feminists, who share this unease, have moved towards accepting the importance of looking inside the family and have been debating among themselves about the conceptualization of family relations as an extension of class relations. In general, in feminist literature, economic theories related to these issues stand accused of a general failure to appreciate the multiple functions of a family and the very real play of patriarchal power through gender relations in their performance.

Reproduction and family cover a vast number of topics from various bio-physical and social science disciplines. This chapter deals only with those aspects that interface with economics. Even within that limit, it aims to focus on the interaction between these two institutions and the position of women in that society and economy. My approach is to start with an explicit acknowledgement of the relevance of gender-related power play in understanding the concepts of family and reproduction: my aim is to critically review from that standpoint some of the existing theories in this field.

The paper draws extensively on literature from multiple sources, but to a large extent, its perspective has been influenced by the South Asian database and experiences with which I am most familiar. I have tried to point this out whenever relevant. However, in the present context, relating the issues to a specific set of local institutions is in fact a crucial part of the methodology applicable to the analysis.

Neither the family nor its reproductive behaviour is static in any society and their nature changes radically in the process of economic development. So, while some of the theoretical positions considered here were conceived of as far back as the eighteenth century, they are being considered here in a dynamic context. Boserup's early work, *Women in Development* (Boserup 1970), had provided a framework for bringing together considerations of justice in gender relations *vis-à-vis* outcomes in the general economy in the course of development. It was she who had perceived women not as supplicants for handouts in the process of economic development but as rational beings who have been denied their rightful share of productive resources and well-being (Jaquette 1990). Boserup, however, had left out of consideration the family and women's reproductive responsibilities; nor had she considered the possibilities of an interaction between economic development and these institutions. An attempt is made here to see how the interweaving of all these helps us to understand the trends in women's position in the process of development.

## GENDER AS AN ANALYTICAL TOOL

Since the present analysis is in terms of the gender dimensions of reproduction and the family, it is important to clarify the definition of gender and the purpose that it is to serve. Essentially, gender refers to the whole set of sex-specific social and material, as against physical attributes which each society attaches to being a man or a woman. Consequently, it also refers to the values that are implicit in the relations between men and women. A society defines these attributes not only as a natural part of maleness or femaleness, but also as the morally and socially acceptable one. However, as social constructs, the attributes and the gender relations that they posit can and do vary widely from one region/community to another. They are, moreover, capable of change and correction, perhaps consciously, through specific social actions or contingently, through changes in socio-economic institutions that economic development triggers off. Gender relations thus are a major social force in any society, but they are by no means a naturally determined invariant that has to be accepted as such.

Concepts of reproduction, family, and gender are closely linked with each other; family is the site where reproduction takes place. On the other hand, each society develops an elaborate set of social, legal, and political institutions for supporting the family precisely because it wants to ensure that reproduction takes place as per norms and practices of its choice. The standard patterns of reproduction and the family are, in turn, based on and shaped by the specific notions of gender relations, i.e. of the relative roles, status, and powers of men and women that prevail in that society. And, as the form of gender relations undergoes a revision in the course of development, the shape and norms of the typical or ideal family and reproductive behaviour also keep altering. In general, gender relations are projected to be ideologically derived from the traditions and values that the society morally upholds; *but everywhere, they have a strong material content in so far as these beliefs and practices set the norms for allocation of work between men and women and of access to and ownership of assets and wealth.* These norms are also the sanctions behind the pattern of sexual division of labour that is accepted and practised by any society.

In spite of their variability, gender relations today in most societies are patriarchal, i.e. they justify men having powers over women to subordinate them. Basically, it has been made a part of the cultural consciousness of both men and women that men are the norm endowed with human rights as well as with the capacity for comprehension, judgement, and reformulation of social mores.[1] Women are assumed not to possess such capacities and are therefore expected to remain subservient to the authority and judgement of their superiors, the males. Different cultures have used different arguments to justify this male bias. Lerner, for example, points to the Paulinist tradition in Christianity which justified male superiority on grounds that men were the glory of God while women were the glory of man. Woman had been created of man and for man (Lerner 1993). Mernissi, on the other hand, shows that Islam considers men and women as potential equals but justifies male control over women on grounds that women have dangerous capacities that need to be subdued (Mernissi 1975). For Hindu society, Bhattacharya traces the roots of the pattern in mainstream India back to Aryan texts, which had placed women in the same category as the *shudra* (a low-born) or a dog (Bhattacharya 1989).

In general, gender relations are formulated with the purpose of controlling women's sexuality, their bodies and their labour. Most societies put some controls on all three; but there can be wide differences in the relative emphasis laid on each as well as in the instruments used for achieving the control. Also, some of the controls tend to lose their hold or become more class-differentiated in the course of capitalist development. This issue of the controls and their interaction with the economy at the household and macro-levels is of crucial relevance for the later part of this chapter.

The conceptualization of gender in this form is based on substantial factual evidence that is available for almost any country, both from official sources and from field studies in different disciplines. For example, official data for India over a long time had been indicating some persistent disparities *vis-à-vis* men in the position of women in India; this data has now been analysed by experts in several fields who all agree that such disadvantages of women are not natural but the result of a systematic, gender based bias. This bias is large enough to show up in many macro-measures; there is a marked difference in the chances of survival of girls as compared to boys, their achievements in education and training for marketable skills are significantly inferior, and their status as workers and decision-makers compares very poorly with that of men (See, for example, GOI 1974; Dreze and Sen 1995; Agnihotri 1995; Banerjee 1985; Visaria 1999). Similar evidence of a gender bias to a greater or smaller degree is available for most countries and cultures. This sex/gender dichotomy, i.e. the distinction made between biological differences and social relations of power between men and women was first highlighted by Beauvoir (1972) who argued that 'a woman is not born but made'. Although Beauvoir's hypotheses about the origins of gender-based subordination have been criticized on several grounds, her basic conceptualization of gender as a social institution created through a culture of patriarchy has been widely accepted.[2]

## REPRODUCTION

One can distinguish between three socially significant processes in human reproduction; these are: biological reproduction, reproduction of the labour force, and social reproduction (Eldholm, Harris and

Young 1977). Social reproduction refers to the ways in which social practices, values, etc., get passed from generation to generation. The construction of gender roles and providing social approval for its practices is one of the more important parts of that process. In this chapter, that process is taken as the starting point and for that reason, I will not discuss social reproduction any further but confine myself to the other two aspects.

In standard economic literature, the term reproduction is not in common use[3] despite the fact that it is the main determinant of the quantity and quality of the supply of human labour in a given economy and also of the ultimate demand for its products. These aspects are connected both with biological reproduction as well as with the reproduction of the labour force and they have been a subject matter for discussions by classical political economists and by neoclassical economists.

## BIOLOGICAL REPRODUCTION

Biological reproduction consists only of the processes of child-bearing and breastfeeding which, by nature, are exclusive functions of women. In discussing the determinants of variations in the size of the population around a 'steady state' level, classical economists from eighteenth century onwards assumed that this reproductive activity was entirely a natural phenomenon with no scope for human discretion. They were trying to explain the fact that this 'natural' process had not led to a continuous growth of the total population to an untenable level. In other words, their models were about the mechanism that could control this inevitable explosive growth in the number of people. Malthus' theory of population (Malthus 1798), for example, assumed that fertility, or the number of children born to a woman, was naturally determined and constant over time. It was an outcome of 'passion between sexes which (is) necessary and will stay in the present state'. Given this, (Malthus' affiliation to the Anglican church made him reject the use of contraceptives), there was no question of individual choices regarding the number of children that each couple would have; therefore, all populations would inevitably tend to grow. In Malthus' analysis, the main determinant of the actual size of the population in any country was not the fertility rate, but the rate of mortality. Given the assumption of diminishing returns to labour, a rise in the population would mean a fall in the real wages and therefore in the standards of living. That would lead to a rise in the rate of mortality through 'misery and vice'. The subsequent fall in the size of the population would once again raise real wages and lower mortality rates: the cycle would go on till, at the optimal level, the rate of population growth would be zero. The only way fertility rates could be variable and influence the overall size of the population in Malthus' model would be through delays in marriages. But in Malthus' analysis, this could postpone the tragedy only if the whole class of workers rather than the odd couple were to follow the prescription. The model thus gave no scope either for individual choices regarding fertility or for social factors such as the pattern of gender relations influencing those choices.

Malthus' theory fell into disfavour in the First World when it became apparent that demographic trends in this century could not be accounted for in that framework. With rising incomes and prosperity, the much more common pattern has been for *fertility to fall, not to rise*. Also there have been sudden shifts like the baby boom and baby bust in the USA in the 1950s and the 1960s which too suggest that there are other forces at work than the iron law of wages.

In developing countries, however, there has been a resurrection since the 1950s of the spectre of Malthus and overpopulation by bodies like the Population Council; policy makers in several of the countries including India were persuaded about this imminent danger so that they accepted that population regulation was a state function. India under Jawaharlal Nehru was perhaps the first country to adopt an official family planning policy (Karkal 1997).

## Regulating Fertility

Nevertheless, the current trend has moved considerably away from Malthus even in the developing countries. It starts by recognizing that even in primitive societies, fertility is seldom allowed to take its natural course. Most societies have their own conventions and ways of regulating when and how many children of what sex are to be born and raised. This regulation, furthermore, is a matter of social, political as well as personal choices. Societies mainly differ in their stands regarding who is entitled to make the choices. For each society, thus, the question is: *who does the regulation—the woman, the couple, the household and kin, or the state?*

Traditional patriarchal societies, like the Indian one, have entrusted these decisions to household authorities to regulate fertility in their own lights. Measures such as early marriages of girls, taboos on widow remarriage and on children born out of wedlock along with well-established conventions regarding childbearing and childrearing practices or even female infanticide, all help the family to have the desired number of children of each sex. The measures also effectively limit or even deny women's agency in these matters. In general, for successful implementation of such controls, gender relations are developed in a way that make women an unresisting instrument at the command of family authorities.

On the other hand, an autocratic regime as in China completely converts fertility decisions into a matter for state diktats; the state reserves for itself the power to punish those who break its orders on this point. Other societies have relied more on persuasive measures, providing or withdrawing incentives to women for having or not having more children. Rules for maternity leave, schemes for mother and child welfare, tax rebates on incomes, or even giving presents for accepting contraceptives are some of the measures tried for influencing individual couples' fertility decisions towards levels compatible with state priorities at that juncture. Individual couples, according to Malthus, were slaves merely to their own passions; in reality, they, particularly the women, are at the command of the various authorities whose interests are at stake in the determination of the fertility pattern.

### Home Economics

From 1950s onwards, there was a growing response from mainstream economists to this renewed interest in population growth; this came to be known as the 'Chicago-Columbia' approach. This approach acknowledged that fertility was not automatic and that families had discretion in determining the number of children they had. Therefore, they undertook a micro-level analysis of fertility decisions within the family. While Samuelson (1956) and Leibenstein (1957) were among the earliest writers of this new genre, Gary Becker's work is the better-known and oft-quoted work in this field which is now known as Home Economics.

Home Economics is now a well-established branch of main-stream economics; it deals with the relations between family members and their decisions, particularly about the number and quality of children they are to have. Becker defines a family in terms of the 'altruistic' relations between its members (Becker 1981): this implies that the utilities of family members are interdependent and positively related to each other (Becker's family is a nuclear one, consisting of parents and their unmarried, and presumably minor, children). Parents' utility depends on their own life-cycle consumption, and separately, on their degree of altruism per child, the number of children, and the utility of each child. The couple chooses optimal values of its own consumption, the number of children, and the amount of capital transferred to each child, while taking account of the costs of rearing children and of the dependence of their utility on the utility of the children (Becker 1988, p. 4). Becker uses a supply-demand framework though his main emphasis is on the demand for children by parents. That is to say, he does not consider problems of infertility, etc. Having children is neither automatic nor problematic and each couple decides on the number of children they are to have as per its own calculations of maximizing utility.

In his earlier writings, Becker was dealing with the problem that while Malthus had predicted a positive relation between incomes and fertility, actual fertility rates, particularly in Europe, had been dropping continuously throughout this century, even when incomes were rising. Becker argues that the effect of rising incomes is offset by the substitution effect arising from the costs to the family of having children. Becker talks of two kinds of costs, the cost of improving the quality of children and the cost of the time of the mother. Of these, parents' pursuit of quality of children is the major cause why we do not, in general, get a positive relation between income and fertility. In Becker's model, the altruism per child is negatively related to the number of children, i.e. the positive effect of each child's own utility on the parents diminishes as the number of children goes up.

> When quality per child is an argument in parents' utility function, the shadow price of the number of children depends on the expenditure on quality and the shadow price of the quality depends on the number of children. This means that anything that increases expenditure on quality of children would also raise the cost of the number of children, generating a further substitution effect away from quantity of children to quality of children. (Ben-Porath 1982, p. 55)

Becker's argument about the cost of quality of children has since been developed into an extensive literature about investment in human capital. Becker also developed a macro model where investment in human capital is the main determinant of the rate of economic growth (Becker 1988).

## Gender Relations in Home Economics

It is actually the treatment of the other cost, the cost of women's time, that is of more interest to this paper. Since Becker first wrote about it, the idea has been developed more systematically by authors like Willis (1974), Ben-Porath (1974), Becker and Lewis (1974), and Mincer and Pollachek (1982). The argument is that the loss of market earnings of mothers due to demands on their time in childrearing represents a measure of family investment in the human capital of their children. Therefore, as market opportunities for women's employment improve, the opportunity cost of women's time rises and inflates the cost of having children. This dampens the demand for children in general.

Becker is one of the few economists who explicitly include into a family's stock of available well-being the output of the nurturing work that goes on within the household, both of the cooking/cleaning and of the affective kind: it is the latter which gives people love and security. That is to say, in Becker's theorization, the income of a family consists of both the money income earned by market activities and the value generated by home-based, non-market activities. Given that, why should the argument about the rising cost of children in terms of a mother's time be only in relation to her market activities? Having more children adds to housework; it also affects the physical condition of the mother. However, models regarding household decisions about the number of children to have do not regard these non-market, women-specific items as costs to be included in calculating either the losses incurred by having children, or the costs of investment made in them. Nor is the fact that these costs increase with the numbers considered a possible reason why families may opt for having fewer children. This contradicts Becker's position that production of well-being through intra-household activities is also a part of a family's total income. *If the additional gains through women's housework are supposed to be a consideration for the family's welfare, then the cumulating costs of having more children should also go in as a negative welfare or a cost for the family.*

That they are not regarded as such indicates that in the Beckerian world too, women-specific costs that do not have a male equivalent are automatically degraded. Unless women earn an independent money wage, their positive or negative contribution to the family's state of well-being is not valued adequately. Goode in his comment on Becker's paper on marriage (Becker 1974) says that, 'Becker's paper sometimes goes awry not because it uses economic reasoning in non-market areas, but because it fails to take note of powerful non-market variables' (Goode 1974). But this neglect can also be due to the implicit assumption that women's work inside the household is not a cost but a source of pleasure for them. This in turn means either that Becker too assumes that a woman's biology is her destiny, or that, as an inherently inferior member of the family, costs specific to her can be disregarded.

## Policies for Regulating Fertility

However unreal these assumptions, it may be argued, in true Friedman-like manner, that assumptions by themselves merit little scrutiny and theories should be judged by their success in generating and satisfying empirical predictions (Friedman 1953). This theorization has in fact triggered off a spate of very systematic empirical work relating fertility to women's work, schooling, income, and wage rates in many countries.[4] In their turn, the findings have been repeatedly interrogated for guiding population policies particularly in developing countries.

In the Indian context, the possible impact of women's literacy and education on fertility has been widely studied though the resultant literature continues to give mixed signals (see, for example, Gurumurthy 1990; Basu 1992; Cassen 1994; Jain and Nag 1986; Basu and Jeffery 1996; Basu 1996). A straightforward statistical analysis such as that of Gurumurthy (1990) finds that among the Yennadis, a tribe of Andhra Pradesh, the few opportunities of education for women have had little impact on their fertility. In a more sophisticated analysis, Basu and Jeffery (1996) suggest that the relation between schooling for girls and their fertility rates is by no means a direct or an infallible one. After allowing for the fact that the interaction between women's education and fertility has behaved differently at different stages of economic development (see Jeejibhoy 1991), they suggest that *women's autonomy* is the main channel through which schooling can affect fertility. Based on a detailed review of available empirical work from several South Asian countries, Basu and Jeffrey re-examine each of these terms—schooling, fertility, and above all, women's autonomy. Schooling as it is available to most girls in South Asia can often reinforce discipline and docility among women and reduce their autonomy. On the other hand, that schooling and marriage are still mutually exclusive in this region means that more schooling does postpone girls' marriages and, thereby, their years of childbearing.

The need to introduce the concept of women's autonomy into this debate underscores the inadequacy of the home economics kind of analysis of fertility. There are societies, where women, educated or not, are traditionally subject to others' decisions about when she is to be married, whether she is to participate in wage work or not, and most definitely, how many children at what age and at what intervals she is to bear. Her education can only make a difference to this position if, for some reasons, it does increase her say on these matters. Admittedly, studies from various regions and times, when taken together suggest that there is no single or uniform indicator of this autonomy which is common to all times and areas (Caldwell 1987); even within the same country, a simple variable like women's access to outside paid work does not work unambiguously. Nor is the effect of higher levels of education always towards enhancing this autonomy. But as Basu and Jeffery put it,

> The consequences of schooling for particular aspects of women's autonomy must be specified in much more details before we can readily accept the role that is claimed for it (Basu and Jeffery 1996, p. 22). And simultaneously, 'female education needs to be pushed . . . to cross the threshold beyond which the net effects on female autonomy are all positive and, by extension, those on fertility are all positive. (Basu op. cit., p. 70)

Dreze and Sen have also argued that it is through its effect on women's agency that education and other variables such as women's mobility can affect fertility most effectively. In fact for them, women's ability to make free choices is the most relevant variable; they demonstrate this by comparing China's coercive methods with the more superior one of voluntary actions of women in some parts of India, especially in Kerala, in response to improvements in levels of their education and mobility as well as their access to health services (Dreze and Sen 1995, Chs. 4 and 7).

## REPRODUCTION OF THE LABOUR FORCE

The analysis that is focused on fertility ignores the other reproductive task that is generally carried out within families[5] and is equally important for the perpetuation of a society. This includes all the processes that nurture human beings from birth onwards and ensure that they are given the necessary equipment for carrying out their roles in the economy and the society. Each child born in a family is given the physical and mental inputs required for her to become an adult member of the society; each worker member, similarly, is given the everyday inputs that replace the energy lost during his daily chores. Households also look after their members when they are ill, unemployed or old. A welfare-oriented state may provide some of these functions, but if it abstains from any of those, it is assumed that the household will automatically do the work. Household members are entitled to these services even if they do not contribute to the kitty. In any case, no wage is paid for the work involved and no price is charged for the supply received. In other words the household is engaged in functions that produce use value and not exchange value.

Standard economic theory, however, considers the household strictly as a unit of consumption; its consumption is limited to what can be purchased out of the incomes earned by its members in the market economy. The household sends its workers to sell their labour in the market economy. In return, the members get incomes, which, the economist assumes are pooled and then spent on market purchases of goods and services. From the point of view of national accounts, a household's total consumption is supposed to be limited to what it can buy out of these incomes. If it undertakes any production for its own consumption within the household, that output is not considered a part of the national product; similarly, engaging in such tasks is not considered an economic activity and it does no make the person a productive worker unless at least a part of that output is exchanged in the market. International conventions for measuring country-wise national product do make an exception in the case of subsistence agriculture in developing countries even when the entire output is produced and consumed by household members. But others like gathering freely available materials including water, fuel and fodder, storing and processing of food and other raw materials, rearing animals, growing vegetables or making clothes, all of which add significantly to the household's real income, remain out of economic calculations.

Moreover, economists ignore the huge range of activities that provide comfort and nurture within the household to its members— care of the children, of the sick and the old as well as the daily services of cooking, cleaning, etc., which are essential for restoring labour power.

Generally, it is assumed that, in a developed market economy, most of these goods and services, even operations of child care, nursing, etc., would be provided by the market at a price. However, it has been estimated, admittedly with some rather grandiose assumptions that, if the money values of all such intra-household activities for 'reproduction and maintenance of household members' had been included in it, the 1990 estimate of the US GNP would have gone up by no less than 30 per cent. A similar calculation for Pakistan showed that its GNP would have gone up by over 80 per cent (Cloud and Garrett 1997). Another author has argued that, since more and more women in the USA are taking up wage work, an increasing part of the work they earlier used to do for free at home is being replaced by market purchases (e.g. eating out rather than at home). As a result, these activities, which were earlier left out of national income calculations, are now being valued and added to the GDP. That is to say, the GDP is being overvalued by additions to it of the value of work that had earlier been ignored. Therefore, the actual growth of the US GDP was estimated to be slower by at least one percentage point in the 1990s (Madrick 1997). A calculation on a similar basis showed that, corrected for this bias, the GDP for Norway between 1970 and 1990 was actually smaller by about 20 per cent (Aslaksen and Koren 1996).

## WOMEN AND THE SEXUAL DIVISION OF LABOUR

In almost all known societies, these functions done within the household are assigned exclusively to women even though none of them require any qualities that are specific to the biological features of femaleness. Such conventions rest on what is called the 'sexual division of labour' (SDL); the SDL has a long history going as far as testified by the myth of man the hunter and woman the home-maker. Engels felt that this was because such nurturing tasks were really an extension of biological reproduction and therefore it was 'natural' to assign them to women. But he argued that, in the domestic mode of production, this had not denied women a role in the productive work (and therefore, presumably, a status equal to men) since both kinds of tasks were located close to home. However, with the accumulation of private property, alienation of workers from their tools and separation of the sites of productive and reproductive work that had undermined women's economic position. When productive work came to be located away from home, they could no longer combine it with housework (Engels 1975; Mies 1986). Engel's remedy for women's exploitation under capitalism was for women to join social production through socialization of the tasks of nurturing, and disintegration of the working class family.

On the other hand, home economics is the one branch of neo-classical economics that considers goods and services produced within the household for the use of household members as a part of the latter's total 'income'. But it does not discuss its valuation or its inclusion in the GDP of any country. Becker's *Treatise on Family* (Becker 1981) has a chapter on the 'Division of Labour within Households and Families'; which analyses the way the work of intra-household production is to be allotted between different members. The discussion is garbed in terms of comparative advantage of different members in different skills and specialization of training for different tasks: but Becker admits that 'Although the sharp sexual division of labour in all societies between the market and household sectors is partly due to gain from specialized investments, it is also due to intrinsic differences between sexes' (p. 21). In other words, here too, it is the biological element, reinforced by rational economic calculation, which acts as the crucial variable in explaining the sex roles.

## The Feminist Position

The feminists' analysis of the sexual division of labour, however, starts from the premise that the roles assigned through it to men and women are not *complementary*. 'Rather, we can turn the argument on its head: only in a society where men and women constitute unequal genders is there any reason why gender should be an important organizing principle of the social division of labour, with the exception of the physical processes of childbearing' (Mackintosh 1981, p. 5).

Contrary to the Marxist position that the capitalist mode of production is responsible for women's subordination, many of us hold that *unequal gender relations are independent of the prevailing mode of production*. More important, women's participation in wage work does not automatically emancipate them from the work burden associated with reproduction of labour power (Pearson et al. 1981). Under capitalism, when reproductive and productive activities get separated in space, it is the women who are automatically made responsible for the former. This means that women's responsibility for such work is a part of an already established pattern and women have no power to question this division of labour. Anthropological evidence from a wide range of countries and cultures shows that the division between tasks for males and females is not the same in all societies. But common to all is the fact that there is always such a line and its demarcation is always a male prerogative (Rosaldo 1974).[6]

Studies from India show that earning a significant (i.e. over 40 per cent) of the family income does not relieve women from these tasks (Banerjee 1985b, 1993; Batliwalla 1985; Tom 1989; Ghotoskar 1995; Workers' Solidarity Centre 1995). These studies relate to West Bengal, Karnataka, and Maharashtra and cover workers in a wide range of occupations and modes of production from domestic workers, home-based workers, family helpers in cottage industries, workers in factories of multinational corporations (MNCs), and also in public sector banks. Fieldwork for these studies had been done at different times in a long time-span from the mid-1970s to the mid-1990s. In other words, it is a remarkably stable and persistent pattern. Also, the situation is not much different in advanced industrial economies of Japan and South Korea where most young girls complete high school. Over 80 per cent of women in their early twenties were in the labour market; but most of them would leave their jobs when they get married because housework and childcare were still regarded as exclusively women's jobs (Banerjee 1999).

## SDL and the Nature of Women's Work

Mackintosh's argument that was quoted above rests precisely on this observed stability of the SDL. This outcome cannot be explained except by the existence of a relation of power between the genders. This power relation moreover has to be internalized by all members of the society. Parents of daughters socialize their children to accept and follow it. In order to avoid disputes and protests by the losers, the society builds many myths around women's role in the household; all these portray this work as acts of love rather than any kind of a chore. Whatever material benefits the woman gets as a member of the household are not tied to her doing the work, or doing it well. Also because it is not to be regarded as work or a cost to the woman, households in general are indifferent to her efficiency in doing it and do not allot resources for tools that could lighten that burden. Until the women's movement in India started talking in the 1970s about the enormous burden on women of fetching drinking water from distant sources, public policies for drinking water supply had focused mainly on providing everybody with a source of safe water but not necessarily a convenient one. In other words, households and the society set down their requirements of the level and contents of housework expected from the woman and it is left to her to find ways of doing it, whatever may be the cost of it to her.[7]

Apart from the injustice implied in this characterization, it means that women's work has no definite shape or sequence to it. Instead, their skill lies in being able to switch from one task to another whenever required. This may be one reason why women's labour is regarded as *flexible* because they are not expected to specialize in any particular skill but to accept whatever work is assigned to them and mix it in with their other duties. It also means that even when women take up productive work, it has to be of a kind that can withstand being intermixed with several others and are amenable to frequent stops and starts. That is why, in many parts of India, women were marginalized in the productive economy when more and more of their productive tasks became commercialized and the workplace moved away from home (Mukherjee 1987; Banerjee 1988; Banerjee and Mitter 1998). That is not to say that the constraints were entirely on the supply side, and that it was ever difficult to find women to work in factories. But it meant that among the women who did come forward for these jobs, a very high percentage were widows and deserted women (Sen 1999); and even today, among wage worker women in India, there is a preponderance of those from poorer households (Visaria 1999) where women are compelled to find work. On the demand side, the idea that women find it difficult to work outside their homes has probably dominated employers' perception of female labour in India and made them reluctant to give work to women.

For household-based enterprises too, the tasks allotted to women tend to be of the same kind. In some cases, this may mean that households find it difficult to switch to other, more productive technologies for their enterprises if that involves having to release women from their household responsibilities. If the well-being of the decision maker in the household depends on both the services of women at home as well as the returns from the enterprise, then the additional returns from adopting the new technology have to be sufficiently large to compensate for the loss to him of the comforts that depended on her housework.[8] In our work on the sericulture industry of West Bengal, we found that the sericulturist householders preferred to continue with the inferior nistari variety of seed cocoons in spite of the government efforts to push the superior bivoltin seeds. This was at least partly because of the householders' unwillingness to change the nature of women's work. Although production would have gone up, the superior crop would have needed the much greater and undivided attention of the family women; they would no longer have been able to intermix that work with their routine tasks as they had traditionally done with the nistari crop (Banerjee 1993).

## Measurement of Reproductive Work

As mentioned before, in economists' calculations, most part of reproductive work does not get recognition as being productive since there is no relation of exchange involved in the production and consumption of its output. However, there is now a growing awareness of the labour involved in it for women and the contribution it makes to the households' well-being. As a part of the campaign for women's rights, there has been a fairly strong movement in the West, especially in Germany, demanding wages for housework. In developing countries, this demand has never really caught fire; markets are not always as well-developed and a section of the economy continues to be non-monetized. Nevertheless, in India, there has been an active campaign against the fact that, despite their large work burden, women are perceived as unproductive dependents of men. Efforts are being made to get the policy makers to recognize the size of the contribution that women make, especially through their activities of gathering and foraging, processing, and preserving. These often prove crucial for the survival of the poorest households but get neglected because they are invisible, being hidden inside the household and obfuscated by images of the happy housewife engaged in labour of love.

In order to counter this, two kinds of efforts have been made in India. Since 1978-9 the National Sample Survey Organisation (NSSO), in its five-yearly surveys of employment and unemployment, has included questions for the officially non-worker women about other activities that are routinely undertaken by them. Here, participation in the standard housework tasks of cooking, cleaning, and childcare are put under the category 92, while other tasks, which add to the household's command over material goods and services are categorized as the 93 group. In states like Punjab, which are known for their marked bias against acknowledging women's work, the 93 category has netted about five times as many women as have standard queries about women's productive work (Sen and Sen 1985). While these efforts have been welcomed by the women's movement, a section of them along with the official statisticians are unhappy about the use of their results. This is for two reasons: the queries do not or cannot elicit unambiguous answers about whether or not the work was full-time or part-time. Therefore adding these participation rates to standard work participation rates is unwarranted. Secondly, they are asked only of women who are not in the official labour force. So they throw no light on the extent of women's double duties—for gainful activities as well as for housework.

The other method consists of small, intensive studies of groups of women by participatory observation methods, where the researcher spends considerable time with them to actually observe and note down the amount of time that women devote to various tasks of housework (Jain and Chand 1985; Anwar and Bilquees 1976; Freedman and Wai 1988)). Goldschmidt-Clairmont (1987) collated many such time use studies from countries and concluded that, in those countries, women's contribution to domestic activities ranged from two and a half times to 14 times that of men. She also found that because national accounts did not take into account the output of domestic activities, the GNP figures fell short by not less than 25 to 50 per cent.

The problem with this method is that it requires large amounts of trained observer time and the quality of the results depends on the quality of the fieldworkers, with the better quality workers being more costly. Also, generalizations from a few small studies done in some areas at some time to a macro-picture is also fraught with problems; the pattern of housework probably changes from the busy season to the rest of the year. It surely changes from place to place since the local environment makes a difference to the availability of water, fuel, and fodder. It must also keep changing over time and so on. This method therefore cannot be used in the regular data collection work of official agencies.

Collecting such data by either of these methods leads to a bigger problem, the problem of valuation of the contribution. If the intention is to highlight the quantum of the contribution of women through housework to the national income, then the amount has to be converted into its money value. The process is complicated by several problems. A large part of women's work is valued for the love and affection embodied in it. Even more difficult is the problem created by the fact that women internalize the socially sponsored myths about their work; therefore, in many cases they do not perceive themselves as workers and their tasks as work. If asked to recall their time schedule, they are unable to report it correctly. Also in many cases, the work cannot be separated in time from their leisure activities. All in all, unless their daily routine is observed, or at least probed with detailed questions by a third party sensitized to the issue, it is not possible to get a full record of their activities (Bhattacharya 1985).

Two methods have been suggested for this. One is to value women's time spent on work by its opportunity cost. Usually this is taken to be equivalent to the wage rate that the women would have earned had they been working on a paid job. The second method involves valuing the products of women's work at their market prices. In the examples mentioned above for the USA, the authors have used a somewhat complex variation of the income method, allowing for variations between women in their human capital endowments. Mukherjee had made an estimate of the value of women's reproductive work in India by a method mixing both the income and the output methods (Mukherjee 1986). Goldschmidt-Clairmont (1982) had found that, the wage method put the value of those activities in a range of 25 to 50 per cent. Valuation by the output method in one example from Lahore city in Pakistan gave a figure of about 35 per cent of the area's domestic product and from Nepal, an estimated 30 per cent of the household income.

I feel that while such exercises are very valuable for dramatizing the much neglected contribution of women to household survival, they are of value neither for rebuilding estimates of the national product nor for providing a correct assessment of the burden that women bear. In countries like India, there is a high rate of unemployment among women which means that the opportunity cost of women's labour may be set at zero. On the other hand, women's wage rates may be low and/or unemployment among them in a particular region may be high precisely because, *given their load of housework, the choices of wage work for women are severely limited.* The market for women's labour is far from perfect. They are subject to family taboos about their choices of work. There are prejudices on the part of employers, as mentioned earlier. And most women who enter the labour market come there in a state of desperate need, so that their supply price remains depressed. In such a situation, assessing women's contribution by these depressed wage rates is unlikely to give a realistic estimate of the value of the work.

On the other hand, a common feature of women's work is the poor, inefficient tools and technologies they are saddled with because they do not have access on par with men to resources that the family considers valuable. As a result, the product of a day's work usually yields very little in money terms. The valuation will certainly not reflect the amount of energy and time that she has to put in for those products. More important, a common characteristic of women's work is the cumulation it involves of tasks loaded on them. Valuing the product of each task separately does not take account of this piling of work. The wage method too would not allow for the long hours unless housework time is valued at overtime rates. If women were to be compensated for their work by these methods, it is possible that they will end up being losers by a large margin. To give one example: if an irrigation scheme were to stop the water supply to a village and make the women spend a longer time to fetch water, the pooled compensation that all the women may get for the present value of that time they would need is hardly likely to be sufficient for them to build an alternative water supply scheme.

## Reproductive Work, SDL, and the Labour Market

Becker's position about the relations between SDL at home and in market work is rather circular and not at all clear. The levels of investment in skill training are supposed to be one reason for male-female wage differentials; but the training given to boys and girls is supposed to follow the pattern of inherent traits which differ because of original biological differences. So the question remains: is it these biology-based differences that determine the nature of training given to men and women and thereby the wage differentials between the two, or is it the existence of such persistent differences in earnings (either due to the nature of the demand for labour or because of discrimination by employers) that leads to parents investing less in girls' training and therefore to the perpetuation of those differences (Ben-Porath, op. cit., p. 53)?

Rozenzweig and Schultz (1982) have examined the related question: do parents distribute available resources for child upbringing in a way that compensates for the children's genetic traits (or disadvantages)? Or do they follow the signals given by the market about the relative valuation of those traits and thereby try to maximize the returns to their investment? Findings based on their model indicated that parents appear to accept and follow the lead given by the market. Does that mean that the assumption of altruism, which defines the Beckerian family, is no longer applicable? If parents give a preference to the sons' welfare over the daughters' for these market-oriented reasons, their behaviour then fits better into a model where parents do not practise altruism but merely try to maximize their lifetime income and for that, pool together the present values of their own and their children's expected incomes. Folbre (1984), also questioned the conclusions arrived at by Rozenzweig and Schultz on the grounds that the model had moved away from the explanation of maximizing household welfare, since the welfare of the girl-child (as reflected in her chances of survival or of a good life) were being sacrificed in the interest of a larger future income for the others. Incorporating a taste for discrimination within the joint utility function that families maximize appeared to give an equally robust explanation. Objections like these were dismissed by Rozenzweig and Schultz in their rejoinder (1984) in the same issue of the journal on the grounds that although somewhat 'unreal', their model did have a perfectly adequate predictive power! Incidentally, that claim was also not warranted in the case of their explanation for the regional variations in sex ratios in India. As we have demonstrated from historical time series data on the same issue, the correlation between women's workforce participation rates and survival rates of the girl-child does not hold for other points of time. Instead, those variations in the region-wise treatment of the girl-child can be better explained in terms of several cultural practices (Dyson and Moore 1983; Banerjee and Jain forthcoming).

## The Household and the Market: Where Does SDL Originate?

The more important issue relates to the interrelations between the pattern of SDL in reproductive work and women's position in the labour market. Hartmann (1979) has traced the history of paid work in the USA from the seventeenth century onwards to show that in the USA, male artisans and skilled workers had used the guild system to bar women from getting into and being trained for any of the better paying jobs. This way they had confined the women to unskilled, poorly paid work. As a result, women remained dependent on men for the maintenance of their children and of themselves. Men could then force an unequal SDL within the home and put the entire load of housework on women. Walby has traced a more or less similar pattern in the non-agricultural economy of Great Britain since the sixteenth century. Under the country's laws of inheritance, women had been denied any rights to land and had been handicapped in the agrarian economy. In the process of industrialization, they were again confined to low, home-based skills because they could not become members of the guilds of artisans. The same tradition was later carried into factories where women and children got identified with unskilled work. By the beginning of the twentieth century, women had been pushed out of factory jobs and their largest single occupation was domestic help (Walby 1990). Both Hartmann and Walby thus argue that it was the inferior position of women in the labour market that accounts for the unequal SDL in reproductive work.

I have argued elsewhere (Banerjee 1999) that in the case of India, the process has probably worked differently. Indian women were also handicapped by laws that denied them rights to inheritance on par with men.[9] But more important is the fact that, even among subsistence farmers and artisans, the tradition has always been for families to arrange early and universal marriages of all children; marriages in general are patrilocal and the women move to affinal homes, where their labour, mobility, and sexuality are under the control of the husband's family. Moreover, women are taught only those productive skills that are traditionally regarded as their tasks in the family occupation. They are expected to carry out those tasks along with the housework; but they are allowed to seek work outside the household economy only if and when the household needs it and that too usually after the birth of several children. Thus, it is their position within the household that has always determined both their access and preparedness for the labour market.[10]

It can be shown that even today, these traditions play an important part in determining the nature of Indian women's labour supply as also their bargaining power in the labour market. Elsewhere I have shown that the supply function of women's labour in India is significantly different from those of women in other developed countries and also in several developing countries. Not only is their age-wise work profile different but so also is their status at entry into the labour market. For example, it is a common practice in most ESCAP (Economic and Social Commission for Asia and Pacific) countries east of Bangladesh for women to go to work as soon as schooling is finished (not before the age of 15), and for women's workforce participation rates to reach their peak between the ages of 20 to 24 years. In most of those countries, this peak in recent years has been as high as 60 to 80 per cent of the age group. The average age at marriage has been increasing rapidly and it is a common practice in those countries as in the developed countries for women to take up jobs before getting married and to work for several years to acquire some financial resources as well as work experience.

In contrast, in India, women's workforce participation rates in 1993-4 were less than 30 per cent in the age group 20-4 years; they reached their peak not before the age group 40-4 years (NSSO 1997, Table 6.2.1, pp. 80-5). In 1987-8, less than 15 per cent of the unmarried Indian women were working (*Sarvekshana* 1990, Table 30, pp. s64-s69 and pp. s206-s211). Equally relevant is the differential in the levels of educational attainments of men and women, which, as is well-known, has proved very persistent in India. In developing countries of Asia outside the Indian peninsula, these gaps are fast being made up (Banerjee 1999a). One can similarly point to the relatively slow urbanization of women in India and their concentration as workers in agriculture uptil the 1990s. In contrast, in nineteenth century Europe and, in this last quarter of the twentieth century, in Latin America, West Africa, and South-East Asia, the rate of rural to urban migration and transition from agriculture to industry were much faster for women than for men.

It is not surprising that there are these differences in the situations of women of different countries. Since gender is itself a social construct, its form is region and culture specific. It is further modified by the forces of economic development; in the case of reproductive work, its contents, as noted before, change as the economy becomes more commercialized. The interaction between these two forces—economic development and patriarchy—gives rise to innumerable possibilities about the way women will be positioned in the labour market. The Indian case is just one illustration of that.

The problem is that, so far, these inter-country variations in women's positions have been obscured by the urge felt by the supporters of gender equity to generalize about inequality between men and women across countries and cultures. Therefore, even at the cost of contradicting their own arguments about the social nature of gender, many feminists are trying to find more commonalities in women's positions everywhere than the mere fact of gender-based subordination. This tendency has been particularly strong in the analysis of women's employment, especially in the literature on the 'feminization' of the workforce. Several economists have analysed data from a large number of developing countries to show that women's industrial employment was positively and closely linked with the trends in per capita national income. This was particularly true of countries where exports had been an important instrument of growth (Standing 1989, 1999; Cagatay and Ozler 1995; Horton 1999). On that basis, it has been suggested that development is a good predictor of trends in women's employment and vice versa. Following these ideas, there has been much speculation about the possibility of a similar 'feminization' of the post-liberalization Indian industrial workforce. Many researchers have accepted this logic unquestioningly, so that the debate about women's employment in the 1990s has been mainly about the advantages and disadvantages for Indian women in this apparently imminent situation. In the meanwhile, though the actual trends in the 1990s in Indian women's employment are extremely disturbing and negative, they are being sadly neglected.

## THE FAMILY

In the last two to three decades, economists then have taken up the analysis of the concept of family, though their treatment so far, has been fairly limited by the assumptions behind it. In Marxist analysis, the family was a carryover from the pre-capitalist, domestic mode of production where households were both units of production and consumption. In a capitalist economy, its survival among the working classes was the instrument of the capitalist for extracting further surplus from the worker by making the family and women's unpaid domestic labour responsible for the reproduction of labour power. The working class family was not motivated by the concern that the bourgeoisie had for a system of ensuring legitimate transfers of property. Therefore, it was expected that workers would try to bypass the institution of the family and make the state take over the responsibilities of reproductive work. Jane Humphries (1977) has shown that, in reality, the nineteenth century working class family in England was the main support system for the non-working members of the working class, and the workers had fiercely resisted its break-up precisely because they were dissatisfied with the form of reproductive services (shades of Oliver Twist!) that the state under capitalism had offered.

In neoclassical economics, the issue has not always been treated systematically. In many aspects, as in the labour market, the assumption is of firms dealing directly with an individual; similarly, the consumer is an individual using her purchasing power, whatever its sources, along with her preferences to determine her actual purchases. On the other hand, in determining liability to personal taxes, most governments take into account the payee's family size and the number of dependents. Similarly, for official estimates of the distribution of income in an economy, the usual unit is a household: in the current public estimates and schemes for those below the poverty line, the calculations are on the basis of households in each consumption expenditure class. The estimates of the number of persons below the poverty line are made by multiplying the number of households by the average size of the household in that expenditure class. In none of these analyses is there any consideration about interpersonal relations and distribution within the household. This has some serious policy implications: it is assumed that handing over resources to the head of the household automatically results in all members getting an equitable share in them. No further attempt is made to see whether or not the weaker members did get their share of those resources.

Home economics, on the other hand, claim that it unpacks the family to take account of the relations between members, of the work going on inside it, and its division among the members. It is supposed to consider the process of arriving at both production and consumption decisions. In fact, Becker has an elaborate theory about how marriages and choice of partners are made (not in heaven!), and also about the benefits of polygyny (Becker 1976). Home economics portrays the family as if it is a firm engaged in a process of rational decision making. Just as the firm maximizes profits, the household maximizes the joint utility of the family; the assumption of altruism as an essential aspect of intra-family relations is necessary in order to get round the very tricky problem of interpersonal comparisons of tastes and preferences. In an 'altruistic' family, the head takes decisions on behalf of all members and is, by definition, a benevolent dictator who ensures that each decision by each individual member is in the interest of the collectivity. If it is not, i.e. if there is a selfish, 'rotten kid' in the family, the head can compensate for his actions through changes in allocations to him out of the rest of the family's pool of well-being. Inexplicable behaviour due to differences in tastes is allowed for, but are treated as idiosyncratic and trivial (Amsden 1980).

In his earlier models, Becker did not assume a benevolent dictator but instead that decisions about marriage and the subsequent division of labour within the household would be between equals and supposedly unexploitative; either partner, if he or she feels that the exchange involved is not satisfactory, need not enter the contract. Once the marriage has taken place the contract is assumed to be perfectly enforceable. Therefore the ex ante contract at entry to marriage is no different from the ex post outcome. This is why his two models are really not different since the partners in marriage act as if they are a single agent.

The home economics analysis has been challenged on many points; for example, as against the bland position that income within the household is pooled for disposal by the beneficent head, several reviews show that there is a marked difference in the welfare of individual members depending on who makes the spending decisions. Fathers seem to spend more on what have been called adult goods (smoking, alcohol, etc.) than mothers who spend more on food, clothing and education for children (Agarwal 1994; Kabir 1994). A similar inequality in the distribution of the responsibility for reproductive tasks has been discussed earlier in this chapter.

Most of all, the inconsistency involved in treating the family as a firm (where self-interest has the dominant role) and yet basing the analysis entirely on altruism has naturally come under attack. As Folbre says, Becker can 'allow for rotten kids but not for rotten parents, rotten husbands or rotten wives' (1984, p. 253). In a later paper Folbre reviews the evidence regarding distributional inequities within the household from many developing countries (Folbre 1986). Also, as Kabir remarks on the assumption of taste differences being idiosyncratic,

> . . . when (a) subordination of personal needs in favour of the well-being of others appears to be systematically the property of the less powerful category of individuals (women and children), while the beneficiaries of such preferences appear systematically to belong to another more powerful category (men), and when (b) the consequences of such behaviour are life-threatening levels of ill-health and malnutrition, then the notion of voluntaristic decision-making becomes patently absurd. (Kabir 1994, p. 107)

## THE BARGAINING MODELS

Several economists who share a common starting point in the critique of the Beckerian model have been grappling with alternative approaches to deal with the complexities involved in understanding intra-family interactions. These models characterize intra-household relations as outcomes of some sort of bargaining. The approach includes elements of cooperation because household members accept that they would all be better off that way than by not cooperating; but there is an array of possible cooperative outcomes of the kind that depend on which member gets what share. This can be about the division of consumption goods and services, about the division of the load of work involved in their production, and about the use of time by each member. So long as members know that breakdown of cooperation will leave each worse off than with cooperation, they seek a solution through bargaining. When the position reaches that point where making one better off is at the cost of making another worse off, the solution involve conflict of interests of different members. Depending on the threat points or the fallback position of each, the conflict will be resolved favouring one or the other. If, at a later stage, the fallback position of one changes, then there will be a renegotiation of the solution. Doss (1996) provides a competent review of the different groups of models and brings out areas of further research as suggested by the review.

The bargaining models have added significantly to the tools for analysis of intra-household relations and the institution of marriage. In feminist writings, the framework has been used profitably to account for some observed situations. Agarwal (1990), for example, has used it to explain why the rate of desertion by men of their wives in rural India tends to go up in times of calamities and famines. Hartmann (1987) similarly has discussed the relation between the increasing rates of divorce and singleness in the US and women's rising educational standards. However, in this approach, the formalized models particularly focus exclusively on individual interests and assume that these are clearly and unambiguously perceived. As Sen argues, 'this assumption misses crucial aspects of the nature of gender divisions inside and outside the family' (Sen 1990, p. 131). What persons see as their due and as their interest itself depends on the perceived notions of what is their appropriate role in that society and what they legitimately deserve as their share. These perceptions are very much produced through what Sen has called *social technology*, i.e. the social arrangements which lay down the social rules about who does what (SDL), who gets to consume what and who takes these decisions in a given social institution like the family. The information about the particular kind of social technology under which the bargaining goes on needs to be incorporated in the models. In other words, *formulating the bargaining problem has to be not in terms of unambiguously known self interests but in terms of their perception by each member in a given society.*

It is important therefore to accept that: (*a*) within the household there is no automatic optimal distribution and what will come about in reality will depend on the relative bargaining strengths of members. (*b*) In the case of some household members, even if the solution is apparently acceptable, this may merely be because they have been socialized to accept an inferior share as their just desserts. (*c*) Therefore, for policy-makers and social reformers, it should not be enough that household members have accepted a particular resolution of the conflict. They should judge its desirability in terms of some objective measure of the well-being of the subordinated members such as their longevity, their comparable nutritional and educational status, etc.

What then are the factors that determine the actual bargaining strength of each member? Sen sums these up in four groups of interlocking asymmetries. These are: (i) the differences between the options facing each member should the negotiations break down (a person's fallback position), (ii) the perceived significance of her contribution to household prosperity, (iii) the degree to which she identifies her interest with that of the household, and lastly, (iv) the ability of some members to exercise coercion over others. Sen emphasizes the need for the contribution to be visible to all for it to influence a person's bargaining power.

Agarwal (1997), writing on this topic has focused on some dimensions, which are 'critical in determining a person's bargaining power, but often get treated as exogenous and outside the realm of analytical specifications' (p. 6). She is particularly concerned about the hierarchy between the various determinants—are some more important than the others? She also explores the links between the factors influencing intra- and extra-household bargaining powers of a person. Her treatment is exhaustive and especially relevant for analysing the position of South Asian rural women. Many of the factors she brings out in fact arise out of what Sen has called social technology—the social arrangements which are especially powerful in shaping perceptions within the household of what constitutes work as well as entitlements of different members. In the Indian context, perhaps these are much more important in the short run than the visible or invisible contribution of the woman. These, moreover, play a very basic role in allowing and condoning the use of violence within the family. As

Agarwal points out, 'women's roles and modes of behaviour may be outcomes of past ideological struggles. To shift what has long been taken granted by a community into an area of contestation and discourse (from 'doxa' to 'heterodoxy') may therefore require bargaining' (p. 19).

Within a given cultural milieu, it is not clear how the bargaining process would work over time. Obviously, the methodology allows for changes in a person's bargaining position as illustrated by examples of how women's status is enhanced when they start earning a money wage. So, is the process of change a continuous one? That is, does one look for a steady curve to depict a person's changing bargaining power? That portrayal does not appear to fit the facts, which show that women's burden of housework remains almost unchanged even when they start contributing substantially to the household's prosperity. Does it then work through continuous and gradual changes in the relative importance of various determinants? Or can a sudden and critically large shock to a particular variable alter the entire picture? All these questions are very critical for formulating movements and policies. For example, in India, though there has been much discussion on the theme of patriarchy and its roots within the household, all policies and movements have focused on bringing about a change through creating employment opportunities for women. One can argue very cogently on the basis of past experience that employment projects, that do nothing to alter the intra-household SDL and power structure, do little to empower women.

Bargaining models are methodologically formulated in terms of individuals, but the framework has the potential for 'accommodating the idea of gender asymmetry as the product of structural rather than purely individual inequalities in power, privilege and resources' (Kabir 1994, p. 112). In other words, the framework can be used to analyse the prevailing gender relations at a societal rather than merely personal levels. However, in order to understand what structure is relevant in a particular situation, a researcher has to start with a fairly clear idea about the basic structures of that particular society. It is possible that a scholar working on West African families may not be equally thrilled with the analysis of Sen (1990), Agarwal (1997), and Kabir (1999) as are those of us working on South Asian gender relations. Even a highly abstract theoretical formulation in this case seems to be affected by the point from which the theories are being initiated.

## THE TRANSACTIONS COST APPROACH

The transaction cost approach has not been used very often in the analysis of households perhaps because it focuses mainly on the role of the family as a governance structure for economic activity. But I feel that in a country such as India, where social arrangements substitute for legal provisions in governing many long-term relations, the approach is a particularly valuable one. It looks at marriage as an institutional arrangement that is both flexible enough to allow for sequential decision-making in the face of changing eventualities and rigid enough to give some security to each member from self-seeking behaviour of others. In other words, it does guarantee even for the weaker members a degree of social security that other, less formal relations cannot provide (Pollak 1985, p. 595).

The analysis rests on the assumption that families or interpersonal, long-term relations are necessary for the production of an important range of public and private goods (including children) that people consider essential and which cannot all be produced in market relations. As in all production processes, the production of those goods and services will be efficient if there is specialization in those skills by some one member. But the inter-personal relations that form the basis of these non-market production arrangements are too complex to be provided for through some explicit contracts that can work over a long period. One-period bargaining models provide us with the solution at a given point of time, given the threat point of each member then. The same framework can in principle also show how the position can change through some shifts in particular variables. But that theorization cannot deal with the question whether or not the outcome will be efficient in achieving the original aim of producing those joint benefits. It cannot also deal with the eventuality of continuous deterioration in the relative bargaining position of one partner: what is it that then keeps the relation alive in some form? Specialization in 'marriage specific' skills creates the hazard that the bargaining position of the specializing member will become increasingly vulnerable through time. Working in the home creates non-transferable skills; also, the specializing member misses out on opportunities for acquiring the kind of human capital that is essential for working in the market economy. This in turn reduces the bargaining strength of that member by cutting into her ability to compete for market opportunities. However, in spite of these changes in the relative bargaining positions of the contracting members, the contract itself may continue; this is because there are transaction costs imposed on the partner with the stronger bargaining powers, partly through social censure, but also in having to make afresh suitable arrangements for the production of those goods and services that had been supplied by the other member.

The approach is particularly helpful for understanding the nature of intra-family gender relations, especially in a patriarchal society like India. As mentioned before, Indian families can and do put a great premium on the comforts that are generated within the family by the woman who undertakes to perform a whole range of unspecified home-oriented functions. For that purpose, a woman is expected to specialize only in marriage specific skills: she is neither trained for nor allowed to develop skills that are valued in the market. Although it is known that coming late and unprepared to the labour market has very adverse effects on her position in the labour market and therefore on her bargaining position within the household, families consent to this. They do so because there is an understanding that husbands will not act on the basis of their increasing bargaining power because the breakdown of marriage-based arrangements after several years of marriage is not without costs to them. It also provides one explanation for the fact that staying in the marriage in the face of enormous maltreatment is an important value for most women. Marriage remains the one kind of governance that provides them with some strength in gender relations when their bargaining power has been eroded through long years of identifying their own interests with the household.

## WHAT SEEMS TO BE THE FUTURE?

Some recent developments especially in the US society, have given rise to a new spurt of theorization about intra-household bargaining. As mentioned earlier, even in countries where the age at marriage was not customarily low, women had accepted the bulk of the load of housework because returns to their outside work were much lower compared to that of men. This system of specialization had meant that household operations were done efficiently although at the cost of gender equity. What then happens when women get educated and look for careers in the labour market?

Wells and Maher (1999) have constructed a dynamic model in a non-cooperative bargaining framework to deal with such an issue. Any contract between the partners is incomplete in the sense that no third party can enforce it. The contract that the parties enter at marriage is renegotiable from time to time on the basis of the current state of affairs. In models where the household acts as a single maximizing unit, partners engage in complete specialization in marriage, so that the surplus from marriage is maximized. The distribution of that surplus between partners is according to the ex ante supply and demand conditions of the grooms and brides in the marriage market. The Wells and Maher model, however, imposes two further conditions: that the earnings of husbands and wives are similar and follow the same trajectory, and, secondly, there are learning effects early in the careers of both. That is to say, for building a career, it is important for both to avail of the on-the-job training in early years.

In such a situation, Wells and Maher argue that the marriage contract will have to be continuously renegotiated so as to accommodate the requirements of the wife's career. So, falling wage differentials will be associated with an increase in women's labour force participation accompanied by a fall in fertility. They also show that children will be born later in the reproductive cycle of the mother. What is more, given the persistence of the pattern of SDL within the household, women will continue to bear a disproportionately larger burden of housework, given their wage rates and labour force participation level.

I find this speculation interesting for several reasons: one is that the links between fertility and women's wage work are being qualified, and rightly, not just by the level of participation rates but also by the nature of the jobs. Unless there are learning effects of continuously staying in the job in the early years of women's careers, working will not by itself lead to postponement of marriage and childbearing. Secondly, for the husband, allowing a woman to have a career will mean that the size of the shared surplus from marriage will be reduced (because the woman does not and he will not specialize in those tasks). The increase in his share of the well-being from the increase in the wife's market income may not be sufficient to compensate him for the cut in his share of the marital surplus when its total size gets reduced. Thirdly, if the woman's having a career does not change her share in the housework (even when the total load of housework is cut down by use of gadgets, etc.), can she compete equally with men in the job market? If that is not the case, either the employers will remain prejudiced against employing women when male workers are available, or women will be forced to remain single and sacrifice the comforts and security of married life while their male counterparts can enjoy both careers and home life. Either way, it is a lose-lose game, as far as women are concerned.

## NOTES

1. Witness the fact that well-known social reformers of India, particularly in the nineteenth century, were men; even when change is to be brought about in social practices, it has to be men, not women who have to set the new norms.
2. Beauvoir had argued that being preoccupied with the tasks of childbearing and nurturing, women had lost in the race with men for knowledge and a place in history. Beauvoir thus located women's subordination in their bodies and physical functions. In order to gain their rightful position, women would have to rise above these and become subjects of history. She has been criticized for accepting men's history as the norm and treating women's work or behaviour as the deviant, making them the 'other' of history (Braidotti 1991).
3. The New Palgrave Dictionary of Economics does not mention the term reproduction, though it has sections on demography, fertility, and population, including on optimal population and population cycles.
4. See particularly *Journal of Political Economy*, vol. 82, no. 2, part II which gives papers presented at the conference on Economic Approaches to Fertility organized by the National Bureau of Economic Research with the Population Council. Several of them present empirical studies of relations between fertility and variables relating to women's wages, education, and the economic impact of marriage.
5. In this chapter, the terms household and family are used as perfect substitutes for each other.
6. Analysis of Indian census data has shown that, that women's employment in the industrial sector shrank in absolute terms between 1911 to 1961 was, in the main, due to men taking over many of women's occupations when these were commercialized (Sinha 1972, Ch. 5). Empirical studies have shown how, at the time when occupations get revalued because of changes in market conditions, men displace women from those that have been upgraded (Banerjee 1985a).
7. The SDL and women's limited access to the labour market in India has sometimes been ascribed to a notional division of space into two parts, the private and the public, with women being confined to the former (Bennett 1992). This ignores the enormous amount of economic activities that are actually done by Indian women. What women lack is not mobility in the public space but *autonomy* to take decisions about their actions, whether at home or outside.
8. This is formally similar to Bhaduri's (1973, 1979) argument regarding the landlord's resistance to adopting better technologies when he is also the moneylender to the tenant. If better technologies reduce the tenant's need for borrrowing, then the landlord's combined income from the tenant as both rent and interest may go down.
9. Agarwal (1994) has argued that even among communities like the Nairs of Kerala or the Khasis and Garos of north-east India that gave land rights to their women, the actual control and management was left in the hands of a male relative. Women were still confined to doing reproductive tasks.
10. The Rozenzweig-Schultz paper can be critiqued on another very important point. On economic grounds, a girl's parents in India do not have any incentive to invest in a

girl child since her income, if ever it was positive, would always accrue to the husband's family. Their only gain may be if the latter curtail their dowry demand in the case of a working woman; but the fact that a girl has been working before marriage is also known to go against the girl in the marriage market.

## REFERENCES

Agarwal, B. (1990), 'Social Security and the Family: Coping with Seasonality and Calamity', *Journal of Peasant Studies*, vol. 17, no. 3, pp. 341-412.

——— (1994), *Field of One's Own: Gender and land rights in South Asia*, Cambridge University Press, New Delhi.

——— (1997), 'Bargaining and Gender Relations: Within and Beyond the Household', *Feminist Economics*, Spring, vol. 3, no. 1, pp. 1-51.

Agnihotri, S.B. (1995), 'Missing Females: A Disaggregated Analysis', *Economic and Political Weekly*, 19 August, pp. 2074-84.

Amsden, A. (1980), *The Economics of Women and Work*, Penguin, Harmondsworth.

Anwar, S. and F. Bilquees (1976), *Attitudes, Environment and Activities of Rural Women: A Case Study of Jhar Sayal*, Pakistan Institute of Development Studies, Islamabad.

Aslaken, J. and C. Koren (1996), 'Unpaid Household Work and the Distribution of Extended Income: The Norwegian Experience', *Feminist Economics*, vol. 2, no. 3, pp. 65-80.

Banerjee, N. (1985), *Women Workers in the Unorganised Sector*, Sangam Books, Hyderabad.

——— (1989), 'Modernization and Marginalization of Women Workers', in K. Sangari and S. Vaid (eds), *Recasting Women's History*, Kali for Women, New Delhi.

——— (1993), 'Women in Sericulture', paper prepared for the project on the Sericulture Industry of the Centre for Studies in Social Sciences, Calcutta.

——— (1998), 'Household Dynamics and Women in a Changing Economy', in M. Krishnaraj, R. Sudarshan and Abu Salef (eds), *Gender, Population and Development*, Oxford University Press, New Delhi, pp. 245-63.

Banerjee, N. and S. Mitter (1998), 'Women Making a Meaningful Choice', *Economic and Political Weekly*, vol. 33, no. 51, 19 December.

——— (1999a), 'Women's Work Under Patriarchy', in K. Sangari and U. Chakravarty (eds), *From Myths to Markets*, Manohar, New Delhi.

——— (1999b), 'Can Markets Alter Gender Relations?', *Gender Technology and Development*, vol. 3, no. 1, New Delhi.

Banerjee, N. and D. Jain, 'Women's Experience of Development', in N. Krishnaji (ed.), *Essays in Honour of A.K. Mitra*, forthcoming.

Basu, A.M. (1992), *Culture, the Status of Women and Demographic Behaviour*, Clarendon Press, Oxford.

——— (1996), 'Girl's Schooling, Autonomy and Fertility Changes: What Do

They Mean in S. Asia?', in R. Jeffrey and A. Basu (eds), *Girls' Schooling, Women's Autonomy and Fertility Change in S. Asia*, Sage Publications, New Delhi.

Basu, A.M. and R. Jeffrey (1996), 'Introduction', in A. Basu and R. Jeffery (eds), *Girls' Schooling, Women's Autonomy and Fertility Change in S. Asia*, Sage Publications, New Delhi.

Beauvoir, S. De (1972), *The Second Sex*, Penguin, London.

Becker, G.S. (1974), 'A Theory of Marriage II', *Journal of Political Economy*, vol. 82, no. 2, part II, pp. S11-S26.

——— (1981), *A Treatise on the Family*, Harvard University Press, Cambridge, MA.

——— (1988), 'Family Economics and Macro Behavior', *American Economic Review*, vol. 78, no. 1, pp. 1-13.

Becker, G.S. and H.G. Lewis (1974), 'Interaction between Quantity and Quality of Children', in T.P. Schultz (ed.), *Economics of the Family: Marriage, Children and Human Capital*, Chicago University Press, Chicago and London.

Ben-Porath, Y. (1974), 'Economic Analysis of Fertility in Israel', in T.P. Schultz (ed.), *The Economics of Family: Marriage, Children and Human Capital*, University of Chicago Press, Chicago and London.

——— (1982), 'Economics and the Family: Match or Mismatch? A Review of Becker's A Treatise on Family', *Journal of Economic Literature*, vol. 20, no. 1, March, pp. 52-64.

Bhaduri, A. (1973), 'Agiricultural Backwardness under Semi-feudalism', *Economic Journal*, vol. 83, no. 329, pp. 120-37.

———, (1979), 'Agricultural Backwardness under Semi-feudalism: A Reply', *Economic Journal*, vol. 89, no. 354, pp. 420-1.

Bhattacharya, Sudhir (1985), 'On the Issue of Under-enumeration of Women's Work in Indian Data System', in D. Jain and N. Banerjee (eds), *Tyranny of the Household*, Shakti Books, New Delhi.

Bhattacharya, Sukumari (1989), *Pracheen Bharat: Samaj O Sahitya*, Ananda Publishers, Calcutta.

Boserup, E. (1970), *Women and Development*, Oxford University Press, Oxford.

Braidotti, J. (1991), *Theories of Gender*, University of Utrecht, The Netherlands.

Cagatay, N. and S. Ozler (1995), 'Feminisation of the Labour Force', in *Gender Adjustment and Macro-economics*, Special Issue of *World Development*, vol. 23, no. 11, pp. 1883-94, Pergamon, U.K.

Cassen, R. (1994), *Population and Development: Old Debates, New Conclusions*, Transaction Books for Overseas Development Council, Washington, DC.

Cloud, K. and N. Garrett (1997), 'A Modest Proposal for Inclusion of Women's Household Human Capital Production in Analysis of Structural Transformation', *Feminist Economics*, vol. 3, no. 1, pp. 151-77.

Doss, C.R. (1996), 'Testing Among Models of Intra-household Resource

Allocation', *World Development,* Great Britain, vol. 24, no. 10, pp. 1597-609.

Dreze, Jean and Amartya Sen (1995), *India: Economic Development and Social Opportunity,* Oxford University Press, New Delhi.

Dyson, T and Moore, M. (1983), 'Female Autonomy and Demographic Behaviour in India', *Population and Development Review,* vol. 9, no. 1, March, pp. 35-60.

Edholm, F.O. Harris and K. Young (1977), 'Conceptualising Women', in *Critique of Anthropology,* vol. 9, no. 10, Chicago.

Engels, F.C. (1975), *The Origins of the Family, Private Property and the State,* International Publishers, New York.

Folbre, N.C. (1984), 'Market Opportunities, Genetic Endowments and Intra-Family Resource Allocation: A Comment', *American Economic Review,* vol. 74, no. 3, June, pp. 518-20.

——— (1986), 'Cleaning House: New Perspectives on Households and Economic Development', *Journal of Development Economics,* vol. 22, no. 1, pp. 5-40.

——— (1988), 'The Black Four of Hearts: Towards a New Paradigm of Household Economics', in Dwyer and Bruce (eds), *A Home Divided,* Stanford University Press, Stanford.

Freedman, J. and L. Wai (1988), 'Gender and Development in Barani Areas of Pakistan', quoted in World Bank (1989), *Women in Pakistan,* Washington, DC.

Friedman, M. (1953), 'The Methodology of Positive Economics', in his *Essays in Positive Economics,* Chicago.

Ghotoskar, S. (1995), 'Impact of Technological Change on Women Workers in the Pharmaceutical Industry in the Bombay Thana Region', paper presented at the National Workshop on Women and Technology, organized by UNU/INFECH, New Delhi.

Goldschmidt-Clairmont, L. (1982), *Economic Evaluation of Unpaid Household Work,* ILO, Women, Work and Development Services, no. 14, Geneva.

Goode, W.J. (1974), Comment: 'The Economics of Non-monetary Variables', in *Journal of Political Economy,* vol. 82, no. 2, part II, pp. S11-26.

Government of India (1974), *Towards Equality: Report of the Committee on the Status of Women in India,* Department of Education, New Delhi.

Gurumurthy, G. (1990), *Culture and Fertility Behaviour of Yanadis.* Himalaya Publications, Bombay.

Hartmann, H. (1979), 'Capital, Patriarchy and Job Segregation by Sex', in Z. Einstein (ed.), *Capitalist Patriarchy,* Monthly Review Press, New York.

——— (1987), 'Changes in Women's Economic and Household Roles in the Post World War II US', in L. Beneria and M.C. Sing (eds), *Women, Households and the Economy,* Rutgers University Press, N. Brunswick.

Horton, S. (1999), 'Marginalization Revisited: Market Work and Pay, and Economic Development', *World Development,* vol. 27, no. 3, March, pp. 571-82.

Humphries, J. (1977), 'The Working Class Family, Women's Liberation and Class Struggle', *Review of Radical Political Economics*, vol. 9, no. 3, Fall, New York, pp. 25-41.

Jain, A.K. and M. Nag (1986), 'Importance of Female Primary Education for Fertility Reduction in India', *Economic and Political Weekly*, vol. 21, no. 36, 6 September, pp. 1602-8.

Jain, D. and M. Chand (1985), 'The Household Trap', in D. Jain and N. Banerjee (eds), *Tyranny of the Household* in Shakti Books, Vikas Publishing House, New Delhi.

Jaquette, J.S. (1990), 'Gender and Justice in Economic Development', in I. Tinker (ed.), *Persistent Inequalities*, Oxford University Press, New York.

Jeejbhey, S.J. (1981), 'Women's Status and Fertility: Successive Cross-section Evidence from Tamil Nadu, India', mimeo, Family Planning Association of India, Mumbai.

Kabir, N. (1994), *Reversed Realities*, Verso, London.

Karkal, M. (1997), 'Nehru and the Population Policies in India', paper presented at the Seminar on *Women's Perspective on Independence* organized by the Indian Association of Women's Studies, 9-12 August 1997, Baroda.

Leibenstein, H. (1957), *Economic Backwardness and Economic Growth*, Wiley Publications, New York.

Lerner, G. (1993), *The Creation of Feminist Consciousness*, Oxford University Press, New York.

Mackintosh, M. (1981), 'Gender and Economics, the Sexual Division of Labour and the Subordination of Women', in K. Young, C. Wolkowitz and R. McCullagh (eds), *Of Marriage and the Market*, reprinted by Routledge, London, 1986.

Madrick, J. (1997), 'Why Mainstream Economists Should Take Heed', *Feminist Economics*, vol. 3, no. 1, Spring, pp. 143-9.

Malthus, T.R. (1798), *Principles of Population, as it Affects the Future Improvement of Society, with Remarks on the Speculation by Mr. Godwin, M. Condercet and other Writers*, Penguin, Harmondsworth, 1970.

Mernissi, F. (1975), *Beyond the Veil*, Wiley Publications, New York.

Mies, Maria et al. (1986), *Patriarchy and Accumulation*, Zed Press, London.

Mincer J. and S. Polachek (1974), 'Family Investment in Human Capital: Earnings of Women', *Journal of Political Economy*, vol. 82, no. 2, pp. S76-S108.

Mukherjee, M. (1983), 'Impact of Modernization of Women's Occupations: A Case Study of Rice-Husking Industry in Bengal', *Economic and Political History Review*, vol. 20, January-March.

Mukherjee, Moni (1986), 'Bread and Roses', *The Journal of Income and Wealth*, vol. 8, no. 2, New Delhi.

Pearson, R., A. Whitehead and K. Young (1981), 'Introduction: The Continuing Subordination of Women in the Development Process', in K. Young, C. Wolkowitz and R. McCullogh (eds), *Of Marriage and the Market*, reprinted by Routledge, London, 1986.

Pollak, R.A. (1985), 'A Transaction Cost Approach to Families and Households', *Journal of Economic Literature*, vol. 23, no. 2, June, pp. 581-608.

Rosaldo, M. (1974), 'Women, Culture and Society: A Theoretical Overview', in M. Rosaldo and L. Lamphere (eds), *Women, Culture and Society*, Stanford, Stanford University Press.

Rozenzweig, M.K. and T.P. Schultz (1982), 'Market Opportunities, Genetic Endowments and Intra-family Resource Distribution: Child Survival in Rural India', *American Economic Review*, vol. 72, no. 4, September, pp. 803-15.

——— (1984), 'A Rejoinder', in *American Economic Review*, vol. 74, no. 3, pp. 521-2.

Sen, A.K. (1990), 'Gender and Co-operative Conflicts', in I. Tinker (ed.), *Persistent Inequalities*, Oxford University Press, New Delhi.

Sen, G. and C. Sen (1985), 'Women's Domestic Work and Economic Activity', *Economic and Political Weekly*, vol. 20, no. 17, 27 April, pp. WS 49-56.

Sen, S. (1999), *Women and Labour in Late Colonial India*, Cambridge University Press, Cambridge.

Standing, G. (1989), 'Global Feminization Through Flexible Labour' *World Development*, vol. 17, no. 7, Special Issue, July 1989, pp. 1077-95.

——— (1999), 'Global Feminization Through Flexible Labour: A Theme Revisited', *World Development*, vol. 27, no. 3, March, pp. 583-602.

Tom, I. (1989), *Women Workers in the Unorganized Sector*, Usha Publications, New Delhi.

Visaria, P. (1999), 'Women in Indian Work Force: Trends and Differentials', in A. Sharma and T.S. Papola (eds), *Gender and Employment in India*, Vikas Publication House, New Delhi.

Walby, S.C. (1990), *Theorising Patriarchy*, Oxford, Basil Blackwell.

Wells, R. and M. Maher (1999), *Time and Surplus Allocation Within Marriage*, mimeo, MIT, Cambridge, MA.

Willis, R.J. (1974), 'Economic Theory of Fertility Behaviour', in T.W. Schultz (ed), *Economics of the Family: Marriage, Children and Human Capital*, University of Chicago Press, Chicago and London.

Workers' Solidarity Centre (1995), 'Impact of Technological Changes on Women in the Pharmaceutical Industry in the Bombay-Theme Region', paper submitted to UNU/INTECH under the project 'Impact of New Technologies and Globalization on Women', Maastricht.

# Contributors

*Amiya Kumar Bagchi*
Director, Institute of Development Studies Kolkata
Former RBI Professor of Economics, Centre for Studies in Social Sciences, Calcutta

*Amit Bhaduri*
Professor, University of Pavia, Italy

*Aditya Bhattacharjea*
Reader, Delhi School of Economics, University of Delhi

*Nirmala Banerjee*
Retired Professor, Centre for Studies in Social Sciences, Calcutta

*Nirmal Kumar Chandra*
Retired Professor, Indian Institute of Management, Calcutta

*S. Inderkant*
Professor, Osmania University, Hyderabad, India

*Saibal Kar*
RBI Research Officer, Centre for Studies in Social Sciences, Calcutta

*Sugata Marjit*
Professor, Centre for Studies in Social Sciences, Calcutta

*R. Radhakrishna*
Director, Indira Gandhi Institute for Development Research, Mumbai

*C. Ravi*
Faculty Member, Centre for Economic and Social Studies, Hyderabad, India

*Prabirjit Sarkar*
Professor, Rabindra Bharati University, Kolkata

*Eu Chye Tan*
Associate Professor, University of Malaya, Kuala Lumpur, Malaysia

*Chul Gyue Yoo*
Assistant Professor, Sung-Kong-Hoe University, Seoul, Korea